T0198638

ONCE DECLARED
DECLARED
Moot

ZIGLAR HARPAR

authorHOUSE®

AuthorHouse™
1663 Liberty Drive
Bloomington, IN 47403
www.authorhouse.com
Phone: 1 (800) 839-8640

Published by AuthorHouse 06/22/2018

ISBN: 978-1-5462-2412-9 (sc)
ISBN: 978-1-5462-2413-6 (e)

Chapter 1

My name is Ziglar Harper (Ziggy), born to one Darlene Harper. I was born in Baton Rouge Confederate Hospital in Baton Rouge, Louisiana. We lived in Allendale. I remember my grandmother on my mother's side... we lived next door and I can't remember her having harsh words to say about anyone unless someone mentioned the name of my grandfather, who still lived in Arkansas.

My mother had seven siblings. We were really close to my mother's side of the family, but I never got to meet my grandfather... regrettable.

Whenever my grandmother would do anything, she would always talk about Singleton and Mr. Rogers; those were the times I would really get to see, or should I say hear what was really on my grandmother's mind.

One day I asked my grandmother who Mr. Singleton and Mr. Rogers were because she always talked about those two men. My grandmother looked at me, smiling with no fronts (she had no teeth). She told me that Mr. Singleton and Mr. Rogers were two slave masters who lived during her time.

After speaking with my mother many years later about Mr. Singleton and Mr. Rogers, my mother looked at me and started laughing and said Mr. Rogers was my aunt Ebony's father, which gave me some insight as to why my grandmother was so critical about them.

Growing up, I still remember the meals my grandmother used to cook. Oh, yes, I remember standing in the kitchen where she cooked those homemade biscuits and gravy the way she used to make her hot water cornbread that went well with her fried green tomatoes. Those were special times.

When I was 18, I went to live with my grandmother for 18 months in

Inglewood, CA. Not long after returning to Norfolk, VA, my grandmother passed away. My grandmother was special to me.

There were six of us in my family, my oldest brother, Jimmy Jr., oldest sister, Celes, and my brother, Louis, all had the same father. My brother, Todd, and I had the same father, and my younger sister, Regina, had a different father. My brother and I didn't know anyone on our father's side of the family. Hell, we never even got to know him. I never understood that. The only real memory I have of my biological father is how he would come around occasionally, and when he did, he never spent any time with my brother and me.

I loved the summertime with the other kids on the block. We used to go to a neighbor's yard and get old tires from the cars he worked on. We would go to the end of the block and hide in the ditches, and whenever cars came, we would roll the tires in traffic and run real fast back to our hideout. That was just one of the things we did, just being kids. Not soon after, our parents would call us in for the night. My sister, Celes, would get us ready for bed. We would all go over to my grandmother's and sit around on the living room floor playing Monopoly and watching TV, just having fun as kids did. Back in those days, you could leave your front door open and let the nice breeze just blow through the screen door.

The only thing you had to worry about in those days was constant racism. It was hard to get the police or the EMS to come out to neighborhoods when help was needed.

I loved those summer nights. Once we'd fallen asleep, my uncles would carry us home, where my mother would put us to bed.

While I was sitting on the porch one day, at about age 10, a neighbor called me over to her house and asked me to help her rearrange some furniture. She was one of the ladies who used to play cards with my mother while music from the 45s was playing on the turntable and the kids singing along. As I entered her house, she told me to take a seat in a chair that sat in the corner. She disappeared into her bedroom. When she returned to the living room, she was wearing a see-through nightgown. This was my first encounter with the opposite sex. When I said see-through, I meant SEE-THROUGH! It wasn't strange that I was at her house. This wasn't the first time I had helped. I'd helped her cut her grass from time to time, and she would pay me, but today something totally different was about to take place.

Once we finished moving the furniture, she gave me a glass of ice-cold lemonade. After we finished our drinks, she asked me to follow her. We ended up in the bathroom. I could see she had already ran water in the tub, with bubbles at that! As she turned to me smiling, she slowly turned around and let her gown drape off her body. I have never seen something so beautiful. Although nothing happened, it was on this day that I first discovered the beginnings of my sexual nature. Occasionally, she would call me over. She made me promise never to tell anyone and, until this writing, I kept my word. I never revealed it until this day, though I didn't know what I was doing at the time. I think I liked it... Let me stop playing: I know I liked it. This continued until we moved.

Every kid has a best friend as a child. Mine was named Andre. His grandmother lived directly across the street from my grandma, and we used to stand on the porch and try to hit each other with rocks. One day I will never forget while throwing rocks. I hit him dead in his eye. His mother ran across the street yelling, "GO GET YOUR MOTHER!" When my mother came outside, she told my mother that I just hit her son in the eye with a rock. I knew I was in trouble. I got a beating that night. Every time I saw Andre after that, I would apologize to him. Of course, his mother told him that he couldn't play with me anymore. I don't blame her for not wanting him to play with me. After all, I did blind his eye, even though it was an accident. To this day, I still feel bad about it. He was my best friend, and I will always think of him that way. I wish him the best in life, even though I have never seen him again.

The year was 1974. I was 10 years old, I didn't know it, but some serious chains of events were about to unfold in my life in a way that would alter my being for an eternity!

After my mother and Gilbert got married, we moved to Jefferson Heights. I can't help but wonder if the accident with my friend prompted our move; after all, our mothers were friends. We moved into the ugliest colored light-green house you could have imagined with a screened-in porch. It was one of those houses you could easily turn into a duplex, even though it had only one floor, but it was home.

It wasn't long after we'd moved in, we started talking to our neighbors.

On one side of us lived Mr. Roy Lee Johnson, his wife, Ms. Sissy Johnson, and their four children. On the other side was the Jackson family. I really liked our new neighbors.

As time went by, their daughter, Sheila Johnson, and I found ourselves liking each other. My little brother and I played around in the neighborhood with the other kids from time to time. Sometimes I went into Sheila's house with her. Her sister, Adela Johnson, would always run us out of the house. We would run out laughing. Adela would yell, "Don't come back in here!" Adela was older than Sheila, so Adela took on more responsibilities in the house; you know how the oldest always ends up doing the most work. Sheila also had two brothers, Frederick Johnson and Dante Johnson, both of whom liked my sister, Celes, who was 16 years old.

I think Frederick was the first one trying to talk to Celes. He would sometimes come over and sit on the porch. Every now and then, I would come and mess with him. Not long after, it seemed like Dante would be the one dating Celes, and so it was.

I really loved the summer. We had flowers growing in our backyard where the bees would hover and feed. We would take jelly jars, put holes in the top and put flowers in the bottom as lures. When we caught bees, we'd hold them for a day or two and let them go before they died. One day, while trying to catch bees, I got stung. That's when I found out I was allergic. I dropped my jar of bees and ran as fast as I could into the house. My whole neck and throat were swelling. I could hardly breathe. My mother rushed me to the hospital. I was really scared. For a while I thought I was going to die. After I got home, my brothers and sister laughed at me. That's not the only time I had to be rushed to the hospital as a kid.

One day around the age of 11 while playing with my money, I messed around and swallowed a nickel. Yes, once again I couldn't breathe. I was so frightened I didn't know what to do, but I knew that if I didn't do something quick that I would probably die. All I could think is how mad my mother would be, but I knew that I had to do something; I was getting light headed. Finally, I got up the nerve to run in the house. As I approached the living room through the kitchen, I pointed at my throat trying to tell my mother that I just swallowed a nickel. My mother looked frantic and started yelling, "How in the world did you do that boy?"

My mother would always cook a delicious meal; I don't care what it was. It was good. The only thing I didn't like were three desserts. Whenever she cooked bread pudding, rice pudding, or coconut cake, it meant more helpings for my younger brother.

My first year at Jefferson Heights Elementary School, at the age of 11 was fun in the beginning, that is, until a white kid named Willie-Lee started making trouble. Come to find out, he was jealous of me because I could out-do him in P.E. on the chin-up bars. Remember now, this was in the South. Whatever competition it was, Willie-Lee couldn't beat me in anything, and, of course, he didn't like that. It was a time when racism was still very blatant, and it was unacceptable for blacks to excel in anything over whites.

As my first year at the new school came to an end, two major things took place in my life. The first was Sheila talking me into shooting hooky from school. We stayed in a house on the next street as lunch approached. We were going back and forth about who was going to their house to make us some sandwiches. She knew that I couldn't go to my house. I couldn't even cook, and besides, she knew she had a better chance. And since this was her idea, she'd better get me something to eat. We stopped laughing. I had never skipped school before. She left to get us something to eat. When she came back, I was happy to see her. She came back with some bologna and cheese sandwiches and some Kool-Aid.

"Did anybody see you?" I asked.

"No."

"Are you sure?"

"Yes!"

We passed the time playing cards. When we saw the other kids walk up the street, we knew school was out. Listen, I had no idea that our mothers knew we'd shot hooky, but when I got out of the bathtub that night, my mom came in before I could dry off. You know what happened next. A major beating that I've never forgotten. Once again, I was mad at Sheila. I think I stayed mad about three or four days that time. She was still my baby, but she never got me to shoot hooky with her again.

The second important development happened when jealous Willie-Lee went too far and put his hands on me. After enduring many days of his racial slurs, he hit me with a chair. As I went to hit him back, the teacher stepped between us. I told her, "Just like lots of other times, this boy keeps picking fights with me. He hit me with this chair; I'm going to hit him back."

"You'll do no such thing," she said, pointing a finger in my face.

"Why do you always take up for him, when he's wrong?" I asked, acting like I was walking away. She moved, and I hit him with the chair. Afterwards I was escorted to the principal's office. She told the principal that the chair hit her! She never even attempted to tell what took place. She was not going to mention Willie-Lee at all. While I attempted to tell what happened, they both motioned for me to be quiet. The principal told her that she could go back to her class. When she left, I tried to tell him how this kid, Willie-Lee, had been harassing me and calling me out of my name, and each time she would just tell me to go back to my seat, be quiet, and not to get up until she told me to. Sometimes she would put me in the corner facing the wall, and Willie-Lee would continue taunting me. I thought telling him, since he was the principal, that he would do the right thing. How was I to know otherwise? I was only a kid.

That night, I got another beating. Yes, that's right: wet!

When the school year ended, my mother started taking me to a doctor. He put me on medication. I had no idea what was about to happen. I didn't really understand racism. All I knew is that we were treated differently by white people. Back during those days, I guess our parents just did whatever the white man felt was best for us opposed to our parents taking a stand for their children.

I can remember asking my mother, "Why do I have to take this medication? I don't like it."

She responded by telling me that if I didn't, the white people would threaten to lock me up if she didn't make sure that I took it.

Even then when trying to explain to my mother what was taking place with the white kid, Willie-Lee, she seemed to have less interest in what I had to say, and from that one act the rest of my school years were an uphill battle and a constant struggle. The older I got, the more I began to understand a lot that my grandmother used to talk about. The mistreatment and societies biased opinions got clear and painful. What a world!

Once again it was summertime: nothing but fun and play. They were giving out forms for parents to sign for anyone who wanted to learn karate.

After my mother had given me permission, I was only allowed to go for about three weeks because the other kids in the neighborhood started complaining that I was using karate on them, so my mother stopped me from going. That was something I really loved doing.

We were made to go to church every Sunday, Sunday school services as well. We didn't mind. Just kids having fun. I remember one time when Sheila, yes, my sweetheart, supposedly got caught kissing this guy in the back of the church. For the next two days, I was mad at her, so when we saw each other, I would go the other way. As I looked back, she'd catch me looking. I would start laughing and walk faster and faster. When she started to chase me, I would run, but then I would let her catch me. We would both be laughing: You know how it is, being kids. Trying to make up for what she had done, we made a pact. She was to go in the house and take a shower and I was to get a milk crate and stand up to the bathroom window and watch her as she took a shower. At my first look, I jumped off the crate and ran to my backyard, laughing to myself as I peeked around the corner. I tiptoed back, looked around and stepped up on the crate again. I had no idea who it was in the bathroom, but I knew it wasn't her. I almost broke my neck running. Later, she had to sneak out because she'd already taken her shower. We met at the back gate where they had a fig tree that slightly hung over on our side of the fence. I was at the fence waiting for her. She'd set me up that time, and once again I was mad. She got out on me, just one of the games we used to play on each other. She was still my girl.

I remember the last time I stood on that crate, her sister, Adela, caught me looking through the window. Adela yelled out to me, "Ziggy, get your nasty butt out of that window!" Ann was one of those girls who didn't curse. As I ran away, she yelled, "I am going to tell your mama!" But she never did. After that day, I gave her no trouble.

As the day began to wind down, we would all go to the corner where this white family lived in this big white house. The yard was like a hill. We would go down there with cardboard boxes and slide down the hill. Once we were tired, we would just lie under the tree and enjoy the nice cool breeze, listening to the whistling of the leaves from the wind. Those were very joyful moments for me. I used to love that hill.

The first time I met Jason was at the corner store. I knew he was kin to

Sheila's family, but I didn't know how until later. Sheila had an older sister named Ruth Johnson, who had a son named Jason. From the day we met, we stayed in trouble. If there was something I wouldn't do, Jason would do it, despite the fear of a good, old-fashioned beating. I would just shake my head at him sometimes because the beatings he got were far worse than what I got. He just never seemed to care. We would sometimes find IOUs. An IOU was money left over from food stamps with the amount written on it. It was credited to the store. In those days you didn't receive change back from food stamps; you got an IOU. That's right: IOU, baby.

One day Jason and I were hanging out after leaving the store and walking down the alley. After we crossed the street, we continued down the alley. We passed two guys standing at the corner. Jason told me that they were homosexuals, and that he was going to throw rocks at them. I told him that I didn't think that was an innovative idea. He just laughed as we walked back toward the street. When we got there, he started throwing rocks. Then he broke out running, so I did too. We were laughing and joking as we got to the next street. Right at the end of the alley, one of the gay guys was hitting the corner. He had taken off his wig and heels and was just about to catch us. He was so fast, I could not move. All I could do was point to Jason and say, "It was him." I guess he knew that because he ran right past me, and he was on Jason's ass. I didn't see Jason until later that day. He said the guy never caught him. I told him he was crazy. He just laughed.

~" Blind faith; blind utterly."

Chapter 2

One day, when Jason decided that we were going to smoke a cigarette in the bathroom, I really knew he was crazy. All he kept saying was, "Big Mama is going to be gone for a while. She had to take one of the other kids to the doctor." I still remember it like it was yesterday. There we were, standing in the bathroom, trying to smoke a cigarette. I never inhaled, but Jason did.

Suddenly, there was someone knocking on the bathroom door. Big Mama called out to Jason, as she always called him, "Jasonnnnn."

I would always laugh, but that day was different. I almost did laugh. Both of us were trying to blow the smoke out the window. See, Big Mama didn't smoke; she and Ms. Grace chewed snuff. Yes, that's right: snuff. I tried to ease out of the bathroom. The door opened outward, so as I closed the door, big Mama was standing right there. I really had to do number two then. Big Mama got to yelling and cursing and scared the living you-know-what out of me. I ran home really fast. I went to the bathroom to brush my teeth, trying to get the smell off my breath. I couldn't talk in anybody's face.

As the day passed, I waited for my mother to mention something to me. I knew deep in my gut that she would be told before the day was out. This was just one of my mother's specialties, making me think I'd gotten away with it. Yes, as I thought, as soon as I got out of the tub, she was waiting for me. And you know the rest. The following day I got teased by Sheila, and, of course, you know I had to laugh with her.

While Sheila and I stood in the driveway on the side of my house, we could hear some music and noise. We looked at each other and ran to the side street. We knew who it was: Jon. Most of the kids on the block wanted to be like him, and I was one of them. See, Jon could do the things that were "IN" at that time, mainly dancing. Not only could he dance, but he could dance well on roller skates as well, which was a big deal at the time. All the girls liked him. Even my girl, Sheila. Yes, she liked him too, so I had to keep proving my love to keep her.

Jon and his family lived two doors to the left of my family. There were his mother, little sister, and his brother, Jonnie, who was around my age, 12. Jon was older. He was around Dante's and the other guys' age, like the rest of the young guys in our neighborhood.

As I said, all the girls liked Jon, so I tried to get to know him a little better. I had to start by talking to his brother, Jonnie. After talking to him for some time, I could see that he wasn't a bad guy at all. See, people didn't talk to Ronnie because he was an albino. You know kids my age and how we could be. We all stood around as Jon put on a show for us. On this day we had a new spectator. It was a girl from the new family on the block. She seemed to admire his skating skills. I had no idea that this would be the last time I saw Jon skate.

After dinner that evening, my brother, Todd, and I went out on the porch. Suddenly, we heard someone screaming. People started coming to their doors, looking out. Moments later we saw Jon running across the street to his house. Not long after, the police arrived. We walked to the sidewalk, and we could see that they were putting Jon in the backseat of the police car. We later found out he was accused of raping the new girl on the block. Right then, I lost respect for the old boy. I'd thought he could get any girl he wanted. I guess I was wrong. So was he. He just took it. Dummy. The last I heard he was wearing wigs when he got out of prison. Unbelievable.

When I was 12 years old, my mother and stepfather had a bad argument that led to physical contact between the two of them. My stepfather used to put his hands on my mother, but this night was different: My stepfather had made a pass at my sister, Celes. During all the commotion, my mother told my sister, Celes, to call Uncle Ray-Ray. My sister sounded very upset, so that prompted my uncle Ray-Ray's wife, Fannie, to call some of my other uncles, my uncles T. J. and Williams. They all drove from Motown to Jefferson Heights.

Once my mother's brothers arrived, I knew stuff was about to hit the fan. I was standing in the doorway with one of my siblings that night. I was always happy to see my uncles, but especially that night, because I knew they were there to put a stop to my stepfather's ass-kicking. I literally hated him. I wanted so much to express myself, but I could not, so I held it in. My uncle Ray-Ray was beating that ass. I've waited for this night for a long time. It's about time, I thought. I've seen too much already. Looking back on it, I see that my stepfather was abusive. Whenever we got into trouble, we would get the beating of a lifetime. I don't think anyone in the family got more or harsher beatings than I did. He would wait until I got out of the shower, and before I could dry off, he would start beating me with an extension cord. He used to hit me so hard that my skin would swell up just to the point of bleeding. I was tired of him beating on my mother as well as tired of getting beatings myself. I wanted to do something myself, but I was only a kid. In the middle of all the commotion, we heard a loud boom. As I turned and looked on the porch behind me, I saw Aunt Fannie lying on the floor. She had fainted and hit her head against one of the chairs on her way down. I giggled. After all, we really didn't like her because she made it plain that she didn't like us. We used to see Uncle Ray-Ray just about every weekend until he married her. After she came into his life, she wanted him all to herself.

My stepfather was told not to come back to the house until my mother had gathered her things and left. A few days later, my mother purchased a station wagon, and before I knew it, we were on the interstate with our neighbors, Sheila and her family, in another car. My question to myself was: "Why are they leaving, too?" My mother told us that we were going to California where we had family. I knew why we were leaving but was unclear as to why Sheila's family was coming too?

~" Life is not all you think it could be when you first start living and neither will it fail to surprise you with where you end up..."

Chapter 3

After nearly two days of traveling with everyone and everything that we could fit in the wagon and a trailer, we pulled up to a highrise in one of the worst neighborhoods in Jersey City, New Jersey. Now I realized why the neighbors had packed up and left with us; we weren't really going to California with our family. We were moving in with Sheila's family. But what was more ironic was that the neighbor's sister and her family moved with us too so that put four families into a two-bedroom apartment. As I stood on the fenced-in, seventh-floor terrace, I couldn't help but continue to wonder why our neighbors would leave their home. It never seemed like their parents fought, but, then again, who knows what goes on behind closed doors? The most I remember about staying with Chris' family was the lack of space and the extensive line to use the bathroom. But the lady of the house always put a smile on my face with her sweet Jiffy cornbread and Kool-Aid that went well with any meal that she cooked. Her cornbread was the best that I ever tasted.

Another day had come and gone as I walked out onto the terrace. How was I to know that this was the beginning of a chain of events that would unfold and alter my view and perspective of life forever? We'd been told repeatedly by the family we'd moved in with how bad the neighborhood was. The family we moved with from New Jersey, whom we now referred to as our cousins, lived in tight quarters, and we were always together. My cousin, Tee-Tee, and I had to decide to either stay on the seventh-floor terrace until we moved or get our fight game together. Of course, we had to get our fight game up. Who knew how long we were going to be there? I'll tell you, the fight game here was different from home. Back home you could get a one-on-one fight; in Jersey City, you could get jumped at any time! Truly, I had my share of fights there. Finally, we moved into a house on North Street, a two-story house where a girl I ended up liking lived upstairs with her family.

I had a hell of a crush on her. Little did I know, one of my cousin liked her as well, but I couldn't let him know that I was kind of shy when it came to girls. Hell, I was only thirteen. My cousin, two years older than I, made a move on the girl, just out of spite, and we got into a fight. My mother told us to break it up and made me come into the house where I was put on punishment for three days. Unfortunately, that gave my cousin the time he needed to move in on my girl. For a while after that I was angry at him, but like everything else, I got over it. (Family must stick together.)

It was the beginning of the new school year, and my mother enrolled me in North Junior High where I met my next girlfriend, Maria. Wouldn't you know it, it just had to be in a class that I didn't like – Science – but after a few weeks of having her as my science partner, I really began to like it.

More than for anyone else, trouble seemed to follow me. The Spanish boys didn't think it was a clever idea for me to date her because she was Hispanic, and I was black. I thought that she was worth fighting for. After all, her family accepted me, and we really cared about each other. I'd had my run-ins with the Spanish crew to be with her, but how was I to know that one day after school would be my last fight for the one I loved? Three Spanish boys gave me the worst beating I had ever had. I had a fractured jaw, a closed eye, a busted lip and a broken finger. My mother was so furious that she took me with her to the school and raised hell! My mother then stated that the neighborhood was too fast and that we were going to move that night.

After dark fell, I raced all the way to my girlfriend's house, which was about four and one-half blocks away. I remember spending the night with her in my arms. We knew that this would be the last night we spent together. She cried.

During my walk home, I wanted to cry myself. All the fighting with the Spanish boys had only brought us closer, and I never thought it would end. Boy! That was the longest walk that I had ever experienced in my life. For the next two years, all I could do was think about her. However, we promised to keep in contact with each other, but we were just kids. I never saw her again.

One night while living on North Street, chilling with some friends, I wondered why my sister and her boyfriend stayed in the bedroom all the time. I guess it was just a typical thought of a typical 13-year-old. Anyway, as I sat there with a cigarette in my mouth trying to be "cool," not actually smoking (just faking), my mother crept through the back door without any warning. After all, the lookout was at the front door when he should have been at the back door. I was embarrassed and scared at the same time. I was so scared that I put the cigarette in my pocket while it was still lit.

My mother said, "I see that cigarette. Think you grown, don't you boy? You better not set my house on fire. Put that cigarette out and go to your room. I'll tend to you later!!"

I waited all night, trying to stay up. As soon as I fell asleep, she tore my ass up! I wasn't the only one who got in trouble either. She caught my sister and her boyfriend. I don't think that I need to say what happened after that.

My brother, Jimmy Jr., because he was the oldest, thought he could hang with the fast crowds of New Jersey. He always hung with this crowd along with his girlfriend. One summer evening we while we were hanging out on the porch as usual, my brother's friends pulled up in front of the house, and as they pulled my brother from the back seat of the car, I could see that something wasn't right. While they were bringing him up the steps, it seemed that he was speaking in tongues. When they got him into the house, he started acting crazy, like something was all over him. Then he started taking his clothes off. I thought it was funny, but I found out that he and his friends had been taking acid, and he was having a bad trip. Who would have thought that he would never be the same again?

~" Many people use the hurt and pain that one person caused them to punish us all."

15

Chapter 4

The year was 1978. I was 14 years old and was enrolled in Guilford Middle School. Wouldn't you know it; I just had to end up with the wrong crowd to hang with. The guys I hung around with most were Rabbi Gills, Leni Howard and "Scary Grant." We called Grant Bowers "Scary Grant" because every time we got into a fight, he'd be the first to grab his Kango hat and run.

Someone had drilled a hole from the back side of the boys' gym to the girls' locker room. I don't know who did it and really didn't care. All I know is that I used to skip a class every now and then to go watch the girls. Mind you, once you skipped that one period, there was no way to leave the back of the boys' locker room without getting caught. There were always truant officers around, so we had to stay in the cubby hole. Upon leaving, you had to be careful not to bump into Mr. Williams because he was notorious for wearing his low-cut running shoes just to catch someone, but he never caught ME! The rest of the school year was pretty much the same day to day.

Nearly every weekend during the summer, there was someone having a party. On one Saturday night, I saw the girl who would be the next love of my life at the Y Dance. Her name was Miracle, and she was the prettiest girl you ever wanted to see. She had natural shoulder-length black hair. She had brown skin with dimples and a smile out of this world, and she was totally bowlegged. I was so scared to say anything to her. I had butterflies in my stomach. Wouldn't you believe it took me all night to get up the nerve to go over and talk to her? As I approached her, I said "Hi, how are you?" As she began to respond, all hell broke loose, and (wouldn't you know it) it was my crew. So, I turned and looked at her and her cousin, and I pulled her by the arm, shouting, "Let's get out of here." After I went back to join my crew in the fight, sweet thoughts of her still crossed through my mind.

Three weeks passed without a sight of her. I asked my brother, Todd, if he perhaps knew the young lady in question, since he went to Kempsville High School, and I went to Lowell High School. I knew she didn't go to my school, so she either had to go to Kempsville or Grass Field High School. I asked my brother, Todd, to check on that for me. The whole week he said he couldn't come up with anyone with that description.

That following Saturday he asked me to come hang out with him and his crew. I told him that his crew wasn't like mine and to go ahead. "I'll get with you youngins later. I'm going to hang out with my own boys."

Moments later My brother came out of the house and told me that he thought I should reconsider going with him. Again, I told him to go ahead. As he got to the end of the block, I yelled out, "Hold on!" I was kind of curious as to why he was so persistent on me going with him, so I had to check it out.

I caught up with him and we walked and talked. Just as we were getting to where we were going, I was about to turn around for the second time. It was a long walk from where we lived to where we were. Finally, we walked up to this house. He knocked, and this guy answered the door. After they embraced each other, my brother introduced me to his friend, Ziggy, Randy, who then yelled out, "Camila! Todd is here to see you!" We were asked to take a seat in the living room.

Moments later this female comes walking from the back bedroom, and right behind her was the girl I'd approached at the dance. I didn't get a chance to get her name then, but I made my mind up to have her name and number before I left tonight. As I stared, she began to pick up the phone and start dialing. I jumped up playfully grabbing my brother in a headlock. Then I leaned over put my arm around Camila (even though I didn't know her) and whispered, "You know her?"

She laughed and said, "Yes, she's my cousin."

By this time Miracle had walked back to the bedroom. I asked Camila to call her for me. She turned, looked at my brother, and said, "Todd didn't tell you?"

"Tell me what?"

"He knew all week long that he was supposed to bring you over to meet her."

When Camila said that, I got real nervous, just as I did that night at the dance. As they proceeded from the back room, Camila introduced us. I had no idea her mother was on her way to pick her up; therefore, we really didn't get a chance to talk. So, we made plans to meet there next weekend. We said goodnight. I watched her as she walked out the door. My heart was pounding. We talked everyday till that weekend.

When my brother and I got there, Miracle hadn't arrived yet. With every passing car, my heart would beat faster, then slow down. Finally, there was a knock at the door. Camila opened the door, and there she was, so beautiful, one in a million. She walked over. We reintroduced ourselves, and she said, "You're that troublemaker; that's what I'm going to call you."

God knows I didn't want her calling me troublemaker. We sat, talked, listened to music, and ordered pizza and sodas. Of course, Miracle and Camila had to pay for the pizza. I was so embarrassed and pissed. I had lost all my money that day shooting dice. I told them that the next time I came over I would pay. I was relieved to hear them say okay because I really didn't know where I was going to get any money to pay for the pizza.

Miracle and I continued meeting at Camila's house for the next few weeks, but the walk home on that first night is one I'll always remember. It was about four o'clock a.m., and my long walk home didn't seem so long that night. Thoughts of Miracle were on my mind all the way home. Walking from thirty-Seventh Street to my house was about sixteen long blocks. But time flew because I was on cloud nine with sweet thoughts of the first date with the young lady I thought so much of.

The next couple of weeks were great, and our relationship started to grow. We often walked hand in hand, watched movies, and went to teen parties. We hung out together a lot as teens did. one Saturday night we were at the Elks Lounge Hall at a party. I had hoped I wouldn't run into Fay Johnson and Marcella, who were rivals of me and my boys, but there they were. (We were the Colley Ave Boys, while the Elks Hall was in their territory, which was Churchland Ave.) I took Miracle by the hand and started walking around and dancing, trying to dodge the rivals. I really didn't want Miracle to see me fight. Things were going great between us, and I didn't want to spoil it.

I eventually bumped into Marcella on the dance floor. As we got ready to fight, Miracle grabbed my arm and said, "If you don't stop right now, I will not go anywhere else with you."

I told her and Camila to go ahead, and I'd catch up with them. Fay Johnson and Marcella were at the door, and I knew that I had to fight. I just didn't want them to see me get my ass whipped. As I tried to leave, blows started flying! As I fought my way out the door, I was happy to see my crew. My boys joined the fight. Fay Johnson took a two-by-four and hit me with it, holding it in both hands and pushing it into my face. The blow was so hard that it cracked two of my teeth, one at the top and one at the bottom. I start bleeding from my mouth. We fought for eight blocks. I was so tired I didn't know what to do, but I knew I couldn't hit the ground because if I did, that would have been the end of me. It ended between 21st, 22nd street and Colley Ave. One of the guys went to swing on me, and I turned and knocked him down. As I was bent over with the palm of my hands on my knees, I could see the police drive up. They walked over to me and asked if I was okay. While they were leaving, I could see people looking, and amongst them was my brother, Todd, and cousin Tee-Tee. This fight was the talk of the town for the longest time.

For the next four days, Miracle was mad at me. When I did go see her, it was obvious nothing had changed. As soon as I walked through the door, I asked if her mother was upset with me? I liked her mother. She was down to earth. Every time I visited she'd ask me to look at the clock. Her philosophy was, "The earlier you come, the later you get to stay. The later you come; the earlier you leave." Of course, I chose the latter. "But I couldn't help but wonder whether this philosophy was hers or Miracle's. Whenever I was a few minutes late, Miracle would always interrogate me. "Where have you been?"

I would just smile, give her a kiss, and attempt to plead my tardiness. "Nowhere, just hanging with the fellows for a few." Once I got that first smile with those pretty dimples, the rest of the night would be smooth.

When I first started going to Miracle 's house, I wouldn't eat there. I was shy about eating in front of her mother. One day when I arrived, she came to the door smiling. She always smiled, but this smile had a different expression, and I knew something was up. I said, "What's going on?"

She didn't say anything; she just kept smiling and led me to the dining room where her mother was sitting. We spoke to each other, and then her mother proceeded to tell me that I better lose that shyness, have a seat, and eat. "I cook well, and I'm sure you'll enjoy it, and you need to eat. You're here more than at home."

I was relieved to hear this for more than one reason, the biggest being that we didn't have much to eat at home, sometimes not much more than a bowl of rice. My mother was raising six kids on her own, not to mention the expense of the three-bedroom house in which my mother and baby sister, Regina, had to share a room.

I didn't understand why my sister and her boyfriend got to share a bedroom because my mother was kind of old-fashioned.

My brothers and I shared a room. Even after my brother, Louis, moved out of the house, it was still crowded. There was no privacy.

Miracle didn't have this problem. It was always peaceful there. She had one brother, and he lived in THE BOTTOMS with her father, while Miracle and her mother had a big two-story house on Maple Avenue. Those who don't know what THE BOTTOMS are, let's just say it wasn't a place you would want to spend too much time at. There is a lot going on, and when you go to that part of town, there is always trouble. Although you could find trouble all over, THE BOTTOMS had the worst of it and still does.

Miracle's father and brother lived alone. The first time I met them it was kind of awkward. Her brother lived an alternative lifestyle. Not many black gays were out in the open at this time. Although I have nothing to say about alternative living, being around gays wasn't my cup of tea. Occasionally, Miracle would go to her father's house, and I would accompany her.

We still hung out at Camila's house from time to time. There was a guy named Rob who was a friend of Camila's family. He had the hots for Miracle long before I came into the picture. Ole Rob, he always seemed to have a pocketfull of change, while I, on the other hand, was struggling and had none. I had to find a way to earn money for two reasons: to help my mother out and to out-shine Rob.

My sister's boyfriend worked at Larry's Paint & Body Shop. I asked him if he could get me a job working there after school? He said he'd see what he could do. For the rest of the school year, I would inquire about the job. As soon as school was out, he asked me if I still wanted to work with him? Heck yeah, I did!

My mom had to sign some papers, and soon after, I got the job. The summer was great, even though my mom would get most of my pay. I only kept a little money for myself. Back in those days, twenty dollars was a lot of money!

The summer passed, and another school year started. I talked to my boss, and he let me continue to work after school. I was going to Lowell High School. It was four miles away, and by the time I got to work, I'd lost an hour.

A couple months after I spoke with my guidance counselor about the job situation, she got me one at the Burger Shop, which was better because it was around the corner from my high school.

Another school year was over. The summer arrived, and I loved it, but for me it was short-lived. Miracle and her mother moved back to Carolina. I was heartbroken.

~" *Many of us spend our whole lives trying to be somebody in the eyes of others, while feeling like nobody in our own.*"

Chapter 5

In 1979, we lived on 14th Street, the only block that still had the railroad tracks still in the streets. The summers on 14th Street were good. We would always play hide and go seek, and you know what happens when you find the girl you like. Mindy had a cousin named Stacey. Every time they would come over, my heart would skip a beat. She was short, with long hair and a pretty face. Another guy who lived down the street, named John, liked her as well. I used to hate it when she would braid his hair for him.

One day I was coming back from Day & Nite, the corner store up the street, and I could see Stacey and her little sister getting out of the car. When I saw her mother pull off, I knew that It was possible that she may stay the night, as she did sometimes. It was nice outside, everybody hanging out. I could see Stacey, Mindy, and everybody were out on the porch. My bike didn't have brakes, so I would use my feet to stop by putting it on the front tire.

Yup! I pushed so hard that the bike stopped on a dime, and I went flying, along with the bread. I was so embarrassed. Everybody laughed. I didn't come out for the rest of the day.

One day hanging out at the pool hall on 16th Street J.T. and Jr. had gotten into it, but it wasn't the first time they had words. Even though Jr. stood every bit of 6 feet and then some, J.T. was only about four foot five if that, but he had skillful hands, and everybody knew that. Jay Lewis was his boy. Jay could have played with the NBA; he was like that. No one in the neighborhood could touch him with that basketball. In fact, after his scoring that summer, a scout came from New York. All I know was they wanted him to go back to school and get his GED, and from there he would go to their camp. The summer games at World War One Recreational Center was the good ole days. I never played on any of the teams they had because I was too young, but I always hung with them: J.T., Jay, C.J., Lefty and finally Chris Lowell. They were the baddest team in the neighborhood.

On the street I lived was a vacant house where we would sit and drink beer, talk, mess around and just hang out as usual. There was this one kid named Mike Wilson. J.T. had kind of taken him under his wing. Mike never liked me. I couldn't understand because he didn't have any problem getting girls just like I didn't. One day we got into it, but he knew that he couldn't do anything with these hands. J.T. jumped in and held me. While he was holding me, Mike had broken an empty 40-ounce bottle, and before I could get loose, that chump cut me on my left upper arm. I started talking mess to J.T. for holding me while he did that. I didn't talk to J.T. for a while after that.

My sister's husband and I were close (or at least I thought so). He used to take me with him when he went to see this girl named Marci. He took me this time for her roommate named Carlotta. Other times he had taken my cousin, J.T., but she had told my brother-in-law that she didn't want to see J.T. anymore because he was ugly. On our way to their apartment we stopped by the store and bought some beer and wine. I don't remember what kind of beer, but I surely remember that "Thunder Bird." I really couldn't stand the smell of it. I would get sick, but I thought to myself, here I am with this woman, and she was looking good, at least until she smiled. I then noticed she had a tooth missing in the front. So, I asked her where the bathroom was so I could go and get my laugh on. When I returned from the bathroom, my brother-in-law was sitting at the table by himself. I asked where the girls were. He said they were in the bedroom talking. He was coaching me on what to say. This was the late 70s. I was only a teenager, and they were all in their twenties.

After playing cards for a while my brother-in-law and Marci went into the bedroom, and Carlotta asked me if I wanted to play strip poker. I said yes. After all, I had had a few beers and some Thunder Bird in me after she had mixed a pack of Kool-Aid with it. Anyway, she said the winner gets to tell the loser what the winner wants them to do. I was all for that. She got me down to my t-shirt, boxer and socks. I had her down to her panties at that time. I was ready. I told her that we don't need to play anymore. "You won, so what do you want me to do?"

She got up and said, "I'll be back."

As she walked away, I noticed she had a hole in her panties (you know I had to look at that ass). When she came back from the bathroom, she took me by the hand and led me to her bedroom. That was the first time I realized what the real thing was. She put it on me. The sex was good. That went on for a few weeks, of course, until they found out where we lived and showed up unannounced.

When they pulled up in the car, I was sitting on the porch with some neighbors of mine. At first, I thought this was cool, the girl who's been putting it on me was here, but then it occurred to me that my sister was here too. "Oh, shoot!" I jumped up and ran into the house and told my brother-in-law that Marci and Carlotta were outside.

He looked at me, his eyes as big as a 50-cent piece, and said, "You bull shitting?"

I told him, "No, for real!"

He told me go talk to them, and he was going to keep my sister in the room. I was to tell them that he wasn't here. As I headed back into the front room, I heard my mother talking to them at the door. I ran back through the house out the back door to the side of the house, and I heard my mother telling them how old I was. She told everything. My sister and her husband had it out that night!

One day after my brother-in-law got off work, he asked me to go and get him something to eat from this soul food restaurant that was five blocks away. I took my time getting back, with no special reason, but what was about to happen to me I would never have imagined in a million years. I walked in the house and he asked me where I had been and what took so long.

Before I knew it, he had slapped me. I took a step back and said "Man, why you slap me?" He looked at me and said his food was cold. I thought to myself, Chump, you go and get your own DAMN food from now on. For a long time, I didn't say anything to him.

A few days later, my cousin, J.T., and his friend, Lee-John, were in a car accident with some family members of J.T.'s girlfriend, Mindy. She had two brothers: Jon and Boo, who were cool with me.

Lee-John was the only one with some sense. He sued the insurance company. From the accident his two front teeth got knocked out. He also had a broken arm and leg. He spent two months in the hospital. When he got his money from the insurance, he bought a new car and always flashed money around. Now Lee-John moved across the street with the people who he was in the accident with, but this was unusual. The people across the street were the parents of Mindy, and Mindy was J.T.'s girlfriend. J.T. and Lee-John had been best friends for many years. In fact, Lee-John had just come up from Louisiana about eight months prior. He used to live upstairs with J.T. and his family. There were Miss Grace, Tee-Tee, Will, Patricia, Jonathan, (J.T.) Lee-John, Eli, Joy, and her two kids in a duplex on 14th Street in which my family and I lived downstairs.

After he got that money, it was like he didn't even know them anymore. A month after he got there, there were rumors that he and Mindy were sleeping together. Lee-John and J.T. had it out. After that, they were never friends again. Lee-John moved back to Shreveport, Louisiana. Money will sure change a person. That mess was crazy.

It's back to school now. My grades weren't that good, and I was still missing Miracle. They went downhill quick. I really missed her a lot … how we used to go for walks, play hide and go get it, which was a game where one of us hides and the other looks. Once they find you, they get to kiss you. Those were some good days.

There is always one girl no one wants to find. Well, I just happened to run across her one day while we were playing. I turned and immediately ran the other way! You would have thought I saw a ghost! Then everyone would come together on the front porch and she's yelling, "Ziggy, you know you saw me!"

Knowing I was lying, I said, "No, I didn't," laughing my ass off. The only way out was to say you quit, but I didn't want to because I didn't get to kiss the girl I wanted to yet. But I had to since I wouldn't kiss the other girl. So, I went into the house and got that big block of "government cheese," which made the best grilled cheese sandwiches ever.

~" Many people cannot recognize when others are being persecuted against, until it starts to happen to them."

26

Chapter 6

Before the school year had begun, we moved to 46th Street. One night we had a party, something we always did for holidays and birthdays. Some of us were in the kitchen playing cards and drinking. Suddenly, somebody said, "Frederick is coming," and he had that look that we all knew and respected. Everybody knew that when Frederick got mad, it didn't matter if you were the one who pissed him off at that time or not. Sometimes Frederick would have flashbacks, even being sober.

It started on 16th street at this little pool hall where we all hung out, and Frederick had been drinking like the rest of us. Anybody could be suspect.

Before I knew it, everybody started running. Where I sat in the kitchen there was no exit behind me, just the sink and a window along the wall. Feeling cornered, I quickly tried to talk my way out by saying anything to take his mind off this ass-whooping he was about to give me. When I realized nothing was working, I tried to make a run for it but couldn't make it. I wasn't quick enough, and the area in the kitchen was so small. I had nowhere to go. When he grabbed me, I called out for help, still trying to get away. Thanks to the spilled liquor on the floor, we started slipping and sliding all over the place. He couldn't get a good grip on me. That was the only thing that saved me.

When I finally got loose, I ran through the house and all the way through the cut to 25th Street because he was still behind me. Everybody was laughing. I would've laughed too, except it was me he got this time. Frederick is a good brother-in-law; just keep the alcohol away.

One day we were hanging out on the back porch. Todd and I got into a fight, just one of our many in life growing up as brothers. He could never beat me...ever! We ended up in the kitchen, and everybody was trying to break it up. At that time, they took him outside. But before they took him out ... when they were trying to separate us ... he stole on me. Once outside, he put his face up to the window and start tormenting me and stuck his tongue out. Before I knew it, I'd hit him through the window. I didn't even realize the window was down. My mother was furious. Yet again, she had to take me to the hospital. After the doctor finished stitching up my arm, he said that I wouldn't have much use of my right arm because I had ripped my veins and tendons, but it healed okay.

There was a guy named Mikey that lived down the street from me. We never hung together, just spoke in passing. One day we were just hanging out on the porch when all kinds of police pulled up to their house and brought Mikey out in handcuffs. After everything came down, we learned that Mikey and his boys had just robbed a store or something. One of his buddies got caught and told on everybody. Mikey's family bailed him out, but as the court date got closer, he went in his mother's bedroom, into her closet and got her .38 Special and committed suicide, shooting himself right in the head.

I had just passed his house. I thought I heard something, but I wasn't sure. I continue walking to Ivanka's house, which was just two doors on the other side of my house. She was just a friend, but she knew what I was trying to do. I was returning from the store picking up some beer and top papers. Moments later we heard police and an ambulance. That's when we walked outside. His mother, sister, and everybody just seemed to be screaming and crying. It was a dreadful day for that family. Ivanka brought that up for the rest of the day.

Yeah! Ivanka, with her high yellow self. In fact, there were a few good-looking women on that block. But there was one that I think was infatuated with me. She was very beautiful and aggressive. I found myself spending a lot of time at her house. Her mom worked the evening shift. Most of the time, it was just Ivanka and I. She had some female friends who would occasionally stop by. I didn't mind that. After all, they were all women. The only thing I regret is that I never hit it. At times it seemed like she was trying to give it to me, but she would pull back and would say something like, "You're not my man ... you can't handle this," and stuff like that. Who would have ever thought that I would never get it?

I will tell you why I missed my chance. Some friends talked me into taking my mother's car. So, I stole the keys out of her purse, and we went riding uptown, which is about six or seven miles down the road. We were just teenagers doing teenage things, like going to see teenage girls.

How would I know that this would be my unlucky night? Here I was, leaving the girl who I'd been trying to get for a while now. Instead, I was standing there talking shit with one of my school buddies, and the other three guys were talking to some girls. I was pissed off. The father of one of the girls came to the door and yelled, "If y'all don't get your ass away from my house..." Somebody yelled, "Forget you!" Boy, was that the wrong thing to do. That man came outside with a gun in his hand and fired one time in the air. I jumped in the car and yelled, "Everybody who isn't in is left!" Everybody was jumping all through the windows. I was pulling out of the lot. Everybody was laughing. Suddenly, something hit us from the back. This fool was driving backwards and bumping us, he bumped us through two lights. Finally, he ran us off the road into a ditch. It had been raining early that day. We tried everything to get the car out of that ditch. We put two by fours under the back tires and still couldn't get it to move. Mud was everywhere. Aww hell, just what I needed, state troopers were everywhere. My buddies ran all through the woods and left me.

I was arrested because I didn't have a license. When my mother found out, she was furious! They put me in juvenile hall. We went to court, and because it was my first time in trouble, the judge was willing to let me go home, but then my mother told the judge to lock me up. I couldn't believe it. The judge asked my mother if she was sure, and she said yes. All the while, I was looking at my mother trying to get her to change her mind. My mother wouldn't look at me until they were taking me out of the courtroom.

~" Nothing can be started, created, changed or finished without first having the thought to do so."

29

Chapter 7

I was transferred to The Youth for intake. During my time there were two male staff officers that worked together on the day shift in our pod, they were cool. One was good in basketball every time we went to the gym to play ball everybody tried to get him on their team. Not to call any names the other one would smoke marijuana all day. About a month later I was transferred to Kid St. learning center where I spent the next seventeen months locked up.

During my time there I went to school but kept getting in trouble; however, I did get a certificate in interior & exterior painting. There were two guys who I got along with, named Antoine and Gillian. Antoine and I were in the same Dorm F. We worked out five days a week we would do a deck of cards twice a day. Whatever you pulled that's how many you did. Face cards were 10 and jokers were 20. We were cut! Gillian was in a dorm down the hill. Gillian and I were on the football team he was the quarterback and I was the running back and punt return. I was a young kid going through the motions the thing that bothered me the most, is when the judge asked my mother did she want to move forward with this case or drop the charges and take your son home? The fact that she moved forward and allowed me to be taken away was a down point in my life. The entire time I only receive one visit and the counselor made that possible realizing why I was acting out. During the visit I was hoping she could tell me why she sent me away, the day passed, and I was still left with that question; my counselor saw the hurt in my face after that visit I lost all interest in school. The only thing I missed was playing football, but no school no football. So, my counselor worked it out so that I can go to a group home in Richmond City, Virginia. It looks like things were beginning to look up for me, or so I thought. Just about every day at the group home I had to endure constant name calling, talking behind my back, sly remarks. The racism was non-stop. One day I stood up at the dinner table and told them that today would be the last day that I would be discriminated against. As everything began to get out of hand I went all out. Flipped the dining room table and commenced to kicking asses! I was later taken to the detention center! So much for things looking up. It was about two or three days that I refused to come out of my cell as I had often did before. I'd sit and stare up at the ceiling I couldn't help but wonder back to my court day repeatedly. Asking myself "why would my mother do such a thing," who am I kidding! She has been telling me all my life "I'd never amount to anything, and how I look and act like my father" and when she looks at me she gets sick".

There was this one counselor who treated me decent. He tried talking to me to see what the problem was. He said that the only way that he could help me is to know what was bothering me. I was so embarrassed to tell him. "I found myself protecting the very person that was source the problem and this dysfunctional family of mine." After all she was my mother and I still felt the need to protect and honor her name. I was returned to The Youth intake where you go before going to Kid ST. Learning Center, and there I remained for the next six months.

After returning home from Kid St. Learning Center I went back to hanging with my crew. As usual we got back into the swing of things. We never got in trouble for big crimes, but fighting was our thing and always seemed to resurface when we were together and sometimes with each other. Although we had our share of scuffle with each other it never amounted to much until I had a run in with my boy Rabbit Gills over money. I knew it was time to take a break, so I bounced and went to stay with family in California.

When I came back to Norfolk, from Inglewood, California, that was a very long ride, considering that I didn't know what to expect. My mother was living on 40th St. and Colley Ave. My mother greeted me at the door, gave me a hug, and said she was glad I was home. At that very moment, that day in the court room came back but I quickly shook it off just happy to be home. It was nice to be home again the only thing that I didn't like about the house was that the middle room was my room. You had to go through my room to get to everything else in the house.

My oldest brother Jimmy Jr. had the room off the kitchen. At that time, my mother was taking care of him; he had fallen ill again. My youngest sister Regina was in the room with my mother. My youngest brother would come and stay sometimes, but he lived with his girlfriend and her family.

I was sitting on the porch one day and this girl walked by on her way to the store, and it kind of surprised me because our house sits back a bit from the building on the corner. As she emerged from the store I began to make sure I had my game together. As she approached, my words didn't come out the way I had practiced, but it didn't matter I got her name, number and address anyway. I called her on the phone and her mother answered and wanted to know who I was, where I was from and the whole nine yards. I'm saying to myself, "I'm not trying to get with you; I'm trying to get with your daughter." Finally, she came to the phone and a sweet voice said: hi; this is Samantha Andrews. We talked, and we talked and finally she asked me if I wanted to come down for a while. I asked her was it alright; her mom was asking a thousand questions. She laughed and said, "are you coming?" I said sure, so we spent the entire night on the porch talking. I had the chance to meet her entire family. She had a son name (Tee) which was short for Anthony he was two years old. I especially liked her youngest brother Bryant he was 12. Her older brother Bobby was in college but home for the summer. I also met her oldest sister Angela, she was there a lot but didn't live there. Angela's old man and I became good friends as well.

One day while we were at Mrs. Sissy's house were Jason lived, which was two houses from Samantha's house on the same side. we were drinking and having an enjoyable time. The guys were lifting weights to see who could lift the most, everybody had their shirts off flexing. My buddy Bryant came to the gate and told me that his sister Samantha Andrews wanted me. I told him to tell her that I'll be down in a few minutes. About an hour or so passed. Bryant came again, I said I was on my way. Moments later she came walking up the street as she past I yelled: where are you going? She said the store. I told her to bring me something back. Jason which was my nephew through marriage turned to me and said, "Chump, don't be asking my girl to bring you nothing from the store." I told him that she was my girl and she told me that the both of you were just friends. He just laughed and said we will see when she gets back. Before anyone of us could catch her, she was passing the house I called out to her as she walked towards the gate. She turned around and started walking back to me.

I thought I told you to bring me something back? She reached in her bag and pulled out a bag of chips, nothing to drink? She gave me a kiss I turned around and smile...to rub it in Jason's face. As soon as I walked back in the yard he turned around and stole on me in my face. I said what the hell is wrong with you, chump? At that point we began to rumble. They broke it up I went into the kitchen area. Lolita told me that I was wrong for messing with Jason's girl, I told her that Samantha was not Jason's girlfriend. She told me so and that she and I were dating. A whole lot of commotion broke out. Everybody was jumping on me but what hurt the most was when my mom started punching me and yelling: "I wish you were dead." My entire body went numb, I didn't feel any punches after that.

Once again, those powerful words that killed my very soul, again my mother had me arrested, as I sat in the police car, tears came to my eyes, and I said to myself; this is unbelievable! I often wonder if I was adopted I could never believe that a birth mother could have so much hatred for someone who she had given birth to. So, we go to court my mother stood in court and tried to describe the way that I hit her, I explain to the judge what happened and that I was trying to stop my mother from hitting me, and I never threw a punch at her. The judge dismissed the case.

As soon as I got home I called Samantha. She was surprised she didn't know I was out. (I had spent three weeks in jail.) I hung up the phone went out the back door, as I got to the middle of the block Jason was coming from her house," he had been messing with her while I was gone." We kind of gave each other the eye he grabbed his crotch and that really pissed me off. When I got there, I asked her what he was doing here? and we started arguing I got up to go home; but Samantha started kissing on me. Then she reminded me why I put up with her mess. The loving was good and constantly made me forget about the rest of the bull-crap. I don't know where she learned it, but she was the bomb. Finally, one day she stopped Jason from coming down. So, we continue dating. Samantha knew that I didn't have any kids, but often talked about having my baby. After that every time we had sex I would pull out she knew what I was doing, and she would get mad and here we go again arguing. I wasn't ready for any kids and surely, she didn't need another one. The way her mother used to carry on about her son if I didn't know any better I would have said her mother wanted me anyway.

Samantha's school was giving a dance. This was her last year, so she got tickets and we went. Her mom asked if we wanted her to drop us off we said no, because it was a nice night and we wanted to walk the 48th street Bridge. My reason for that was to stop by the store and get a bottle to drink. Me and my crew drunk half of the bottle walking to the dance. There were other people walking across the bridge as well doing the same thing. I had a couple of my running buddies with me Rabbit and Grant. We just knew we were fly, we had on our brand-new clothes, Chuck Taylor's with our creased Levi jeans and a Polo shirt but it wasn't complete without the Kango. My boys and I started flirting with girls at the dance I knew my girl was there, but I was feeling good after drinking. Every time she walked to the other side of the gym with her friends I was in somebody face, I knew she saw me a couple of times. When the dance was over I went to retrieve the rest of my bottle from the bushes where I placed it before going in. Just as we hit the bridge she stopped me and said she wanted to talk. I told my boys to go ahead. She started arguing about me flirting with the girls at the party. Things got out of hand her mom told me not to come to her house anymore. The next day at work the police came to my job and arrested me and charged me with a shooting. I was devastated to find out that some asshole had shot up the house. I spent three weeks in jail. Samantha's mother ended up dropping the charges in court. There was not really a case anyway I was at work when it happened. When I was released I went to my girlfriend's house, her mother was screaming I know you had something to do with it. All I could do was throw my hands up and say, "I didn't do it."

~" Most people spend more time and energy trying to improve the appearance and performance of the body which was made for destruction; rather than improving the condition of their spirit which was made to endure forever."

Chapter 8

Bobby and I worked for Complicit Carpet Company. In fact, he helped me get the job. We helped finish building, after which he became a salesperson, and I became the assistant stock manager and head delivery man. The general manager, Jim Smallwood, was real cool for a white guy back in those days. There was another guy who worked with us named Luther. Luther and I had become cool. When Tim moved down from Michigan, we helped him move his furniture into his apartment. Tim and his wife had lots of problems and had separated. She had taken their credit cards and ran them up to $20,000. Because of this, Tim drank a lot and used his bitter divorce as an excuse. There were times when I didn't think the old boy would make it, but overall, he was a good dude. Luther and I used to hang at his apartment a whole lot until Daryl came down from Michigan.

Daryl took the place of our assistant manager, Larry. Larry was a good dude but had recently gotten a divorce and was moving back to North Carolina. Daryl was not too fond of blacks. I could tell the first time I met him. After Luther, I, and couple other guys from the store helped him move in, he did something unbelievable.

He had a house warming party that I had no idea I would be paying for. When a customer comes into the store and orders carpets or rugs, if we didn't have it in stock, we would have to order it from the main store in Grand Rapids, MI. Sometimes I would go to Virginia Beach if they had what we needed. The customer would make a down payment, and after the item came in, it was my job to deliver it and take the final payment. Some days after deliveries, I could have up to $6,000 in my possession.

One morning at work the assistant manager, Daryl, told me that two hundred dollars was missing from the delivery money. I told him, "That's impossible. The customers and I counted the money together. I check my invoice, the customer seals the envelope, and I bring the money and turn it in."

Daryl told me, "Well, I don't know what to tell you, but the head office told me to tell you that they will take out $25 a week for eight weeks until it is paid, and if you agree you are to sign this garnishment sheet, but if you don't agree, then I will have to fire you."

I told him, "I'm not signing anything because I didn't take any money."

He went on to say that he would give me until the end of the day. I told him, "You don't have to wait until the end of the day. I quit." He told me that the money was still going to be taken out of my check. That's when I lost it. Stuff hit the ceiling then. The police were called. After they got there, everything was explained to them, and I was told to leave the property. I looked at Tim, the manager, and waited for his input. I couldn't believe this was happening! This guy came all the way down here to take my job from me because he wanted to have a party. Tim just stood there. I turned, got my things and left.

When Friday came around, I went to get my check. When I got my check, Tim called me to the side and said, "Let's walk to the back." He then told me that what he was about to say was to stay between the two of us. From the look he had on his face, I knew it was about the money that came up missing. He said, "Remember that house warming party? Daryl used his credit card to pay for that, and he took money out of one of the envelopes to pay for that credit card."

I stood there in disbelief with watery eyes. I asked Tim if he knew what Daryl was up to, why not say something?

He then started going on about the troubles that he was having in his life and that, for him to get involved, would be detrimental to him at that time being that he had not completed the company's probation period.

I told him, "I have been doing this for nearly a year, and no money has ever come up missing. What am I supposed to do now? I can't pay my rent and have nowhere to go."

Tim asked, "Don't you have family?"

I told him that my mom and I didn't get along, and there were no other relatives living here, and besides what does that have to do with what he did? He told me to give him a call in a couple of weeks, and he would see what he could do for me. I told him that I had thought that we were friends. He said we were, but he couldn't get involved at the time. I walked off. I walked home that day, which was about two miles. I didn't want anybody to see the tears coming down my face.

That night my cousin, Lisa, had a party, which they normally did. Lisa used to solicit guys out of money back home, but I guess you would call it prostituting.

One day her ex-boyfriend/pimp showed up at her house. His name was Jay-boy, one of the blackest chumps you ever wanted to see. Run across that chump in a dark alley, and he would scare you with those yellow teeth, red lips and bloodshot eyes from drinking all the time. Now that Jay-boy was there, she was back to her old tricks. The only difference was that she was not standing on the corner. She was tricking the older guys in the neighborhood. I didn't really like Jay-boy even though he and my brother Todd got along well.

That night, Jay-boy and I had gotten into a fight. I had just left Samantha's house where we'd had an argument. The police were called. As the officer was walking me back to his car, he was reading me my rights. I told him, "I'm not going to jail tonight." Then I knocked him down and started running. I could hear everybody behind me yelling, "Run! Run!" I was running like hell. The next day I went over to Lisa's house, and she told me that she had to jump in front of the police when he drew his gun. She said you couldn't see nothing but my two-tone Stacy Adams kicking it as I ran across the field. I was sharp that night with my pinstriped suit and black and gray Stacy Adams. I looked out for the police all that night. Lisa told me that when the police asked where I lived, everyone said that they didn't know me. I was just someone from the neighborhood. I was very surprised.

Jay-boy and I got in to it again, only this time my nephew, Jason, beat me to the punch and tore into him. Jay-boy used to jump on Lisa all the time, and Jason and I would defend her. Jay-boy finally got tired of the ass whippings that we were putting on him and moved back to Louisiana.

I got another job driving a firewood truck. My mother and the other families had moved to Ohio, so I moved in with Lisa until I could get my own place. Samantha and I had parted. Let me tell you how that happened.

I used to stop by for lunch whenever I was in the area. On this day,

I walked in the house to find the woman I loved sitting at the table with another man. So, her mother immediately got up from the sofa and told me if I started any trouble that she was going to call the police. That was the last thing I needed. So, I quietly turned and walked out of the house, but before I left, I asked for my money that she used to hold for me. When she returned, I asked why. She had nothing to say. I knew it was her mother's doing. Her mother thought it would be better if she dated him because he was in the military. She met him through her friend who was also dating a guy in the military, so her mother was all for that. Anything to get me out of the way.

One night while hanging on the Ave. with my crew at the corner store, I saw a nice-looking girl named Vanessa Carlton. Every time I saw her after that night, I would tease her about her knock knees and tell her how pretty she was. It wasn't long before we start dating. She had a nice body, light brown eyes and those knock knees that I liked. I remember the first night I went to her apartment, her mother, Miss Eley, answered the door and said, "What do you want, negro?" I thought about it for a minute then I asked if Vanessa lived there? At that time, Vanessa appeared at the door and asked me in. I asked if she was sure? She just giggled and asked me to come in. She told me her mother is like that with everybody. I asked if that was supposed to make me feel better.

Vanessa had two boys: Eric and J.D. They were good little boys. So, we dated for a good while. The loving was good. I swear, every time I left that apartment I know I shed four or five pounds. Not from the sex alone; her mother would have it so hot in that apartment, at times I thought I would die. Eventually, Vanessa and I finally moved into our own apartment.

I was still driving the firewood truck. One night after work I tried to open the door with my key, but the safety chain was on the door and I could hear people laughing, talking…the music was playing, so I left the door and walked to the window. As I peeped through the window, I could see people sitting around having a good ole time. Just one problem with this picture: This was my apartment, and I don't remember giving anybody permission for any gathering. At that moment, one of the guys noticed me looking through the window. He got off the sofa, walked over and yelled: "Can't you see we're having a party, negro." Then he pulled the shade down on me. Somebody lost their mind. I don't know what they were thinking. It was already dark, so I looked around and reached down in my book bag and pulled my pistol out and fired four shots through the window. Everybody started running out the back door like bats out of hell. I ran around to the back door and walked in. One guy was lying on the floor. He couldn't run because he had a cast on his leg, so I walked over and kicked him real hard. He yelled, and I kicked him again and told him if he was here when I come back downstairs, I was going to bust a cap in his ass.

He jumped up, grabbed his crutches, and hopped out that back door. I went upstairs and tried the bathroom door. It was locked. I yelled for Vanessa to open the door. Nothing happened.

I kicked the door open, and her best friend, Juanita, was on the toilet. I told her, "Stop faking. You not using the toilet. You better get up before I smack you with this pistol, and get out my apartment." I knew this was all her idea. As I walked toward the tub to pull the curtain, Juanita ran out. I pulled the shower curtain. Another girl was hiding in the shower. She started screaming and hollering. I told her to calm down, that everything was okay. I proceeded to the bedroom, as I opened the closet door, Vanessa was trying to hide underneath a bunch of clothing she had snatched from the rack. I pulled her out of the closet, and before we could get started, the police pulled up outside. I told her to get rid of them, not to say anything about me, and that I'd be back. I ran downstairs and out the back door. I ran two blocks down the street to my friend Camila's house (Miracle 's cousin) where I stayed the night. The next day I went to the apartment, and Vanessa wasn't there, so I fixed something to eat and then went upstairs and packed some of my things because I didn't know what to expect once she got home. She returned home that evening. When she walked through the door she immediately asked me if I was angry, and if it was safe to come in I said sure. She had Juanita with her with that puppy dog look on her face. I told them they could stop looking at each other, and they started laughing. They began to talk about last night. They said I was crazy, but I never had that problem again.

We were told we had to move a couple of weeks later. We moved a couple of blocks down the street. I don't know how it happened, but Juanita ended up living with us. Vanessa and I had our bedroom, and Eric and J.D. shared a room. It was only a two-bedroom house. Juanita slept in the living room. Occasionally, When I came home from work, there would be some guy there to see her.

One night when I got home, Juanita was having sex in my living room. I asked her what the hell she was doing. We then started arguing. I asked the dude to leave, and he left. Then Vanessa came downstairs, and three of us were just arguing. Vanessa took Juanita's side. Things were not getting any better. Ever since her friend moved in with us, things just start to deteriorate, so I decided that it was time to leave.

Deciding to leave town, I put in my two weeks' notice. One day I parked down the block just to see what was really going on. As Vanessa and Juanita left the house, I proceeded behind them. As I got closer, I realized that Vanessa was wearing those house shorts that I liked so much. They were house shorts because everything hung out. I pulled to the side of the road and called Vanessa. She was surprised to see me. I told her to get in the truck. As she was getting in, Juanita was getting in the back. I told her she could walk home. When we got home, I told Vanessa to sit down on the sofa. We had a conversation about the way things were going. She just seemed to be nonchalant about it.

The next day I pretended to leave for work. After they left the house, I went and backpacked my things, left her a note, and hit the highway.

I got a bus to Cincinnati, Ohio and headed to my mother's.

~" It is an exercise in futility to ponder the alternative and mourn over a life that could have been if only one had sided on a different course of action in event of the past."

Chapter 9

During the ride, I thought about the day my sister's youngest son, at the time, had died of crib death. See, the day he died my mother had gone up the street to my sister's apartment. Moments later she came running out with the baby in her arms yelling and screaming that my sister had killed her baby. After the paramedics took the baby, my mother was screaming and yelling at the top of her lungs. The police told me to try to calm her down. As I tried to hug and console her, she yelled that if I didn't turn her loose, that she would hold it against me for the rest of my life. I started to wonder if I was making the right choice. Could I live with her once again when I got there, knowing our previous relationship?

Once I got there, I made a phone call and learned that my mother was living in Cincinnati, Ohio, which is right across the bridge from Guilford, West Virginia. I had to sleep in the living room. My mother, my sister, and my oldest brother weren't doing too well. He had revisited that bad trip he had in New Jersey. For the past two years he had been making these very annoying noises. My mom had to feed him, cloth him, bathe him and take him to the bathroom. Seeing him like this made me know that drugs, especially angel dust, doesn't discriminate and is a friend to no one. My brother hasn't been the same since.

Our neighbors that lived two doors down across the hall were Lashunta and her husband, Ge-Ge. He was from Nigeria. They had a son named Alpheus and a daughter name Annette. Annette was about two years old. Annette used to come to our apartment most mornings and wake me up. She was my little buddy, so my mother would always open the door and let her in. From the first time I met her, we were cool ever since.

Moments later, Lashunta would come knocking on the door asking if Annette was here. She would come in with that see-through nightgown on every time, knowing I could see. I knew she wanted to get with me. She would let Annette out knowing that she was coming to our apartment. I'd been there for about two months, and Lashunta had made it known that she liked me.

Sometimes she would be just a foot from standing over the top of me with that see-through gown on. Ge-Ge attended Charlotte University and would work part-time, so he was gone a lot. She had inquired about me to my sister off the back, but they lived too close for me to mess with her. Besides, my mom and older sister had asked me not to. We only messed around once because I later found out that she was younger than she told me.

Even Lashunta's mother, Margaery, was trying to get with me. She had a nice van with a bed in it. One night we were out in the parking lot in her van. She started talking dirty and telling me what she would like to do to me. I wanted to knock her off, but she was still married, and I'd heard that he was crazy. Whenever she would come around, she would always bring pizza and beer. So, every time she came around I would just eat and have no sexual contact with her. Finally, she stopped coming around for me when she realized that I was not going to sleep with her. I may do a lot of things, but sleeping with a married woman is not one.

I needed a car, and I was still getting unemployment checks, so I bought a Maverick for two hundred dollars. If you wanted to go anywhere there, you had to have a car. Everybody would laugh and joke about my car. After driving about two miles, I would have to pull over and let it cool off and put water in the radiator, which had a hole in it. I put sealant in it that only worked for two days. Come to find out, that joint had two more holes in it.

My sister, Celes, and her husband were living on Ninth Avenue in Guilford, West Virginia. She had attended Charlotte University. I got tired of hanging out over there with them, especially after Jason and I got into a big fight behind Lolita. I know that they spread rumors that my family had a disease to prevent me from sleeping with girls in their families.

That same day Jason came down to our apartment. My sister and her husband were also present. We got into a fight. When he was getting the best of me, no one tried to break it up. Once I got myself positioned right, suddenly I got strength from nowhere and just picked his ass up and slammed him real hard on the floor. I got on top of him and started drilling. My sister's husband jumped in and pulled me off him. My sister then started screaming, "Let him go, Dante! Let him go!"

"You didn't jump in it when Jason had the best of him!" my mother was screaming.

Jason was supposed to be the big bad ass of their family, but I got that ass that day.

That night I left my mother's apartment and start hanging out in Guilford, West Virginia. I had been living in Guilford for a while before my mother moved there, as well as the other families, too. Initially, I had told my mother about Guilford, WV, and suggested that she move across the bridge. At the time, I suggested it to her, I wasn't expecting her to take the idea back to the other families. I was trying to get away from them. That was the purpose of me getting my mother to move. However, my worst fears came true; they moved as well.

I met several girls that were cool, but two I liked: Christy and Darcy. Both were fine as all outdoors! Darcy was bow legged. She was also dating Don Richardson. So, I started dating Christy. She had three sisters, Maliana Bmore, Maria Bmore, and three brothers, Antonio, Earl and Kirk (better known as "Dolo").

The first time I found out how old she really was when her brother, Kirk, approached me at Club Repro. He got out of his car, took his shirt off, and said, "I'm going to kick your ass, chump." I started laughing and asked him what the problem was. At this time, her other brother, Earl, pulled up and got out of his car. Kirk and I had squared off by that time. Earl came up behind me, and I started backing up to keep both in front of me. I kept telling them, "If you want to fight, I'll take one at a time." People hanging outside the club started yelling, "Fight him one-on-one!" So, Earl and I fought heads up. I whooped his ass. After that, Dolo didn't want any, so they left, and I went home.

The next day Christy came over to my house, and I told her that I didn't think we should be together. So, I drove her home, and I told her that I was not going to be fighting her brothers every time I turned around. I told her that she lied to me about her age. She got out of the truck, I drove off.

When I got home that night, my roommate, Shawn, told me someone was in my bedroom waiting for me. I looked; it was Christy. I closed the door and went back to the living room.

Shawn and I shared an apartment that belonged to his half-sister. Although she charged him rent, she would take me in another room and would act like I was paying her, but she would never take any money from me because she liked me. The money Shawn gave her paid the rent anyway.

She never stayed there. She lived with this older guy. There were times she would come by and try to get me to go to bed with her. As bad as I wanted to, the guy she was dating was very well known. It would have been crazy if I did because sometimes he would come by with her when she came to check on the place. Then I'd go out and have a conversation with him. He wasn't a bad guy.

Every time they left she would always give me that look and move her lips as to say: *I'm going to get that*, but when she was by herself, she'd always hug and kiss me. That's why I started coming outside when he was with her. If I were there, she would always feel on me. We were the same age.

Shawn was working at Ratio Burger's. Usually, he would bring food home from work. I didn't have a job. I made my money by driving to Chandler every Friday and Saturday. I used to charge the guys in job core twenty dollars a head, round trip. I used to get six to eight, which sometimes would average around a hundred and sixty dollars. That was good because I had somewhere to go and eat and live rent free. That night I made it a point to make Christy's mother aware that she kept coming to my apartment on her own accord.

We got in my truck and drove to her house. As she went up to the door, her niece, Tracie, answered. I asked if Ms. Lorraine was home. She went to get her grandmother while I was trying to get Christy out of my truck. Ms. Lorraine came to the door, and we talked. I explained that I wasn't aware of her age. I told Ms. Lorraine that every time I brought her home, she'd just come right back. Ms. Lorraine told me that she had heard of it, and she appreciated me coming by and talking to her. She told me that she couldn't stop her, so she gave me permission to date her. So, I told her I would have her home before late.

When we got down the block she jumped me, kissing me, telling me how much she loved me and that she was going to stay the night. I told her, "I think not." I am going to take you home like I told your momma.

When we got back to the apartment, Shawn had a white girl who worked with him there. Shawn was one of those guys that didn't have a girlfriend; he wasn't banging anything in the neighborhood. And I don't think he knew how to talk to women. Anyway, they had drinks. We played cards and talked until it was late.

The white girl was saying that it was time for her to leave. I was trying to tell Shawn, "This your que, man." The girl was giving him all the signs in the world the whole time we were playing cards. I was helping him out by saying trivial things. She was with it, but boy, he dropped the ball.

Finally, she said that it was time for her to leave. When She left, I started messing with Shawn. He was my guy, but he really dropped the ball that time.

Christy went into my bedroom. I asked her if she was ready to go home. She said, "I'm not going home tonight."

I told her, "Yes, you are. I told your mother I would bring you home, and that's what I'm going to do."

She said, "Not before you sleep with me."

I delighted her, then took her home. After that night, she started staying over a lot.

I like keeping my room dark when I sleep. I'm a very light sleeper. One night while sleeping, something woke me up, and I felt something on my leg. I raised my head, and I saw something under the cover coming towards me. I snatched the cover off, and it was Shawn. I said, "Man, what the hell are you doing?"

He said, "Oh! Oh! Oh! I thought you said any girls you bring here, if I could get 'em, it was alright with you."

I said, "Not this one; this is my girl."

He said "Oh! Oh! Man, I didn't do anything. I was just going to eat her out." By that time, Christy was kicking the man in the face and started screaming. They got into it bad. Even though it was late, and I was tired, I got up and took her home.

One day hanging out at the boy's club playing basketball, Smoky and I had gotten into an argument. C.J. Copeland jumped in the fight to help Smoky. This is the second time that C.J. put his self into one of my altercations. He didn't like me because I was knocking off a couple of his cute cousins, and when I stopped coming around, the light skinned one took it hard like many others in the neighborhood. I wasn't trying to be locked down by anybody. I just had that effect on women. I tried everything I could to shake Christy. She just wasn't having it. I told her from the beginning that I was not looking for a girlfriend. You know how they do? Say okay, but all the time in their mind you're in a committed relationship. I was young and handsome. I had that rap game, and I was new in town.

Before everybody moved over on this side, it was okay for me with the women, but once they started that rumor thing, it seemed to go astray.

Since I'd been living over here for some time now, well before they came, some people listened, and some paid them no mind. And I know that's the only reason I was safe from their evil intent.

One day we were playing basketball, and I got in a fight with black Smokey, so that ended that game. The altercation went all the way out into the parking lot. I ended up getting jumped. They didn't like the idea of a new guy in town getting lots of rhythm. I see how women could be trouble no matter how you look at it. I was so upset by the fact of being jumped, even though I didn't lose. I would get jumped because no one there could beat me fighting, and I'd had plenty of fights in Guilford.

I sat in my truck two blocks from the apartment complex where the guys I was fighting lived, and then I just started driving through the complex recklessly. People were screaming, "Stop, your crazy mf. There are children out here." Before I knew it, it look like the whole police force was out there. Somebody was screaming, "Lock that crazy mf up." I was arrested and charged with reckless driving and dangerous use of a vehicle.

Maria or Maliana would bring Christy to visit me in jail. Being there was more whites than blacks, the whites tried to run the jail.

The first guy I got into it with was back on a writ for murder, already been down five years.

Whenever their block had recreation time with ours, that redneck always had something to say that was racist, so one day I told him that he had everybody here fooled thinking he was like that, but he wasn't, and we can find out whenever he was ready.

I used to hit the weights on the yard. That day I had a feeling he was going to try something, so I kept my eyes on him and just like I thought, he did.

He and this other guy started throwing a football to each other. When the guy threw it back, he threw it in my direction. As he got closer, I jumped up, went underneath him, picked his ass up, and slammed him real hard on the concrete, While I commenced to kicking his ass, the deputy pulled his gun (remember, this is Guilford, West Virginia). I hit the ground.

About two days later he got this guy named L.A., another redneck in my block, to jump me. We got to fighting, and I beat the brakes off that chump. They moved him to another block.

After a couple of encounters, I was well-respected in the jail. That's when Vance and I got real tight. Vance was a white guy who was also well-known and respected in the jail. We had become such good friends to the point when my sister came to visit me, she would go and pick up his wife. His wife was pregnant, and that's how he got his marijuana in, which my sister never knew about. From there, we ran things until I was released.

Friday, November 27th, the sheriff came and got me from my block. I asked where he was taking me. He said they need me in court.

As I entered the courtroom, I saw my lawyer. She was fine for a white woman. She turned to me, smiling. Right then and there I knew it had to be something good. But then I thought to myself, *My court date isn't for another two months.* As I stood beside my lawyer, the judge asked me to state my name for the record. He asked me if I could stay out of trouble.

Of course, I said, "Yes."

He said, "Merry Xmas. The charges are dismissed." I thanked the judge and my lawyer.

The more answers we find to the mystery and purpose to our lives, the more questions we are left with.

Chapter 10

I was released from jail. I walked from downtown to the hood. As I got to the Boys Club, it seems like everybody was hanging out. It was unbelievable how everyone embraced me. Little-Cee was about five hundred pounds. I don't know where they got the name "Little-Cee" from, but everybody liked him. He was a good dude, but I think they liked him mainly because he always supplied the drinks. He was one of the few people who worked at the Loading Plant, which was the best job going. He and I had become close after that. See, before going to jail, some thought I was undercover because I just showed up one day. I don't know where that came from.

Little-Cee fixed me a drink. Up the street I could see Christy running towards me. She jumped in my arms, kissing and telling me how happy she was to see me. Little-Cee gave me the keys to his van and told me that I can have it for the night. I grabbed some beers and filled my cup up with some liquor. Christy and I hung out the whole night. The van was equipped with everything, including a bed. From that day on, Little-Cee had given me the nickname, Ziggy Cop.

A few months later, one of Christy' s friends, named Elaine, had met Tyrone Hopper. The Hoppers had come down from Carolina. The oldest one, Jake, was working for the railroad. That's how they ended up in West Virginia. Tyrone and I became best of friends. Every weekend we would all do something together.

By this time my, mother had moved to Guilford, W.V. from Cincinnati, OH. She moved into a three-bedroom brick house on Churchland Ave. I moved in with her and my little sister, Regina.

It had a beautiful view of Charlotte University's football stadium because it was right across the street from our house. This girl I knew that was going to Charlotte University told me that the car she was driving that day was her father's, and he was selling it. It was tight; I just didn't have the money right then. I told her to give me some time, and let me see what I could do. She agreed.

I wanted that car. A man should always have wheels. I convinced my mother to buy the car because I didn't want anyone else to get it.

Soon after, I got a job at the Martin Hotel on the ave. I got that job the same way I got the job at Complicit Carpet Company. I got a job with the contractor when they were building the hotel. Once we finished, everybody who wanted a job there, just filled out an application. I got a job in housekeeping as the stock man.

After working there for a year, this young white kid was hired. I had no idea I was training this guy to take my job. Had I known, I wouldn't have trained him. Not only that, my mother and I would drop him off at home after work because he lived three blocks from us. I was laid off, so I just got unemployment for a while.

I bought that car from my mother for two hundred dollars. It was a seventy-four custom Nova with crushed velvet bucket seats. It was tan on the outside and maroon on the inside. This was my pride and joy.

During our relationship, Christy and I started to have problems. That's when I met Gloria. Three months after I met Gloria, she told me that she was pregnant. I was kind of upset. I wasn't ready to be a father. I had taken all precautions not to impregnate any woman that I had gotten involved with. Come to find out, Gloria had purposely gotten pregnant because she and Christy were in competition for me. Gloria's mother, Julie King, had sent word that she wanted to see me. I didn't know how she was going to react about the situation, so I went to Little-Cee's house to get Stick because Stick was Julie King's boyfriend and the driver for little-Cee whenever he got to drinking, which was pretty much all the time.

Once I entered Little-Cee's house, Stick stared laughing and said, "Julie King is going to kill you." I told him that was why I had come to see him.

When we got there, Julie King told me that I had broken my promise to her. Before we slept together, Gloria had promised to keep up with her pills. I told her that Gloria had led me to believe that she was keeping up her pills too and was doing everything necessary to prevent from getting pregnant. Julie King asked me if I was going to be in the child's life. "I said, "Of course."

Not long after, Gloria and I parted, but we remained good friends. Christy and I started messing around for about three weeks again. Not long after that, Christy told me that she was pregnant. Now Ms. Lorraine had known me for a couple of years. She really laid it on me and told me that her mother (Granny) wanted to see me. Although Miss Lorraine laid it on thick and really got on my case, Granny didn't lay it on me that hard because we were close, and I used to spend a lot of time at her house, especially on Sundays when she cooked that big meal. Boy, was that good eating.

Christy had some family that moved to Guilford from Louisiana. She had a cousin named Charlene that was so fine that everyone wanted to get with her, including myself. After getting familiar with her every chance I could, I would flirt with her. She was flattered, and like any woman, would enjoy getting attention from a man.

It was a beautiful summer night, and we were all hanging out like we usually did in Rotary Complex where they lived. It was getting late, and everyone was going in. Christy lived in the first row of houses when you come into the complex. She didn't hang out with us much because she was pregnant. Out of the blue, Charlene walks up to me, grabs me by my shirt and says, "You've been trying to get with me since I been here. Well, this is your chance."

As we walked toward their apartment, I stopped and said, "I can't do this."

She turned to me and said, "After all this time and the flirting you've been doing, I decided to give it to you, and now you don't want it?"

I told her that I wanted to, but if I did, things between her family and me would never be the same.

After that, she just shunned me. Every time we came across each other she would give me that look that said, "I'm mad at you until you come and get this, bad ass wanna-be."

Although I wanted Charlene, I couldn't bear to put Christy through it again. Reflecting on the first time I met Christy, I also met her aunt Nita at Club Repro, and for about a week or so, I was talking to both.

The following Sunday, Jackie invited me over for dinner. I was watching

TV while she was in the kitchen preparing dinner. I was not ready for what happened next. Somebody was knocking at the door, and in walked Christy. She looked at me, and I looked at her in shock. She asked me what I was doing at her aunt's house. I didn't know what to say. I just held my hands out with my palms up. I don't know if I was glad when Jackie came from the kitchen or not. I didn't know what to do. Jackie came from the kitchen and asked what was going on. I stood up and told them that I didn't know that they were family. And I said Jackie and I were just friends, and she invited me over for dinner.

Christy said, "Friends? Yeah right!"

Jackie said, "That's my niece."

I said, "Oh, shoot!"

As the three of us began talking, I was asked to make a choice. Being undecided, I walked out. But you see who I ended up with.

"One never sees the path of life they have walked in the past more clearly than when they come face to face with the prospect of losing it."

Chapter 11

Buggy's Club on 2nd Avenue and 20th Street was another club in the hood that I used to hang out at. In fact, when Buggy was renovating the building, I got a job working with him. It was a nice club.

One Friday night, Fannie, her sister, Latrina, and a female friend of hers were hanging out at the club. Fannie and I worked at the Martin Hotel on the Ave together. I used to flirt with her to the point that she would flirt back. Fannie was what you would call a stallion because of how good she looked. She was top of the line.

As she entered the club, I was taken by surprise because I had never seen her out. She was married but was separated to a guy named Smokey. I was familiar with him, but we were not friends. He used to come to the boy's club and play basketball with us sometimes. When she spotted me, she smiled, and I smiled back. She leaned over and said something to Latrina, and then they walked over to my table. We spoke, and they asked if they could sit with me. I said, "Sure."

As the night passed, we had some drinks, danced, talked and laughed. We were having an enjoyable time. The whole time I was thinking only two things that could go wrong that night. Either Smokey or Christy could walk through that door. I remind you, this club was right in the hood! I eliminated Smokey because he worked the night shift, 11-7, at the Loading Plant.

As the night began to wind down, my best friend, Tyrone, sent a mutual friend of ours in to warn me that whatever I did, not to walk out of the club with that woman. I ignored that since Fannie and I had never been together the whole time I'd known her, even with the flirting the nine months we worked together. I had always told her that I didn't sleep with married women. That's when she began telling me about herself. I learned that even though she still lived in the same house with her husband, it was nothing else but for the children. I told her that very well may be, but there are some things I won't do, and that's one of them. She went on about how she was saving money to move out. I told her whenever that happened, then maybe we could hook up if everything was final. During our conversation, she told me that she had a house on the west end, and things between her and Smokey were over. She had been living there for the past two months. The boys mostly stay with their father because of their little friends in the neighborhood. We were dancing to a slow song when she told me tonight was the night and invited me to her house.

Fannie stood six feet tall with a butt you could sit a cup on. She had a set of C cups that didn't sag for a woman who had two children. Her hair just passed her shoulders, long legs, perfect lips, big dark eyes, brown skin and a smile that was sure to send butterflies through any man's stomach.

As we proceeded to exit the club, I noticed Earl standing by the door. There was no way that I could avoid him. So, I said, "What's up, man?

He just smiled and looked up at me. Once outside, I see Christy, Kirk and some girl friends of hers. I knew there would be trouble. Christy and I were off and on during our relationship. Currently, we were not together.

I continued to walk the ladies to their car. Before I knew it, Fannie hugged me and said, "I'll be waiting." They pulled off as I proceeded to my car. Christy and her brothers prevented me from getting in my car. She was screaming and yelling obscenities. I was everything in the book, except a saint.

I told her brothers that this was getting old. I asked who was first as they both squared off with me. I threw up my guard, and we are going around and around. Suddenly Aron showed up. He's the oldest brother. He told them to stop and that it didn't make any since that every time Christy and I got into it they found it necessary to fight me. By this time Christy had slashed one of my tires. Instead of fixing the tire, I got Little-Cee to drop me off. Little-Cee was in the club that night as well. He saw me talking to Fannie all night.

Little-Cee and Smokey both worked at the plant. He started interrogating me, so I told him where he was taking me. He stopped in the middle of the street and started laughing so hard, he passed gas and told me that I was living a dangerous life. He said Smokey was going to kill me. I told him that they were separated. He just kept laughing and said, "Smokey don't care about that." Little-Cee was laughing his butt off.

I told him, "Just make sure you answer the phone when I call." With everything that took place, by the time I got to Fannie's house, it was 4:40 a.m.

As I walked up the steps on the porch, the door opened, and I stood there for a second looking at her. She had on a shirt that if she slightly lifted her arm, it would have revealed her private parts. She told me to come in and have a seat. Then she offered me a soft drink. We talked for a few while listening to some slow music. She got in my lap and started kissing me. Then she led me to her bedroom. I looked up at the clock; it was 5:05 a.m. She took her shirt off, and her body was everything I imagined it would be. She stood there smiling. Her body was beautiful. All I could say was, "Teach me how to love you!"

She started laughing.

The next time we came up for air it was 6:25 a.m. We had been going at it for the last hour or so, and I was trying to get the last one before I left, but it was getting to be daylight and close to time for Smokey to get off work. Although they were separated and lived in separate houses, Smokey would still show up unannounced, so I stopped, got up, and asked her for a wash cloth.

She asked why I was leaving. I told her she knew Smokey would be there any minute now. She said this was her house, and Smokey didn't live there. "I thought Ziggy don't run from anybody."

I told her, "Ziggy don't run from anyone, but I'm not stupid."

She asked, "Why are you putting on your clothes?"

I looked at her, and we both laughed. I walked over to the other side of the bed, reached out for her, and she took my hand. I held her beautiful naked body next to mine while considering those deep dark eyes and her beautiful smile. I said, "I'm not running; I'm just avoiding another fight, and you need to get your divorce. I know you are not living together, but the divorce is better."

I called Little-Cee and got no answer. I told Fannie to have a cab meet me a few blocks down the street.

The whole time Fannie was still laughing. She walked me to the door; we kissed, and I told her I would see her later.

As I proceeded down the street, I thought of three ways you can leave a woman after sleeping with her: 1. dissatisfied, 2. rocked to sleep, or 3. with a smile on her face. Due to the small town and how women talk, I was getting so much play. I held the reputation for the last two on lock.

I continued to walk. I had gotten about four blocks, and someone blew the horn. I looked, and it was Smokey. "You don't have to blow; I see you out the corner of my eyes." I knew he did that to let me know he saw me.

I said to myself, *Oh, what the hell.*

I got home and changed the tire on my car. I must have slept all day. My mom woke me up yelling, "Boy! That girl is at the door!"

I didn't know who she was talking about, but I surely hoped it wasn't Christy. That's who it was; she was raising hell. I told her what she did last night was wrong and that we were not together. The only time she did this is when she saw me talking to somebody else. I could just be talking to a girl, and she'd want to fight her. We're apart only when it benefits her, and it must stop.

Now she wanted to fight about me keeping our son, Mario. I never had any problem keeping our son; it's just that every time I kept him, she didn't know how to come back.

The following Tuesday we were all hanging out at the boy's club as usual, and here comes Smokey. He was yelling, telling me to stay away from his wife. I told him, "She's not your wife!"

So, he went into his truck and pulled out his bat. I told him if he came at me with the bat, I was going to defend myself, and if I took it from him, I just might use it. Little-Cee intervened and told us to cut that stuff out. He told Smokey that I wouldn't mess with her again. I said, "You got that man."

"You are free to choose your own illusion of life, create your own sense of reality and live your life as you see fit, but a single experience of the truth can shatter it all."

Chapter 12

Saturday night, me, my sister, Celes, Lashunta, Tonya, Mitchell, Marvin, and some friends of my sister went out to a club named Bobby's, downtown. One of the girls who was with my sister kept flirting with me. My sister noticed it and told me, "Don't mess with her."

I asked her, "Why? Because she's white?" (I know my sister isn't a racist.)

She said, "Why would you say something like that? What does white have to do with it? She's my friend, and I don't want you messing up our friendship, and besides, she has a boyfriend."

I said, "What? She told me they aren't together." I told her not to worry.

Later, that night after the club closed, I doubled back to the girl's house like we'd planned it. I went to the kitchen door where she was waiting. She took me to the living room and we had sex on the floor. After I finished, we talked a little, and I told her that it was getting day and it was time for my getaway. We both laughed. She started asking for more. I told her that it was getting light out, and we didn't want anybody to see me leaving her house. She continued to try to convince me to stay, and I was thinking to myself, *This woman has lost her mind.* I told her that I'd see her next weekend.

I used to go over to my sister's house almost every day. This week when I went, she was very upset with me and told me not to say anything to her. The girl had told my sister that we had slept together. It's wasn't the first time my sister had gotten mad at me for messing with her friends and probably wouldn't be the last. She didn't stay mad too long. When I left, she gave me a hug.

The girl who lived upstairs from my sister started dating my nephew, Jason. Tina was her name. She was a white girl with an ass like a sister. She also had a sister that I tried to get with whenever I was at my sister's, and she's visiting Tina, but I'm glad I didn't. I had the opportunity to meet her mother before sleeping with her.

You see, the way she talked about Jason, I really thought she was racist. She claimed she wasn't; she just didn't think that Jason was good enough for her daughter. I thought to myself, *Hell, I already have enough drama in my life*, so I passed that one up.

It was this other white girl named Charlene that lived around the corner. Charlene was beautiful. She and my sister, Celes, went to the same college. Charlene was in her last year of college. I used to flirt with her all the time. Charlene was a white girl. Her hair came down to her butt. I used to try all the time. Finally, she invited me to her house. I met her mother and her little sister. They were very nice people.

One night while at Charlene's house, we were standing on her porch. She turned and walked to me and said with that soft voice I loved of hers that she really, really liked me, and if I could promise her that I would be hers and only hers that she was ready to lose her virginity to me. At that very moment I thought about someone else other than myself. I was honest with her about my so-called relationship with Christy. I told her that her mother and sister were good people. Every time I came over they made me feel welcome, and I really didn't want to hurt her.

She grabbed my face with both hands and thanked me for being honest with her and told me, "Whenever you feel that you can live with just having one woman, then come see me, but I won't wait forever."

We sat and talked all night. I knew that we were not going to be together. I wasn't ready to be tied down. In fact, I tried get Christy to see that, but she wouldn't go anywhere. So, from that point on, Charlene didn't come around my sister's that much. When I did see her, we would talk a little. I could see the hurt in her face. For months I was telling her all the things that I thought she wanted to hear to get her to sleep with me (not to say she was easy), but it was easy for me because of her beauty. I could be honest. Everything about her made it that easy. I really liked her. That's why I couldn't do that to her. I asked what her mother said. She looked at me laughing and said, "love and hate."

I said, "Love and hate? what that mean?"

Her mother loves me for being honest but hates me for breaking her daughter's heart. We both laughed. I gave her a hug like we always did when we saw each other and said goodbye.

My childhood sweetheart, Sheila Johnson, came down from New Jersey. Just like my sister and her brother got married, as kids we made the same plans, but that was stolen from me.

We all went out to Toss Up, another neighborhood club. Sheila and I were on the dance floor dancing to a song called the Freak. Christy came into the club and called me off the dance floor. I walked over to see what she wanted, and she started asking me who Sheila was. I told her she was family, and she was Dante's sister, just got in town and we were just hanging out. She said, "Do you expect me to believe that stuff?"

I told her that she mad life harder than it must be. She gave me the finger, turned and walked off. I said, "Alright, later."

We went out back to smoke a joint, which I didn't particularly care for because marijuana always made me sleepy. As we were standing there, Christy's brothers, Kirk and Earl, bum rushed me. We fought hard, and I still whipped both of 'em.

I told the guys I was tired of fighting every time she didn't get her way. There was always a fight.

During all the commotion, I didn't know that Christy had hit Sheila in the head with a brick. As I approached Sheila, people were screaming, "She's bleeding!" That's when I realized the blood was coming from her head. I asked her what happened, and she said that Christy hit her in the head with a brick. Sheila was laughing the whole time. I hope she didn't suffer any severe harm. Now the whole family wanted to fight Christy' s family. I'm so glad that Sheila said it was okay because no one was listening to me.

We took her to the hospital, and afterward, we spent the night together. Within weeks her husband Johnny Spudwell had come to West Virginia to plead for her to come back home. He put the word out that he wanted to speak to me. Sheila was staying with her mother, Miss Sissy, so I went over to see what he wanted. He tried threatening me with bodily harm if I didn't leave his wife alone. I laughed and told him that he was not talking to that little boy we once knew. I said, "Besides, she was mine before she was yours anyway, and we both know how you ended up with her."

He laughed and said, "You were a little boy. Yes, I know I was twelve she was two years older than me. So that would have made her fourteen. How old were you at that time? Isn't it true that you were twenty-nine or thirty? You see, I didn't have to pay her aunt to steal her innocence. See, when you did that, you destroyed all the plans and promises we made to each other. I told him that true love is something that you can't buy. Back during that time, she was young and innocent. There were people influencing her to be with you for their own personal gain. Now she's older and can make her own decisions. You can't live with the fact that it's someone else and not you. I looked him in the eyes and told him that this is one fight that he doesn't want. He walked away and that was the end of that.

Two days later he left. I never heard or saw him again. It wasn't the fact she had four kids by him. We had talked about us being together here. The plans we made at such an early age were now gone. I explained to her why it wouldn't work right now. So, we agreed that we wouldn't get into a relationship. She and I had already talked about this, but I wasn't going to let him know that I had already set her free before it got started. Although I did promise her that I would take care of her desires.

A couple of weeks later she had this clown from the hood at her house. As I entered the house, we spoke, and she and I went into the kitchen to talk. I didn't want to tell her what I thought about that dude. I just went along with it, and finally she told me that she didn't want him; she just did it to make me jealous. Whether that was true or not, I knew then that if I asked her to tell home boy to leave, I would be committing myself. So, instead, I smiled and gave her a kiss. As I turned and walked out, she told me not to be a stranger. I told her I'd see her around. I refused to look back. I knew she had that sad look on her face, and I didn't want to make any decisions.

Fall came and went. Jake had bought the club, Toss Up. Because Tyrone and I were best of friends and Jake was his brother, I got the job on the door collecting the money. That only lasted a couple of months. We got into it about a couple of women. The first time I just shook it off. The second time I expressed my thoughts about what he was doing. You see, Tyrone oversaw closing the club, and at times he would have girls come back to the club, but unfortunately, as time went on, I wasn't included anymore.

I had met this girl about two weeks prior that had come in from Maryland to visit her family, the Washingtons, who lived across the street from granny. I remember the first time I saw her. She came out the door and down the steps with those black tights on. She walked up the street to the store. I could see she was drinking a soda. I walked up the street to catch her before she got back. I stopped her and asked her what her name was? She said it was Cindy. You know, that's all I needed was a name like, and it was on. We started talking and from there, we'd been talking for the last two weeks.

One night she told me that she was asked to come back after the club close I asked by who? She said Tyrone. She also told me some of the things he was saying, trying to put me down. This was my best friend, and I didn't want to believe that he was stabbing me in the back like that. So, we set him up. we went back to the club, and about a half an hour later they came out like we planned it. I was waiting in the parking lot. I was leaning on his brother's car waiting on him, and as they approached, I asked what was going on. He replied by saying, "I was just giving her a ride home, man."

I asked him if he ask her to come back to the club after it closed. Of course, he denied it. I told him everything was beginning to become clear now. It was he who caused me to lose my job at the club. For a while now he have been acting a little strange towards me. I didn't know then but now I knew it was all about the women. Without me around, he could go at anyone including mine. As he began trying to explain himself, I stole him. He went to the ground, got up, and I hit him with a two piece. He went to the ground again. He got up, ran, and tried to open the door to the club. I beat him down.

Cindy started screaming, "You are going to kill him! Stop! Please stop!"

I was in a trance. All I could think about was the fights that I fought for him along with everything else. He was supposed to be my best friend. Instead, he was stabbing me in my back.

I walked Cindy home. We sat on the porch and talked for a couple of hours. It was evident that I wasn't going to get any that night, so I kissed her and told her that I would see her tomorrow.

As I headed home, I decided to go to the supermarket to get something to eat. It was three and a half blocks in the other direction through the cut 12th and 13th Avenues, the underpass. As I was walking under the underpass, momentarily disturbed about what I had done to my best friend, I heard a car slam on its brakes.

It was Tyrone. He jumped out of the car yelling he was going to shoot me. For a moment there, I believed him. He had his hands behind his back. I didn't know whether he had a gun or not. There was nowhere to run so my only impulse was to try to talk him down. When I realized my apology was not doing any good, I turned and tried to run. I felt the stabbing and a cut in my back. I then realized that it was a knife and not a gun, so I immediately turned around and struggled with him to keep him from stabbing me again. Finally, he dropped the knife. He jumped in the car. I leaned against the wall to catch my breath. I continued the walk to the supermarket, which was another block. The female cashier noticed the blood and asked if I wanted her to call the police. I said no.

During the struggle with Tyrone, he mentioned that he had just taken a warrant out on me. I asked her to call me a cab instead. I took the cab to Rotary Complex, to my daughter's mother's house. I knew that she was the only one I could trust not to give me up. I knew that the police during the investigation would contact the cab company to obtain the address. So, I got out at the top of the hill. As I approached my daughter's mother's door, I was becoming extremely weak and short of breath. By the time she opened the door, I had dropped to my knees, leaning on the door. She started screaming, and I told her it was alright and to please stop screaming. She asked me what happen and said she was calling the police. I told her that the police may have been looking for me, and I came there because I could trust her. I asked her if she could get some gauze pads.

She put on her clothes and laid her baby on the sofa next to me on the floor. I don't know how long she was gone, but when she returned, she had a bag with iodine and peroxide. She ran upstairs and got the alcohol. Then I told her how to clean the wound and bandage it up.

I hadn't realized how much time had gone by, but on the fourth day, I was sweating in hives. She told me that I wasn't looking too well, and I could hate her if I wanted to, but she was calling the ambulance. My breathing was getting extremely short, so I knew she was doing the right thing. The EMS was asking questions. I didn't answer any of them. I couldn't talk anyway. I was taken to St. Mercy Medical Center Hospital.

The next day the doctor told me that I was very lucky to be alive because I had a punctured lung. Of course, when he asked my name I gave him a false name. He told me that he was keeping me until the next day for observation. As soon as I got the opportunity, I grabbed my clothes, went to the first floor, found a restroom, changed and left. The whole time I was really having trouble breathing. I hitched a ride back to Rotary Complex.

Word got back that if I didn't return to the hospital, I could possibly die with my injury. I must admit I was not in the best of shape. So, my daughter's mother and a friend of hers drove me back to the hospital. Of course, the police were waiting. They read me my rights.

The next morning, I was taken to Clark County Jail. I went before the magistrate, and he set my bond at $1,000. I called Christy's mom and asked her if I could borrow thirty dollars to get out of jail. She asked me why she should help me get out of jail. But in the same breath asked me when I was going to pay her back I told her in two weeks. I called the bondsman and told him I had the money, but he would have to take me to get the rest.

When the court day came, the judge dismissed the charges because after he took the warrant out on me, Tyrone came looking for me to do bodily harm. That was the end of that friendship. After all, that's not the first time we had a conflict about something. He left me when my car got hit taking him to see some female. He told me that he couldn't stick around because he had warrants out for him back home in Carolina, then took off down the street. The other guy had somebody in the car with him, so they believed him instead of me. And what made it so bad, I hadn't changed the title from my mom's name yet, and not long after, she had an accident with my little sister in the car, and the insurance company gave her a real tough time because of that. I had to deal with that because he wouldn't be a witness for me. I had forgiven him for that too many times.

"Reason is often the first casualty of strong emotions."

Chapter 13

I was spending a lot of time at Little-Cee's house. This particular weekend was his birthday. For the past few months he'd been dating this woman named Cherry. She was light skinned, pretty, and very petite. Little-Cee used to get attractive women because he had the best job in town. He had a van, z-28, and a '69 blue and white Cadillac and two homes.

This would be the night that I would betray my friend, Little-Cee. See, after the party that night at his house, some of us went out to the club. After that, we went to Frank's, an after-hours joint. He asked me to drive his girlfriend home; she didn't like the place. Little-Cee and others stayed behind.

When we got to the house, she asked me to walk her inside. Once in, she asked me to fix her a drink. I said, "Haven't you had enough?"

She said, "I'm at home now," and insisted that I make myself one too. She went upstairs and left the bedroom door wide open. She was on the bed on her back. She was wearing a T-shirt that showed all her thighs. She cocked one leg up to where her feet were flat on the bed. At that moment I realized that she had no underwear on. As she began to utter seductive words to me, simultaneously, she turned and got on her knees, pulled the T-shirt up over her head, laid her head in the pillow, and arched her back in a form that I had never seen before. Before I knew it, I had taken my pants off, and I walked right up to the edge of the bed. As I began to talk, she stopped me and said, "Just make love to me real hard." Then she looked over her left shoulder with that yellow face. How could I deny her? We must have rolled around for 45 minutes.

Afterwards, she rolled over, looked up at me smiling, and said, "It's true what they say about you."

I said, "Who are they? And what did they say?"

She just looked at me, smiled, and said, "Boy, you put me to sleep."

I went downstairs, though I was supposed to wait for Little-Cee to take me home. Instead, I made a stiff drink and walked. That was the first time I felt bad about sleeping with a woman. I had just betrayed my friend. For about a week I didn't come around.

A couple of days after, Christy came over, and she immediately started yelling. "You ain't nothing, you no good M.F.! Little-Cee said he's going to shoot your ass. I don't know why I waste my time with you." She went on and on and on. Finally, she left.

It was the weekend, and I decided to go to Simms, another one of our hangout spots. Little-Cee and the gang were there. We talked about what had happened last weekend. Little-Cee was more forgiving than I'd anticipated. At that very moment I learned not to fight over a woman who willingly sleeps with another man. She is more to blame than the man, friend or no friend. In so many words, that was what I learned from Little-Cee. We remained friends. Things were over between him and Cherry. She moved back home to New York.

Christy and her crew were passing by on their way to the store (so she said). I think she was just being nosy. Once she realized Little-Cee and I were still friends, she started a fight by striking me with a blow to the face. This girl was so outraged that she started throwing bottles at me. Little-Cee tried to intervene. At that time Christy started yelling at Little-Cee that he was nothing for being my friend after I'd slept with his woman. She went on about how none of the women were nothing, including herself for messing with me. She just continued, so we loaded up in the car and went to the boy's club to hang out.

About an hour later, Christy, Litta and Kirk showed up. Someone yelled out, "Run, Ziggy! Kirk's got a gun!" As he approached, I could see the gun. Little-Cee asked him what the problem was. He said, "I'm tired of that chump putting his hands on my sister." Little-Cee and everybody who was there said it wasn't true. I hadn't put my hands on her.

Kirk asked Christy whether she was lying or not. She stood there looking stupid. He then told her that even if I was killing her, don't come and get him anymore! They left. Later that night after I got home, Christy was sitting on my porch. So, instead of going home, I went over to Patty's house.

Patty was a white woman who was my sister's friend from the neighborhood. Over time, she and I became real cool. I usually went over there when I didn't want to be bothered with anyone.

The next day, I watched Sunday Night Football. Afterwards, I went home, and when I got there, my mom started fussing me out about leaving Christy sitting on the porch. "Hey," I told her, "I didn't bring her here and didn't leave her here."

My mom said, "One of these days, one of those women is going to do something to you."

I wasn't worried about that. "Before I get involved with a woman, I always have an understanding, and I don't do married women."

She shook her head and laughed. I got something to eat, went upstairs and lay down.

I called a girl named Melanie from around the way. She was fair looking. She had big lips, and she was a thick girl. I had no feelings toward her. She was the girl who I called when I didn't want to be bothered with any questions about anything. She would just come chill and do whatever I said. It wasn't like I was doing her wrong. We had an understanding from the beginning. Like I told any other girl who I met, there would be no strings attached, although some developed feelings anyway and tried to make it more than what we agreed upon from the beginning.

Before she left that night, she told me that my cousin, Will, was trying to hit on her, and that if I didn't care enough to make a commitment, then she might consider taking him up on his offer. I couldn't figure out if she was telling me the truth or just doing this to get me to commit. Was he doing it to show me he could take one of my women? Occasionally, while hanging out, he would make comments about how I treated the women I was involved with. He told me I thought I was a player. I told him, "The only one out here that thinks that is you because you're the only one who has so much time on his hands, you can't help but hate. Don't hate the player; hate the game." Everybody started laughing.

That Christmas, I invited Melanie to our party. As we walked up the street to the house, there were several people on the porch, including Will and his girlfriend, Fay. I said to myself, *I'm going to love this*. I hit everybody off with the shake. I made sure Will was last. Then I asked for everybody's attention. I then proceeded in these words: "I'm now about to show each one of you what I think about two people who wish to develop a meaningful relationship when the one who she's with is unsure about what he really wants. What I'm about to do is only right." I turned to Will, and I grabbed Melanie's hand, and I told her, "In keeping with our agreement from the beginning, I now set you free to develop a relationship with Will." All you could hear was ouch's and ohhh's. Then Will and his girlfriend, Fay, got into an argument.

My cousin, Lashunta Jenkins, came outside, asked what was going on, and said that we were making too much noise. As she turned to go back in, she stopped and told everybody to come inside. About half an hour passed, and Will turned to me and said that I could have Fay. I told him he didn't have anything I wanted, and to show him that I was the better man, I told him he could have both *Melanie* and Fay if they really liked each other. I wouldn't stand in the way. "But make no mistake about it, if I wanted to keep her, I could have her." I finished my drink, grabbed a beer, and went home.

A couple of hours later, Fay came to my house all drunk and upset. She told me that she was too drunk to walk home. I thought to myself, *How did she walk an extra block past her street to get to my house?* I told her nothing was going to happen. She said, "Okay, can I stay the night anyway? Maybe he'll think something went down."

I kind of laughed and said, "Alright." See, Fay was not my type, but more than that, if I slept with her, it would give Will the satisfaction that he had something that I wanted. And that wasn't the case.

~" Most people spend more time and energy trying to maintain the image that they wish to portray to the world, and in the eyes of other men, rather than being who they are, trying to find out why they fear being themselves around others."

Chapter 14

Black-boy was a pimp from Pasadena, West Virginia. We called him Black-boy because he was so black that if he closed his eyes on a dark night, you would never see him with those pink lips. He didn't particularly like me because I took one of his girls, but she pursued *me*. One night at the club, Repro, she and some of the girls that she worked with were shooting pool. They didn't work uptown in the hood; they just came up here to hang out. Her name was Amy Tubbs. She was a very attractive white girl. I approached her at the bar and jokingly asked her *how much*. She turned to me smiling and said that she was not working at the time, and "Besides, a good-looking guy like you paying for sex… Don't you have a girlfriend or two?"

I laughed and told her, "No, my dear, I was wondering how much you would pay me for sleeping with you." She found that to be very amusing. We sat down, had a few drinks, and talked for a very long time. Her friends had later decided that they were ready to go. She gave me her phone number and explained that they all lived in the same house. That included Black-boy. She made me promise that I would call her; I never did.

About three weeks later, she showed up at my house out of the blue. I was very surprised. I asked her how she found out where I lived. I could tell she had really taken to me. She started play fighting and asked me why I didn't call her like I promised. I explained to her that more drama was the last thing that I needed. We sat on the porch and talked for a while. It was getting to be dinner time. I asked her if she would like to join me for dinner. She said, "Sure."

After we finished, we went back upstairs to my room. It was getting late, so I asked her if she thought it was time for her to get back with her crew.

She said, "I was hoping I could stay the night." She reached in her purse and pulled out a fifth of gin. I told her that she was more than welcome to stay. We got our drink on while listening to music. We took a shower together and went back to my bedroom where we got our freak on. I handled my business, and did she ever handle hers.

We continued to see each other for the next two weeks at which point she said she wanted to show me something. We arrived at this two-story house on 9th Ave. We went upstairs and looked around. She asked me if I liked it. I didn't know what to say because it was fully furnished. I said it was nice. She said, "I'm glad you like it because it's our apartment."

I said, "Hold on a minute."

She said, "Please, hear what I have to say before you say anything."

I said, okay."

We sat down on the sofa, and she explained to me that she cut her ties with Black-boy, and that she quit prostituting, and now she worked at a restaurant.

After we moved in, I couldn't go anywhere without her. When I would go to my mother's, they would talk all the time. But what she hadn't told me was that she kept one of her clients, an old, rich white guy who wanted to see her twice a week, and that it wasn't really sex. He used to like for her to put on sexy underwear with high heels on, smoking a cigarette, and whenever she had sex with him, which wasn't often, she always used a condom.

I said, "I work, and you have a job now." There was no need for her to continue. She told me that every time she saw him it was a hundred dollars, and asked if I would let her continue until the beginning of the year, so she could pay off something, then she would give me half each time she saw him. The only bill I had in the apartment was the phone and electric. She would pay the rent and other bills. I told her to let me think about it.

A week later we were hanging out, and she asked me if I'd thought any more about our conversation the previous weekend. All she talked about was paying off her child support. I told her that I really didn't want her to do that anymore, but since she needed to pay off that bill, I told her I'd think about it. I knew that if I didn't agree she would get around to doing it anyway. When I met her, she was making money. No woman I knew was going to give up money for a man with no money.

One day after work, as I walked into the house, I noticed a girl sitting on the sofa. Before I could say anything, Amy walked from the bedroom. Amy introduced us. She said her friend wanted to leave Black-boy and asked if she could stay with us until she got herself together. Even though I said it was okay, I couldn't help but wonder about Black-boy. The last thing I needed was trouble from him. He must have thought I was out to get his women.

Amy took me in the bedroom and told me just as long as I never messed with her friend. I gave her my word that her friend was off limits. Her name was April. She stood about 5'9". She had long hair that came down to her butt, and big breasts that looked firm. The white T-shirt she was wearing revealed everything. She had freckles on her face, and I could see where they ran down to her breasts.

Two months passed, and Amy started up again about our conversation. She just kept on. The next day, I'd finally had enough. I didn't want to, but I agreed. Some nights Amy would have to work late at the restaurant. After dinner April and I went out for a while. When we returned to the house, we had some drinks and started dancing. I went to the bathroom. By the time I got back, April had put in one of my slow jams tapes. Before I could sit down, she grabbed me by the arm and said she wanted a slow dance. I hesitated, but she just kept pulling on me. I said, "Okay, one slow dance." We started dancing, and she kissed me on my neck. As I went to pull away, she kissed me on the lips.

One thing led to another. We ended up sleeping together. Before I slept with her, in the heat of the moment, she promised never to tell. A week passed, and everything seemed to be fine. During the summertime, I would always sit on the porch after dinner. One evening, Amy asked me if I gave any thought to what she had talked about… the three of us picking up and moving to Monongaila, New Jersey. I think she was determined to turn me into a pimp one day. That was never going to happen. Not my thing.

Coming home from work one day I had a bad feeling. When I walked into the house I knew something was wrong. I called out for Amy, then April. "Anybody here!" I walked to the living room, then the bedroom. As I turned to walk back out, I saw a sheet of paper on the bed. It was from Amy. She said that I had betrayed her and that she had loved me with all her heart, and I had broken it. I knew then that April had told what happened.

At that moment, I felt bad about what I'd done. She'd treated me with nothing but respect. It was too late for anything now. I knew she wasn't coming back. I'd had two beautiful women walking around the house with little or nothing on all the time. Amy was 21 years old, April was 20 and I was 23. We didn't know what we wanted. We were young.

I finished out the month, during which time I started talking to Jasmine who lived down the street. Sometimes I would see her in the morning when I was going to work, and she would be on her way to one of those community colleges downtown. I would make small talk then. She knew Amy was my girlfriend. It didn't take her long to realize that Amy and I were no longer together. We started spending lots of time together.

When the month was up, I told her that I was moving back home. She suggested that I move in with her. I told her I wasn't sure about that because I'd just gotten out of a relationship. I had my "understanding" talk with her, so she knew where I stood. I never moved in, but it was like I did. We spent all our free time together. She would never let me stay at my mother's unless she was with me. If I told her that I just wanted to chill at my mother's and didn't invite her, she would start an argument.

To be honest, I kind of liked it. Even though we weren't in a committed relationship, she did things that would tell everyone we met in the streets that I was hers. She was always sweet, never had a bad word to say about anybody. I really dug that about her. She didn't act like most girls our age. She cooked every day we didn't eat out. She told me about her life and how she ended up in foster care. She was very beautiful.

Not long after that I got laid off, so I started drawing unemployment, again.

Dara was a woman who lived across the walk from us, about six steps away. She was seeing James Harris. James was a black police officer who everybody knew. Dara was a brown skinned woman. She had a little daughter and was pregnant. People said it was James's baby. He was an older guy. She told me that she was 25 years old.

James had been with the police department for 15 years and had always worked the night shift. He was the only black officer on the force. He had two sons, Jerome and James Jr. (James Jr. became a police officer and was sent to Chandler, West Virginia.) Jerome, well, Jerome lived on the other side of the law. His dad had gotten him out of trouble for various things, but the fourth time Jerome ended up going to prison and, after that, he just continued to go back. He never did more than two years at a time. His dad still had that much pull. Jerome was good people. Whenever pay per view fights came on, he charged $10 a person, but I would get in for free. When Jasmine was at work, sometimes I would sit outside, and Dara would come out and we would talk.

James used to come by quite often. What I couldn't understand was that he was still married to his wife. In fact, they lived two blocks down the street. The town was not big at all; everybody knew everybody. Now I think that was some crazy stuff... a police officer married, and with a baby on the way by another woman down the street from his wife ... wow! Dara was so pretty, and even though she was pregnant, she was still trying to give it to me. Not only was she beautiful, but pregnant stuff is the best, it's always warm and wet.

Anyway, one-day Dara and I were talking. I asked her when she was going to invite me over for dinner, drink, or something. She laughed and said that I was full of myself. She said she didn't need to make any problems for my little girlfriend. I told her it was not a problem; we had an understanding. Not a problem.

She said, "I better not."

I said, "We're friends, aren't we?"

She said, "Yes, but you don't need to come in my house. We could continue to talk outside, and besides, what if James pulls up while you are in my apartment?"

I said, "James isn't going to do anything to me. I know him from the community. I know his sons." I was telling her that, but in my mind, I knew that chump would kill me if he thought I was knocking her off. But I was willing to take that chance, so we continued talking. I knew by the conversation that I was getting close to getting through the door. Right then, James pulled up. He stopped and talked to me as always whenever he came over. Not once did he ever ask me about my conversations with Dara. He kept it clean. And besides, how would it look if a married police officer got into an altercation about a woman? It wouldn't look good for him. I think that's what gave me my edge.

Christy had come over one day, making trouble, and not for the first time. Jasmine told me that if I didn't do something about Christy, we were through. Well, actually, she put it a little more explicitly, but I see no need to go there. Anyway, it really didn't matter, although I really liked Jasmine. I thought, *I can pack up and leave tomorrow. It won't matter.* Christy would not stop interfering. Finally, Jasmine and I sat down and talked, and we decided to end the relationship. I moved back home with my mom. I didn't get much unemployment, but I had to give my mom some of that for rent.

~" *We all flow in the current of life, some tossed here, some tossed there; but all have ended up where each is supposed to be in life at that moment, according to the choices one has made in the past."*

Chapter 15

My sister, Celes, Lolita, Kim and others would go to the club named Bobby's. It was a club downtown with a mixed crowd. I met a lot of women there. One weekend I met Amanda. We continued talking over the phone for the next two or three weeks. We made plans to meet at Bobby's that weekend. When I arrived, she was waiting just as you enter the club. We hugged and found a table. I called a waitress over and ordered us a drink. She was having Long Island iced tea, and I ordered a white Russian. Before the waitress got back, Amanda went in her purse and handed me some money. I asked, "What is this for?"

She said it was for our drinks. I told her I had it. She said, "No! Don't argue with me. Three weeks ago, when I met you, you paid then. I got it." For the remainder of the night, she paid for the drinks.

When we were ready to leave, she'd had too much to drink and didn't want to drive all the way home. She lived in Lexington, Kentucky 19 miles away, where no blacks lived. Need I say more? I told her she could stay the night with me. I knew that's what she wanted anyway. When I told her that, she had a big Kool-Aid smile on her face.

The next morning, she said that she couldn't get up. I asked what was wrong. She replied, "You put a hurting on me... Now come and give me some more."

I told her, "I couldn't have done too much damage, you want more." I hit it from the back like she liked it. Afterwards, I went to take a shower. When I returned, she had pulled the sheet over herself, and she slept for two hours.

Every weekend she came down to stay with me. I did good, keeping her clear of Christy. It was hard, but I did it. On one of my rides with Amanda to her house, she brought her mother outside and introduced her to me. I had no idea she was going to do that. I thought her mom wouldn't take to me well because I was black, but I was wrong. But I was right about her father though; he was racist.

We'd been dating for six months. One night she wanted to go home and pick up some money from her mother. We had been drinking, but she'd had a little more than me, so she asked me to drive. We made it to her house. She was inside for about 10 minutes. As she was exiting the house, her mom came to the door and spoke to me. Good thing I didn't see her father... or better yet he didn't see me.

On our way back to my house on the interstate, a state trooper pulled up on the side of us. Then he immediately dropped back and turned his lights on. He asked for my driver's license and registration. I handed him my license. Amanda passed the registration. I gave it to the trooper. He came back to the car and asked me to step out to take the test. I asked what I had done to be stopped. He said that I was all over the road. Amanda and I looked at each other. We knew what this was about. I was not all over the road.

I took the test, and he told me that I failed. He took me to a house and said it was the courthouse. We waited for an hour and a half, then he told me that the judge was mad that he had to get up and come down there. I asked myself where the magistrate was. The trooper told me that the judge was not going to be able to make it. I said to myself, *What the hell is going on? I thought I was going to get out tonight.*

He said that the judge would see me tomorrow. I said, "Alright."

We drove from Cincinnati, Ohio, to Lexington, Kentucky. The only thing that separated the three states were bridges and, of course, water. The jail was real small. It might hold a hundred people. Yes, I was the only black in the jail, but I had no problem with the inmates, only the officers. Whenever Amanda would come to see me, they would tell her that I had been released. I knew this because, when I called home, my mom would tell me what she'd said.

You know, it's unbelievable. I didn't get to see a judge or anyone for a whole week, supposedly because of drinking and driving. RACISM!

When my name was called, and I was standing there, the judge claimed he was doing me a favor by giving me time served and releasing me. I said to myself, *What is wrong with this judge?... 'doing me a favor'?*

Don't he know he just violated my due process to see a magistrate when arrested or within 24 hours?

I was ready to leave that place. The judge asked if I had someone to pick me up. I said, Yes, and he said, "We'll hold you until they arrive."

I told him, "On second thought, I can walk."

He told me, "Don't be trying to hitch a ride."

When I got home, I went to see Christy and Mario. She was at the church across from the boy's club. They were having a revival. They had a few choirs from out of town. When I finally found Christy, the first thing out of her mouth was, "Go back to jail and take that white B with you."

I told her that I wanted to talk, not fuss.

After leaving the church, I went back home. I called Amanda to let her know that I was home. She immediately said that she was on her way over. Before I could say anything, she hung up the phone. Now I had to get rid of Christy. I knew it would take Amanda some time to get there. Christy hadn't made it there yet, so I called and told her to come around the corner where her mother lived. Christy immediately accused me of having someone over. I could honestly say that there was no one there. After taking my shower, I went around the corner to see my son, Mario, and Christy.

When I got there, she was sitting on the porch. I started playing with Mario while talking to her. I tried to talk to her about getting our own place. (As usual, my mom and I were not getting along.) I told her that I would get another job. Where Christy's mother's apartment was situated, I could see if Amanda pulled up. Christy had never seen Amanda or the car she drove, so I continued my conversation.

During our conversation, Christy brought up an event that took place just over a year ago. Some of her family on her father's side came down from Alabama to visit, which is where he is from. When they left to go back, she decided that she wanted to go with them, since her father was going. That started an argument. Just over two months later, I got a call from Miss Lorraine saying Christy claimed that one of her cousins tried to rape her. She continued the story and asked if I would help her get a ticket, so she could come home. I helped her get a ticket.

Once she got home, we talked of commitment, but things didn't turn out the way we planned. So, I thought by having this conversation we could really see if we really wanted to try and make this work. We talked for about two hours; then I went home.

But I had come home without a clear sense of what we had decided. I was no clearer of our relationship than when I started the conversation two hours ago. But once it started, it was something different altogether. I thought, *Boy, that didn't go well at all.*

Twenty minutes later, Amanda knocked on the door. My mom let her in. She came upstairs, and she took off her clothes and jumped me. About half an hour into this, my mom knocked on my bedroom door. When I didn't answer, she opened the door and yelled, "Christy is in the living room!"

Good thing my room was up a flight of stairs, so no one could see who was in my room without coming upstairs. I told Amanda to hang on for a minute. I had no problem out of her.

When I got downstairs, Christy had Mario and his bags with her. I normally kept him every other weekend and sometimes through the week. This was not my weekend, but he's my son, and besides, I needed to get rid of her before she asked to come upstairs. So, I acted like I had somewhere to go. That way she would rush out the door like she always did.

She said she'd be back around 10 or 11 o'clock and walked out the door. I took Mario upstairs and asked Amanda to put some clothes on him for me. I played with Mario. We watched TV, and we had something to eat. Finally, I gave him a bath, and he went to sleep. Christy never came back that night. It was not the first time, and I knew it wasn't the last. As usual, Amanda stayed the night.

That morning I went around to Christy's mom's. She wasn't there. At 10:30 we had brunch; then Amanda went home. It was about 1:30p.m. when Christy pulled up with Litta. At this point Litta and I were cool, so we always talked for a minute, and Christy would get an attitude. Litta and I would laugh, and Litta would yell, "Come on, Christy!" I was cool with all the sisters, cousins and the rest of the family, except the two brothers and her mother.

Mario and I were on the porch. She came up smiling, knowing she was wrong again. I didn't say anything; I just let her have her way. What's done, is done.

That night Celes came over to the house. I heard my mom screaming, so I ran downstairs. There my sister, Celes, stood with her eyes closed, black and blue, and her lips were swollen. I asked her who did that to her. At the same time my mom was screaming for my sister not to tell me. Moments later my sister told me that her husband had done that to her, but she told me that he didn't mean it. He had it coming. My mom tried to stop me. I told her to look in the mirror. All the while, my mom was trying to call Celes's husband to let him know that I was looking for him, and no one was going to stop me.

I went to Little-Cee's house and asked him if I could use his gun. He told me that if I used it, not to bring it back. (I had no intentions of using it. I got good hands. I just knew I was gonna get jumped). I set out looking for my sister's husband for three hours. I went everywhere he could be and to every residence of the people we knew. Still I couldn't find him, so I went back home, and my sister and mom were sitting there. My mom asked if I saw him. I told her no, but I would find him. Finally, my sister told me where he might be, after telling me what happened. Some friends of theirs were having a little get-together as always. She said that she and Doug were upstairs, and he was telling her about the problems he was having in his relationship. She said it was an innocent hug, and she was just consoling him, and that was it. I told her that was still no reason to hit a woman the way he hit her. Her face looked bad, and my mom continued to scream at me like I had done something wrong. She had always taken their side, no matter what it was. Here her daughter sits with her face in her hand, and all she can do is defend him for what he's done. She told my sister that she shouldn't have been kissing on another man. I told my mom that whatever she did, he had no right to do her face like that. My mom continued, then she told me to leave her house, and not to come back if I did anything to my sister's husband.

So, he was at my sister's friend's house like she said. I knocked, and she opened the door. I asked for Doug. Her boyfriend came to the door immediately apologizing. He told me what had happened. During that time, my mom and sister pulled up in the car. While everybody was talking about how the whole thing was a misunderstanding, I was furious.

For the next week I went over to my sister's house every day. I told my sister to just give me the okay, and it's a done deal. She told me that it was okay and to forget it.

Eventually, Celes's wounds healed up, and we went out to Bobby's one weekend. Celes and I had a few dances and some drinks.

Finally, Amanda showed up, and she had a friend with her. I had seen her before. We all talked, danced, and got our drink on. When the night was over, Celes went home. Amanda and her friend came with me. My bedroom went from one side of the house to the other. One part was my living room and the other was where I used to write my songs. I turned on some music, and I looked up. Her friend was sitting in my chair playing with her breast. She took her shirt off, and she had the biggest breast I had ever seen in my life. It seemed as if she was seeing if I would be willing to sleep with her and her girlfriend. I was right. They jumped on me. Before I knew it, she had taken off all her clothes and was sitting on top of my legs. Amanda held me down while her friend, Angela, played, and they would rotate. We were at it all night.

The next morning, we had another go around. After they got out the shower, that's when I realized how beautiful Angela really was. As she put on lotion, she stood about three feet from the window, all the while, both smiling. Angela was dark skinned. As the sunlight shined through my window onto her body, it was like silk. She was a pretty, black woman with a banging body, hair down to her shoulders. One of the most beautiful things I had ever seen. I was just loving myself. Once they finished, we went downstairs and had breakfast, and then they left.

Amanda and I continued to see each other for a while. After that we kind of drifted apart. About a month later, she called me. During our conversation, she asked me if I was ready to make a commitment. I told her that I was not ready for that. She wanted to get married. I really wasn't ready for anything like that. One week she called and told me that she was engaged to get married. I told her that I was happy for her. She asked if I was at least a little mad I told her that if she was happy, then I was happy for her. We talked for about three days and, after that I never heard from her again.

"Letting go all that binds you is to finally begin to embrace freedom.

Chapter 16

Things had gotten bad between me and my mother. She had always taken the side of our so-called family. Once again, something happened at Lolita's house. It's her son, Mitchell, the one who could do no wrong no matter what.

Lolita acted like Mitchell was God's gift to women, and he was an ugly mother "you know what." I mean ugly dude. The only reason he would get a woman was because of his sisters and aunt. There were a lot of women in their family, female cousins. After all this time, they were still spreading rumors about my family having a disease. She never stopped about the deal with Dante'. We got into it, and I punched a hole in the wall, I could never get my mother to side with me, never. She went on about how she was not going to pay for the wall. Later that day when I came home I told her that I would pay for it. I gave her the money about two days later.

Three days later I was on my way home, and as I approached, I could see a lot of items on the side of the road. As I got closer, I noticed that those were my things. My neighbors were sitting on their porches. I looked, and everything that I owned was on the side of the road. I took a moment and looked around. I could see that people were mumbling amongst themselves. I was so embarrassed, but most of all I was heartbroken. I just looked one last time at my things, then I turned and look at my mother standing in the doorway. I didn't take a thing out of that pile. I walked off leaving everything. I stayed with Little-Cee on and off. Sometimes I would sleep in my car. I would take a shower over at Little-Cee's house, and sometimes when Miss. Lorraine was at work, I would shower there. It got to the point that I would go three blocks up the street to the hospital. I would go to the elevator that they used to send the trays of food to the floors. Once they finished, I would take the leftover food off the trays and make a meal. This went on for about two weeks. Then Christy started asking me where I was staying and how I was eating every day. I told her that I was eating at Little-Cee's. She knew I was lying.

I asked Litta to watch Mario for a minute. I took her to the hospital with me and showed her how I had been eating. She turned to me with a look in her eyes that told me that she was sorry. I told her I would be okay. She said, "What about your sister?" I told her that I went over there twice to eat, and she told me that her husband said that I couldn't keep coming over there eating. So, I stopped going by. She then asked about Lolita, Kim and everybody else that was supposed be family. I told her they had turned their backs on me too. I didn't go and ask everybody. They all knew anyway, but no one offered to help me out. There were times when Jason, Mitchell, and the rest would come just to make fun of me. You see, I would park my car out back of the apartments where Christy lived with her mom. They would knock on my window sometimes. I would pretend that I wasn't in the car. It was hard to see in my car. I had a dark tint on my windows. I got out of my car smiling but upset. I asked why in the hell they kept come around there messing with me. I was just as crazy as they were. I would laugh it off with them. During this time everybody was wearing the Jerry curl. We would get the kit activator, and it would sell as soon as we hit the block.

Christy would always go in and get items. I could never bring myself to do it. She would always make fun of me. We found a house about two blocks from her mother's apartment. We went there just about every day like it was our house. No one lived there for some time, but it was very clean. No furniture, but the carpet was very soft. That ended when we got up one morning, and the police were standing over us. He said we were trespassing, but he wouldn't press charges, but we'd better not come back on the property or the next time we were going to jail.

That was it. We went looking for an apartment. We talked to Mr. Jasper on 16th Street, and we told him what we could pay. We explained our situation, and he agreed to work with us. About two weeks later we moved in the apartment which was down the street from his home.

In 1988 Litta had gone back to Louisiana with some family members that were visiting. When she returned, she said a guy she had met was coming to pick her up, and they were going to Georgia where the job market was better at that time. She asked me if Christy and I wanted to go. Miss Lorraine was like, "That would be a good thing for y'all to go down there get a job and start your life over."

When he got there, Litta introduced us and told him that Christy and I were the ones she was talking about going with them. I can't remember his real name, but they called him Johnny-b. He stood about 6'3", 230 pounds. At that time, I weighed 162 pounds, but my hands were vicious. The next day as we were leaving, I asked if we could stop by the shop to get something out of my car. I got my clothes out, took one last look at my baby, then we left.

That was a long 12-hour drive. I swear Johnny-b drove slower than Miss. Daisy. We moved into a two-bedroom apartment. They had Re-Re. We had Mario, and Christy was pregnant with our son, Charles. Every day we would go out looking for a job. Everybody did except Christy because she was pregnant. Johnny-b and I were putting applications in some of the same places. After about two to three weeks, Johnny-b got a job first. Within the second week, Litta and I got into it about me driving the car to continue looking for work. We were driving down the street. It got so heated, she pulled on the side of the road, opened the glove box and pulled out a big .38 Special. I guess the move had taken its toll on us. It seemed like ever since we'd been there, Litta and Johnny-b had been fighting just about every day. The police were called, so from that day on, I went out every morning walking looking for a job. There were three jobs that I would make sure that I checked with. Not long after, I got a job at a snack company where I used to stock snack trays. When the father hired me, I explained that I was waiting for a job that payed a little more because I had one son and another on the way. He told me that he understood, and I filled out my W2 forms and went to work. I knew I was being tested to see how honest I was. The workers would purposely leave money in the slots to see my reaction. Proving trustworthy after only three times of going to the bank to deposit the money in his business account, I began making deposits all by myself. I liked working for that family. The daughter and father were real nice people.

Not long after that, I got a job at North End Precast Construction Company. Looks like things were beginning to look up for us. Johnny-b had some home boys who lived in the same complex. Usually they would come over whenever I wasn't there.

One night I went to make a beer run to the store for me and Christy. When I got back, one of his home boys was coming from the back where the bedrooms were. I looked at him as we passed each other in the hallway. I went into our bedroom. Christy had that guilty look on her face. By this time everybody was at odds with each other. I could see Johnny-b doing something like this. I looked Christy in her eyes and told her that if I caught her, that's where they would find her. Lately all we'd been doing in that apartment was arguing. I was saving money so I could move my family out and into our own apartment where I had control of my surroundings.

Finally, I had saved enough money to move out and get our own place. We moved just one block from the old apartment,1300 Hower Ridge Complex. For the first two weeks, every time I got home from working all day, Christy was never there, and no food would be cooked. After about two months, I got Christy a job at this laundromat where I used to do our laundry twice a week. The older lady who worked there took a liking to me. We paid Litta to watch Mario, and Christy would complain about not having any money left over to do some of the things she liked to do. I told her that I was paying everything, and that she had enough money to do what she wanted. Christy just didn't want to work. If I was coming home to a clean apartment, and dinner was ready, I wouldn't ask her to work, but that wasn't the case.

Two weeks passed, and I asked Christy how much she made. At first, she acted like she didn't hear me, so I asked again. She wouldn't tell me anything, so I went up to the laundry mat and I asked the lady. She told me that Christy hadn't worked there for more than a week now. I couldn't believe it. Every day I would ask her how everything was on the job? She would always say "well," but she had been lying all this time.

By the time I got back to the apartment, she had left, so I called Litta and she said that Christy wasn't over there. I knew better because she would have nowhere else to go. Later that night when she finally came home, I told her that we needed to talk. She claimed she had a headache. At that moment she made up my mind for me. I told her that I was going to get her a ticket back home the next day. She hit the fan.

Things had gotten really bad. She was seeing one of Johnny-b' s friends. I had to work, so I couldn't stay home and watch her.

Finally, after two weeks, I got her to leave. She really didn't want to. I told her then she must be moving in with him because I refused to continue to pay rent and bills while she ran around with another guy. When I got home that day, she had taken everything I had and poured bleach on it. I mean all my clothes. She took all the eggs, and threw them against the walls. She took the flour and slung it everywhere. She left a big mess.

I was so tired from work, I just took a shower, went up the street, got something to eat, and went to bed. The next day after work, I cleaned that apartment from top to bottom.

Not long after, a couple of girls moved in the apartment over top of me. After small talk, come to find out they were cousins. Light-skinned Cheryl was attending college; the other one was working. Cheryl had two children, a boy and a girl. Sometimes on the weekend her boyfriend would come up, and each time he would have a couple of guys with him. During this time, Cheryl and I would speak in our passing. I could tell that her daughter was grown by the way she talked and carried herself. She was the oldest.

For the past two months I was hanging with my new friends, Little-T and Joshua. After work we were sitting outside, enjoying the nice cool breeze of the evening. We were out having a beer, and I could hear her with the other children. Little-T lived next door to the girls with his mother. Ever since Christy left, Little-T 's mom had been trying to get me to sleep with her. She started inviting me over for dinner. Initially, I decline, but she insisted. So, I told her that I would be up after I showered.

When I got upstairs, she was standing in the door waiting for me. That made me more nervous. Little-T was sitting on the sofa when I came in. He just kept smiling as we headed to the kitchen.

She would invite me every day after work, so one night I offered money, but she refused. I told her, since she wouldn't let me pay, then she was free to use anything in my apartment that she needed to cook with. She agreed, and from that point on, I gave her my spare key. We always talked at dinner. We were getting close. I knew she liked me, but I didn't know how to advance to her because she was older, or was it that girls my age were always at my fingertips, and I didn't want to give that up? Besides, she was really a nice lady. I would have to give up those things because she deserved it.

Little-T and I used to hang out in front of my apartment. Whenever Joshua wasn't working, he would be over as well. They were my hanging partners. Sometimes Little-T would grab a beer and drink it. I would laugh, but I would always tell him, that if he got caught by his mother, "Don't say I gave it to you."

Cheryl start flirting whenever her daughter wasn't around. One day they invited Little-T and me upstairs. That was the beginning of many nights to come. We used to play act...That always led to sex. Cheryl was my partner. Her cousin wasn't bad looking herself. I started spending a lot of time upstairs with her. It had gotten to the point that her daughter would make little comments to the boyfriend whenever he was there. One day he and his boys tried to get something started. I just ignored it, and finally it stopped. When the boyfriend left, she put something on her daughter and told her never get in grown folks' business while she commenced to whipping her butt.

A few weeks later, she told me that she was moving closer to campus. Also, her boyfriend thought it would be best. That way he wouldn't have to drive so far when he came down on the weekends from Alabama.

That Sunday Little-T and I were leaving out my back door going to the store to get some beer before the game started. As we started walking across the field, someone yelled, "Ziggy!" As we turned around, I could see that it was the cousin. So, automatically we thought that she was talking about Little-T. As I was coaching him, I walked a few steps with him. While I stopped and turned around to proceed to the store, she came out on the balcony and said she needed to talk to me about Cheryl. I walked back, and as Little-T and I were walking up the steps, she told him that she needed to speak to me about her cousin in private. That's when I found out nothing ever happened between them. She was joking as she was telling me about their encounters. I said, "All this time, the both of y'all had us believing something was going down in the next room." I couldn't do nothing but laugh.

We were moving from the kitchen to the bathroom because she was doing her hair. She had always been flirtatious with me as well. She just turned to me and said, "I want to find out for myself." I told her I didn't understand. She told me that her cousin had been telling her about our sexual encounters. She continued by saying that all she got, each time, was wet panties and nothing else. I asked why she never said anything. She said, "And to who?" I could do nothing but laugh. I told her, why didn't she just take control? She laughed and said, every time she tried that, he claimed that he had to use the restroom.

I was cracking up. I couldn't help it because he was telling me that he was getting it. She turned around and leaned back as to sit on the sink. She had on this summer dress that rose up her thighs when she leaned back. She smiled and told me that she wanted me. As I walked towards her, she got up on the sink. I pulled her dress up. At that very moment, Cheryl walked in. I could see her in the mirror. I then turned around and looked at her and was lost for words. I mean I couldn't say anything.

When Cheryl walked off, I went behind her into the living room, as I went to say something, she just put one hand up saying nothing. I apologized and walked out. We never talked after that, and within two weeks, she moved. I never saw her again.

Joshua and his brother lived in the row behind me. We always went out of the neighborhood to play basketball. Sometimes we would take Little-T with us. Joshua and I would always go to the clubs together.

One night we went to club Dominic, and I met a girl named Mavis. When we arrived at the club, we were there for about 30 minutes. There were two women dancing with each other, like ladies do. I kept telling Joshua to go jump in. In turn, he would tell me to jump in. Finally, my boy made a move. After I finished my drink, I walked over to their table, reached out my hand and asked her if she would like to dance. She grabbed my hand, and we all four danced the next two songs. They went back to their table, and we walked back to the bar where we were sitting. Now we were discussing how to end our night. Joshua and his brother shared a one-bedroom apartment. His brother's room was the living room. His brother worked, and he knew he shouldn't wake him up. So, if the woman he's talking to doesn't have her own place, but her girlfriend does, then he'll go with her to her place, or he could use mine. He already knew that my bedroom was off limits; no one sleeps in my bed but me. He knew that the sofa was a pull-out bed as well. In all the one-bedrooms, the bathroom was in the bedroom. That was another reason he didn't want to take a woman home. His brother might get up and need to use the toilet.

As I finished my drink, my intentions were to go and ask for another dance. That's when Mavis walked over to me and told me that I was a good dancer and asked if I would dance with her She stood about 5'11", 145 pounds. She had dimples and pretty brown eyes, which I found out later, they were contacts. So, we danced, and when the slow jam came on, I went to leave the floor. She stopped me, grabbed my hands and guided them and placed them just above her butt. She wrapped her arms around my neck and pulled me closer to her, whereas her head and her chin rested on my shoulder. With her face next to mine, as we continued to double dip with the beat, I began to whisper sweet nothings. She ended up going with me that night, but nothing happened for a week. We spent the next few months together, that is until I got fed up.

What happened? After two or three weeks, Mavis and her daughter, Erica, moved in with me. They lived all the way on the other side of Atlanta, but Mavis worked downtown, and I lived in Savannah, but worked in Athens, Georgia. We thought it would be good. Mavis was older than I was. Her daughter, Erica, was fourteen years old. Everything was great in the beginning. I was working, making good money. She had an excellent job working for the phone company making $500 a week. She had been there about ten years at that time.

Little-T and Erica always got along. I never had any problem with him trying to hit on Erica. He was too busy trying to run with Joshua and me. Joshua would come over sometimes to watch the game. I think he felt like she stopped a lot of things we used to do but, in fact, it didn't; the only thing I stopped was the clubbing, and when I did go out, she was with us.

Erica and I would always go to Sam's cafe every Sunday to eat. Mavis would be doing laundry, cleaning, and cooking dinner for the evening. We would always go by the mall, do window shopping, take our time, as requested by Mavis, so we wouldn't be in the way. One Friday after work I came home, and some guy was sitting in my recliner. Mavis walked in from the kitchen and introduced him as her brother. I really wanted to tell him not to sit in my chair, but instead I let him do it, just to keep the peace. Ever since that day, her brother had been coming over, if he really was her brother.

Sometimes I would come home from work, and Little-T and Elisha would be out at the movies. Lately Mavis had been getting home after me. For the past two weeks no food had been cooked. Come to find out, she'd been going up to the jail, seeing her ex-boyfriend and putting money on his books. Finally, she came clean, and told me that he was in jail for beating her up, and the people in their circle were getting messages back to her from him. That's how she started going up there.

At that point our relationship started going down. There were arguments about her brother being there so much. One day, I came home from work to find her brother asleep in my chair. I kind of slammed the door when I closed it, and he woke up. It was a one-bedroom apartment, and her brother was not going to make this a motel. She kept saying she was going to talk to him. She had a whole week to talk to him. That Friday after work, I walked in my apartment. Her brother had eaten and fallen asleep in my chair again, watching my TV. I walked to the bedroom. As I passed Mavis, I told her to go into the room with her brother.

I reached up on the top shelf and got the shoe box where Mavis kept her .22 caliber. I got three bullets, put them in the gun, and walked back to the living room. I told her brother, since his sister wouldn't tell him, I would:

"You eat before me, drink my beer, and fall asleep in my chair, watching my TV." I fired all three rounds into the TV, while yelling, "But you can't watch my TV anymore!" Everybody broke out running, the police were called, and I was arrested. I spent the next week in jail. I could not believe that it took that long just to see a judge. That Friday, I was taken before a judge and charged with discharging a firearm within the city limits.

I don't know what kind of lawyer they gave me, but this guy could not represent me in a real case. He asked if I wanted to plead guilty, get time served, and go home. I spent seven days in a bull pen with several other guys.

When I got home, the first thing I had to do was call my job and see if I still had one. When I walked in, I could see that my apartment had been broken into; stuff was everywhere. I started to call the police, but as I looked around, I could see that only my clothes were missing. I automatically knew who it was. Little-T used to ask to wear some of my clothes from time to time.

I went upstairs to his mother's apartment looking for him. His mother was glad to see me. All she could do was hug me, telling me what she was preparing for dinner, and that I must stay. I asked her where was her son. She just kept talking, so I had to break the news to her that my apartment had been broken into. Again, I asked if she knew where Little-T was. As soon as she understood what I'd said, she told me go to the pool, and tell him that she said, "Come here right now!"

Once I got to the pool, at first, I didn't see him. Then he emerged from the pool. I stood at the outside fence and waited to see where he had his things. Then he spotted me and tried to walk off leaving the clothes lying there. I walked over and picked the outfit up. The clothes were mine, as I expected.

When I got back to the apartment, his mother was standing on the balcony. As I got closer, I just held up the outfit. She started for the pool. I stopped her and asked if she would wait until he came home. I really didn't want her to embarrass him in front of the other people. "He'll be home in a few anyway; the only thing he has on is his swim shorts."

When he got home, I could see where he was trying to avoid me. His mother was in my apartment helping me clean up. When she went upstairs behind him, I could hear her all in his mess.

At that time, this young girl who lived across the lot with her mother and other family members came over to use the phone. I knew that her mother wanted me to date her daughter because of the things her mother would say in passing, like, "When are you going to take my daughter out?" I would just smile, and sometimes she would call me over. I told her that her daughter was only 18, and I was 23. She would always say, "I give you permission." She used to always tell me that I was a very handsome young man. I would just play it off.

I still went upstairs and ate dinner with Little-T and his mom. We talked about what he did and told him to let this be a lesson for him, and never take anything from anybody. His mother was still all over him. She just kept telling him how wrong he was. That was one of the nights I stayed and watched a movie with them. Little-T and I acted like it had never happened.

I was trying to decide if I was going back to Guilford, West Virginia. I had always kept in touch with Christy for our children. She was still staying at her mother's apartment because she didn't have the money yet to get one. When Charles was born, Litta, Maria, and Maliana were all telling me how much he looked like me, as if I spit him out myself, and I needed to come home and see that.

Little-T's mother was trying everything she could to get me to stay. She told me that she could help me get a job. After all, she worked for the city for the past twenty-some years. After a week, I told her that I had decided to go back to Guilford because I had never seen my youngest son, and I'd lost contact with my daughter's family. She said that she understood, and if I ever wanted to come back, just call her and I'd be more than welcome.

That weekend before I left, Joshua, Little-T, and I went and played what would be our last basketball game together.

Monday when I left, she wanted me to meet her on my way to the bus station. As we hugged each other, she was still trying to get me to stay. She was so nice, and her age had nothing to do with it at all.

That was another long bus ride, kind of reminded me of that four days and four nights ride to Inglewood, California, and back.

> ~" Many of us try to mask the pain in our lives by acting like it doesn't exist, but the ghost of our past will always remind us of all the shame, hurt, regret and fear that we know lurks just under the surface of our thoughts always ready to condemn us all over again."

Chapter 17

How was I to know what awaited me in Guilford. The summer of 1990: It was getting warm again, and the school year was ending. When I arrived at the bus station in Guilford, WV, I got a cab to Christy's mother's house. I walked up and knocked. Tracie answered the door. Maliana, Maria, and Miss. Lorraine were there, and everybody was surprised. We talked for a while. We couldn't call Christy because she hadn't gotten a phone yet.

After we finished talking, Maria gave me a ride to Christy's apartment. Maria took me up to the door. As I knocked, and I walked in, Mario realized that it was me. Then he turned, running back to the kitchen, yelling! "Mommy, it's Ziggy! It's Ziggy!" He came running back to me, and I picked him up.

When Christy walked from the kitchen, she was really surprised. We hugged. After that, I took Mario aside and told him that he was not to call me Ziggy, but Daddy, instead.

From that moment, I held Charles in my arms until trouble came my way. Charles was just three weeks old when I came back. During these few months that I'd been back, Jason and the rest of the guys made it clear that I couldn't hang out with them, as before I left. Nothing had changed, and I still didn't want to be associated with that type of conduct. Now that they were living the good life, they never included me in any of their trips to Cleveland, Ohio. Rather, it was clubbing or to re-up. Now that they were making money, buying cars, and had the girls hanging around all the time, sure they would count me out, and they did just that.

Sometimes I would see them at the neighborhood club. Not only did they make it a point to not be at the same club as me, they would leave if

I was there or showed up. During the few months before the arrest, they made it a point to avoid me by any means.

One of the security guards at Charlotte University had a party. He was from the hood and had asked me to serve the drinks for him that night. That's where I met Melissa White. She was good looking. I directed my attention towards her, and for the next three or four hours, she also flirted with me. I knew she wanted me because she kept coming back for drinks every five minutes. Finally, she leaned over the table and said flirtatiously, "I don't know you, and I don't think you're going to get to know me," trying to get a conversation going. I gave her my smile and told her if she continued to lend me her ear, before the night was over, she'd be in my arms. She looked and said, "You're really confident of yourself!"

I told her, "It's the only way to get what you want."

She said, "I don't think so." While she started to walk off, I leaned over the table and grabbed her by the arm and told her that if she walked away this time, it would be her loss. She looked at me, smiled, and turned while fading into the crowd.

Just moments later I heard a voice say, 'You know what? I like you."

We looked at each other and smiled. I knew then she was going to be mine that night. I made us one last drink, took her by the hand, and we went out the back door. We only talked for a few, then immediately started kissing and touching each other. Someone came on the back porch where we were, so we left and walked about 30 yards to a vacant house. We walked up the back steps to the porch. We continued kissing and talking. Before we knew it, one thing had led to another. We were up there for about two hours not knowing the time.

Someone from the party had told Elaine that I was with a girl.

I asked Elaine who told her that I was with somebody. She told me that everybody saw me leave with her. I told her just because I left with, her don't mean I slept with her.

She then said, "You expect me to believe that you didn't do anything with her? You must think I'm crazy. While you were doing whatever with that girl, Christy was with Mitchell."

I asked her she knew. She told me that she was there at the apartment when Christy got out of the shower.

The next morning, I asked Christy what had happened that night. She and Elaine looked at each other and started laughing. I told her I didn't know what she was doing, but whatever she was doing, better not be done in our apartment because if she did, and I caught her, I was going to put hot balls in both of their butts. She just looked with a smile on her face and said that I was too crazy for her to do anything. I told her, "Try me. I know you will."

Melissa never hung out where we did even though her family only lived two blocks from the starting point of our hang out. She lived on 4th Avenue, and the club Repro was on 12th Avenue. Word was out that Melissa and her friend, Monica, were at club Repro looking for me. For the next week I tried to avoid Melissa. I had already told her that I had a woman, even though it was after we had sex. Melissa knew I had a son by Christy, and she knew how she was, so whenever she wanted to see me, she would send one of her friends, Monica or Sara, to get me.

Melissa was mixed. Her father was black, and her mother was white. Melissa was so beautiful. I mean beautiful. Monica was a black woman herself. Sara was white and on the heavy side of things.

As time passed, I started hanging out with them sometimes. One night we were hanging out together. Melissa and Sara kept looking at me, hitting each other. I asked what their problem was. As Melissa started to tell me, Sara put her hand over Melissa's mouth. Again, I asked what was up. Melissa said that Monica wanted me to hook her up with Marvin.

A couple days later I told Marvin that this girl wanted to meet him. He asked who it was. I told him, and he laughed and then began to talk about how big she was. The next night she asked me if I had talked to Marvin. I told her yes; then she wanted to know what he said. I told her that I could call him for her once we got to her house. She started speeding. I told her to slow down. Melissa and Monica just laughed their butts off.

Once we got there, I called Marvin, but I couldn't get him, so Sara wanted to ride around looking for him. They didn't hook up that night, but they ended up talking. I teased Marvin after they started talking. Melissa and I had been messing around for about two months now.

Currently, things were getting bad between Christy and me again. To make things worse, after hanging out with them, it got to the point that I was spending a lot of time at Monica's house.

One night we had been out drinking, and this night when I went to

Monica's house, before long, she started flirting with me, and I flirted back. In two weeks' time we were sleeping together. Monica was a hairy girl. I really liked women with good hair. It's just something about a woman with that fine line of hair on her belly and that smooth hair that lay down on her arms. Not a lot of hair. Just a little. I had to show Monica things about sex. I really didn't know if she was faking or what, but she learned real fast that night.

I remember Monica before I went to Atlanta. Her mom really didn't let her do too much of anything. You know, those are the ones who turn out to be real freaky. Just about every night I would go over to Monica's house. Her mom worked the graveyard shift at the loading plant. Monica had one brother. He was younger. Most of the time when I came over he would always go to his girlfriend's house. She was white and pregnant. Monica started falling in love. She wanted me around every day, and if I was not with her, she wanted to be wherever I was. Remember, I told you that Melissa would send Monica and Sara to get me. There were times that her mother would get home before I left. Monica would sometimes forget to set the alarm clock, or so she said. When her mother would knock on the door, I would wake in a daze. "Oh, man!!" As I scrambled to get my clothes and hide in the closet, Monica would be laughing. I think her mother knew that someone was in her room, but she never asked to come in and look around. I wonder if she saw me, if she would remember me from years back when she told me that Monica was not ready to start dating. I had to wait until her mother ate and got in the shower before I could leave. Monica opened the closet still laughing, although I asked what was so funny. She said, "If only you could've seen the look on your face." You know I had to laugh with her.

In 1990 I finally landed a job at Charlotte University as a cook. Everything was okay. The supervisor was a white woman named Ms. Cathy. She was an older lady, but she was okay. After about two to three months, we had a new manager that came down to work with Ms. Cathy because the old company contract was up, and the new company who was coming in that he worked for. His name was Dennis.

Dennis was about 6'2" or 6'3", but he was slim. He had a beautiful wife and two boys around the ages of eight and 10. Dennis was from Little-town.

After getting to know Dennis, I realized that he didn't only like to smoke weed, but he had a problem with cocaine powder. When he moved here, he got a house across the street from Jake. Tyrone, Jake, and I all became acquaintances and would go over to Dennis's house and hang out. I used to go over to Dennis's because we worked together. Dennis told me that he heard about my reputation, and if I messed with his wife, he would put a bullet in my ass. I just smiled. He looked at me and said, "I'm serious. I know I can't beat your ass, so I'll put a bullet in it." I told him that he didn't have anything to worry about. His wife was fine as hell. I respected the man, and besides, married women are off limits.

We would go hang out at Jake's Club. Dennis had gotten to the point that he literally needed a hit just to get up in the morning. After a while, we all had gotten real close to Dennis, so we decided to bring it to his attention that he had a problem, and something needed to be done about it before it get any worse. My sister's husband, Dante, was friends with Dennis also.

We sat Dennis down one night, and we told him that we could see in his face that he had a problem, and if he didn't get his self together, his wife may leave. You know most of the time when you try to help someone with a problem such as this, they would always deny the fact they have a problem. We told him that he had a beautiful family, and we knew that he didn't come all this way to lose it for some drugs. It had only been about six months and Dennis was talking about moving back home. I told him that may be the best move he made yet, and besides, his wife didn't like it here anyway. During this time, he and his wife had their fallouts about his drug problem. It was time for him to leave. His drug problem had gotten bad.

My job at Charlotte University had an ad in the paper for a cook position, starting pay, $6 an hour. I went to Ms. Cathy and told her that she could give me that position. I'd been working there for a while, and I knew everything. She told me that she had to hire someone with more experience. I didn't think that was the case. It was the same thing that happened at the hotel. They bring some white person in, I train him, and before you know it, I'm back in the unemployment line.

A few weeks later after being turned down repeatedly, I went into her office and told her that I quit. Dennis got out of his chair and said that he wanted to talk with me. Ms. Cathy stopped him and told him to let me go if I wanted to leave. Dennis continued out the door anyway. We talked, and he told me that I was a good worker, and they needed me because I came in as part of the cleanup crew and had worked my way up to be a cook ... a good cook if I might add. I told him that I was up for a raise for some time now and yet to receive it. Dennis told me that I knew he was waiting for his transfer to come through, and he'd be leaving soon. He said he would like to leave knowing that I still had my job. I told him thanks, but I've been through this before. He told me that he understood because she didn't expect for him to be black with his qualification.

As the cook, I was very popular. For the past two months this one white girl named Jessica, as well as other women, had been trying to get with me. Every time she came through the line, she would always ask for me. But I kind of liked Jessica, I guess because she didn't stop at nothing to get with me. I saw her that night and told her that I quit my job at the University. She told me that if I needed any money until I got another job, to let her know. I told her that it was okay, but I knew if I needed it, all I had to do was to ask. Jessica lived in Kimpsville, which is about 30 minutes from Guilford. I would go visit her from time to time. The last time I saw her, she had transferred to another college. She asked if I would keep in touch. I told her yes, but as time passed, we lost contact, and I never saw her again.

~" Many men have unknowingly sealed their fate by simply deciding on a seemingly trivial matter that has set in motion a chain of events that has changed their lives forever."

Chapter 18

August 28th, 1990, was the beginning of a nightmare for years to come. I had no idea. Christy was at one of her girlfriend's apartments, playing cards, something they did every Sunday. That night, there was a knock at the door. Mario ran to the door, like always. He opened the door and there Marvin stood. I was surprised. After all, I was alienated. I told him to come in. At that time, we embraced each other. He was looking back, so I asked who he was with. He told me that Mitchell was hit by one of the Ann Arbor, MI. boys, claiming that he got hit with a mack-10. I didn't want to go. I only went because Marvin asked me to. I had no idea of what was to happen. I told Marvin he would have to go get Christy. He gave me that "Hell, nah" look. Again, I told him that he would have to be the one to go get her. Moments later, I could hear Christy already. Once she got to the apartment, she looked at me and lost it. She looked at me and said, "You're the biggest fool I ever seen!!"

Christy was going off, and she was right. If anytime she was right about something in our relationship, she was right about that night. What was about to happen, drastically changed my life, and my family paid the price.

I got in the car with Marvin. We drove to Churchland Ave. There, Jason, Mitchell, Carlos, Williams, Robert Gates and Tommy sat on the porch of Tim's house. Everybody was talking. Some had guns. At that moment, I turned to Marvin, "I thought you told me that Mitchell and the boy was going to fight heads-up?"

Marvin said, "Yes."

Moments later, everybody started walking towards Repro. Once we got to Eugene Court Apt., as usual, everybody was hanging out. It was a beautiful night. As we walked through the complex, somebody from the Jagger's apartment yelled out my name. Once I approached, one of the

Jagger sisters said that her cousin from out of town wanted to meet me. Her cousin was doing her hair at the time. She introduced us. We started small talk, as the guys continued to walk...girls hanging around, listening to the conversation...all smiling. Someone outside yelled, "Ziggy! They call you!" so I told the cousin I'd be right back.

A home boy from the hood that lived next door motioned me over to his apartment. He told me that this white girl, who was a friend of his woman, wanted to ask me something. When I walked in, I could see this white girl cutting her eyes every now and then. She was kind of lying on the sofa. I sat down, and my home boy walked back into the kitchen. She told me that she had seen me around and thought that I was a very handsome man. We walked out back and talked about 10 minutes. It was dark out there; the back lights didn't work (like many other things). When I left her, I was just crossing 6th Ave at Shirley's Den. I could hear something like a fire cracker. As I was walking, I could see Robert running across 20th Street, blazing towards Club Repro. I looked to my right a few yards and saw Jason, Williams, and Mitchell. Marvin, Tommy and Carlos were a few more yards down the alley. As I walked towards Jason, he handed me a gun. Simultaneously, the police made a left turn into the alley. Everybody started running. I ran to Granny's house, which was on 10th Avenue. On the porch were Lay-Lay and a friend. Moments later, Jason asked where his gun was. I had thrown it in some bushes. I returned with it and gave it to him.

The next two days everybody was hanging out at Mitchell 's house. From that night, for the next six months, we seemed to be the news. I saw Tommy and Robert on the news one night, showing the fools where they threw their guns in the river. Scuba divers recovered the guns. In a months' time, they were all locked up except Marvin. I had no idea that I was going to get locked up too. True, that night I had walked up there, but I had nothing to do with the shooting or any drug sales.

Marvin came and picked me up. We drove down to Rhonda's house. Not long after, we could see the Feds setting up to move in on Marvin. Marvin and I looked at each other. He said, "Well, let's get it over with." I was with him to drive his car home. We drove two blocks, and they jumped out on us with guns drawn. They were calling Marvin 's name, asking him to throw his heat out the window. We were sitting there with all the guns on us. I said, "Oh Shoot!!! Marvin, what the hell have you done?" They took me and had me sit on the curb. A few minutes later, after they pulled Marvin's car apart, they asked me who I was. I told them my name was Ziggy. They told me that they had a warrant for my arrest. I asked for what. He told me that it would be explained to me downtown. I had no idea this was just the beginning of Mitchell 's plan to use me as a sucker.

Once in jail, we all were given lawyers. Most of us were in the same block at first, but due to constant arguing and fighting, we were split up. I was trying to put my case together. I kept replaying that night over in my head ... how I wasn't even present when all the shooting and drama took place. I had stopped and talked while everything was going down. We'd been in jail for weeks. All the time, I maintained my innocence, so my lawyer gave me a copy of the grand jury indictment. I could see some of the lies that had been said about me. For instance, Robert claimed that someone approached him to purchase a dime of crack and came and got it from me.

Robert was the second biggest dealer in Guilford, WV. at that time. Even though we never got along, I did go into their apartment twice, due to the fact his woman was my daughter's great aunt and my daughter was over there sometimes. (Everybody already knew about the new cars they had; you couldn't hide those. When I walked in, I had to take a step back. Their apartment was laid out. If you were blindfolded and taken for a 10-minute ride, you would think you just walked into a palace.) I don't think Robert had been out for a full year yet.

Also, Mitchell claimed that I was present during some of their activities. He had said I was present during some of the purchasing, cooking, and bagging of the illegal substance. I told my lawyer that the only time I ever was present was when I first got back to Guilford. I saw Marvin at the boy's club and asked him for a ride home. He stopped by Jason and Tina's apartment. We walked to the kitchen where I saw them cooking. I could hear Jason and Mitchell saying to Marvin, "Why in the hell did you bring him here?" Marvin then asked, If I was ready to go. We left, and he dropped me off. That was the first and last time I was ever present for any of the activities. I had never made any trips with them to Ohio, nor was I present on weekends when they rented suites and partied. One more lie trying to tie me in with their drug ring when I really had nothing to do with them or their way of life!

One of the Ann Arbor boys was shot in the heart, as the prosecutor put it. He told me that they couldn't get anything off the bullet because it hit the brick before hitting the guy. I told him he had the wrong guy, and that I didn't have a gun. He told me he had other people saying different. I told him that I never had a gun, and I never shot anybody! My hands had always been my guns; just ask anybody in the neighborhood. "In fact, if we can find one person out there from the age of 25 and up, having nothing to gain, who will come in here and tell you that I was a drug dealer? I'll take 20 years right now." He could never do that. I asked my lawyer to send their investigator to the places I worked, and they would see that when all this mischief had supposedly taken place in Guilford, I couldn't have been present because I lived and worked two jobs in Georgia.

The only thing my lawyers talked about was a woman that I was in a relationship with in Georgia. The investigator had scrounged up but never mentioned about going to check on my jobs out of state. They never even told me the outcome of the polygraph test I had taken. I had no idea I was being rail-roaded.

One day one of the deputies was making his rounds. As he passed by my cell block, he kept eying me, knowing every jail or prison has its own little code. I knew it was something he wanted to say and something I wanted to know. He asked why I wasn't released with the rest of the guys. I said, "What? What other guys?"

He said, "Your co- defendants. I got on the phone and called my sister, Celes. Once I reached her, I asked if everybody was out. She said, "Yes, everybody but you and Jason." I asked her to contact my lawyers and see what was going on. We hung up. I tried from the jail phone, but my lawyer wouldn't take my calls until the next day.

Finally, when I spoke with my lawyer, he told me that everybody took pleas. I told him that we'd been over that already. He told me that if I took it to court, the prosecutor could give me twenty years. I asked, "For what?" At that time my lawyer got short with me. It was evident that I was not going to be defended by these two lawyers.

After sentencing, Ken, Mitchell, and I were sent to Lexington, Kentucky. There I met Kelly Brown and Blue from D.C. It all started one day on the rec yard. We would shoot dice and play basketball for money. During this time in the feds we had corn change on the compound, but like anything else, there was paper money too. After a few days of kicking their butts in dice, Blue tried to start some mess. He claimed I was setting the dice. I told him the only way to set dice was you needed to have loaded dice, and if it served me correctly, these were his dice. At that time, he looked up at Kelly Brown, who at this point was laughing because he put him up to it. The next day on the yard Blue tried to take it further because he knew he had to prove himself, but by this time, I knew who was calling the shots. More DC guys were around that day than usual so when Blue started up, I just sat the dice on the ground and told him to come on and let me give him what he needed so he could learn some respect. I could see everybody making moves. So, I said, "Hold up. That's fine, but let me and Blue go heads up first.

At that moment, Kelly Brown stepped in with his arms out laughing. "Hold on, hold on. He turned to me. From now on I'm going to call you Obama Ziggy."

I was glad he stopped. I knew I was going to lose with all his homeboys being from D.C. I just didn't know how badly.

Instead of going back to shooting dice, Kelly Brown suggested that we play three on three for $20 apiece. No problem I got my money. That was the first time I played ball with them. They suckered me into that one. Kelly Brown was NBA material. Me and the two guys on my team took turns getting our butts kicked. From that day on we were all cool.

Even though we were in the same prison, I never hung out with Mitchell and Ken. One day on the yard four officers was walking towards us. Everybody started asking who they were coming for. The officer walked right up to me and said, "Mr. Harper,"

I said, "Yes, sir."

"Your number please."

They took me to the captain's office. The captain told me that he had to put me in the hole. I asked why because I hadn't done anything. At that time, the captain again apologized and said that it came from the top. I was taken to the hole.

Over the weekend I asked my sister to get a hold of my lawyers. In the meantime, prison life continued. While in the hole, you are allowed one hour of rec time. I spent my time playing basketball on the yard. Through talk, I came to find out the guy in the cell next to me knew some people in Guilford, W.V. When he called the name, it didn't come to mind. Then I knew who it was.

After being put in the hole, getting into three fights, horseflies biting me like crazy the whole time, being complete and miserable for two whole months, and never even being told why I was ever put in the hole, I was transferred to Michigan. Things began to get even worse.

Once in Michigan, I had four fights. My last fight was the worst and landed me in the hole again. I had no idea why I had to fight so much until I was transferred to F.C.I. Beaumont. After being there for two years scrapping daily to stay alive, I left my pod one day, and out the corner of my eye I saw Levart and Blacky. As I approached them, Levart embraced me, and they began to tell me how Mitchell sent the Feds to Cincinnati after them.

By that time, I had a bad record for all the fighting I had to do. Luckily, I'd also had a couple run-ins along the way with some other people that have helped clear my name in prison, once the whole truth was out.

When I first got locked up in the hole, it was Mitchell's doing. He had the prosecutor get the Warden to put me in the hole, so he could go back and forth to court and cooperate with the Feds. He put the word out that I was taking him to court trying to get a sentence reduction for myself, when it was really him trying to shave the years off. I'm thankful for Levart and Blacky because they could show paperwork with him on it. That's why I was fighting for my life. Nothing worse than being the last to know.

My two years there was good. Ozie and I started up a music group. We had one of the best bands on the compound. Every time they had a function they would request our band to perform. That's where I had my first songs copyrighted. Then I was transferred to Bucks County, Pennsylvania. From there to Albany, New York, and finally Lancaster County, PA.

With all I had gone through, I had been searching for something to believe in, something authentic and genuine. See, like most of us, I was raised as a Christian. I also had the opportunity to study the Nation of Islam, but neither complied with their book entirely like the Muslims did with the Qur'an. Like for instance, in the Bible, the scripture tells you to sustain from eating pork. Most people would say that the scripture says that we could eat anything if we bless it in the name of God. The Nation of Islam says that E. Muhammad was a messenger from Allah. But that's not true. The Qur'an teaches us that over 14 hundred years ago (Muhammad) peace and blessings be on him is the seal, meaning the final messenger to all mankind … not to mention all the holidays that are celebrated by the Christians. For instance, Halloween is an outright Pagan practice. For many centuries before Christianity the Pagan cults in ancient Britain and Ireland celebrated this holiday observed on October 31st. They called it (Samhain) which was the day of the dead, as they believed whoever died during that year were allowed access into the land of the dead. It was believed that the world of the gods became visible to mankind during that night, and they played nay tricks on their mortal worshipers, a time loaded with danger, fear, and supernatural episodes dealing with black cats, evil spirits, ghosts, witches and things like that. After the Romans conquered Britain, they added to (Samhain) features of the Roman harvest festival, also held on November 1st in honor of Pomona, Goddess of the fruit of trees. Pagan observances influenced the Christian festival of Halloween, celebrated the same day, October 31st.

A chapel in Rome, on November 1st, in honor of all Saints in 837, Pope Gregory IV ordered its general observance to highlight and honor all saints in this medieval Pagan custom. In Madeira, England, the Festival was known as all hollows. In Europe and America, by the 19th century, witches' pranks were replaced by children's tricks. Celebrating Halloween is a major sin. I picked the one with which everyone knows that are connected to some evil. How could you say that you believe in something but not comply by the book entirely. These are just a few reasons that I decided to follow Islamic practices.

~" Many people try to apply things to other people lives
that they wouldn't want applied to their own."

On November 15ᵗʰ, 1996 I was released from the Federal Prison Victorville. Currently, we were at war with the skinheads. One of the skinheads had converted to Islam. Yes, he was white.

He was in for bombing black churches. The other skinheads didn't like that at all, so they killed him, and we went to war. As time went, by I was told that I was no longer to be involved with this. The community knew that I was up for release any day now. Imam told me if I didn't stay clear of the conflict, he wouldn't have any choice but to place me in segregation to make sure nothing happened to me to jeopardize my release. Yes, the Muslims had that much power. No Muslims were to go anywhere without two or three brothers accompanying each other.

That same year H.B.O. was doing a special on the violence in Victorville Penitentiary for the second time. The first was in 1985. They were doing the story because it was the worst Federal prison in the United States. There was always someone getting killed or overdosing on drugs, guys killing each other over homosexuals. You name it; it was happening. It was nothing but violence.

The Muslims were real tight. I mean it was a real brotherhood. In all the Federal prisons that I was in, the Muslims were always together and looked out for each other. Make no mistake about it; you could always feel the love in the Muslim community.

This year a lot of shit had happened here in Victorville and in the past. There was a Chinese boy from New York who came to Victorville. This Chinese boy looked like a female. He was doing life for allegedly killing his lover who was a representative of some state.

Big time kingpin drug dealer Radcliffe Edwards. It is said before Radcliffe got locked up, he had two transvestites on the streets, and he was paying for their sex change. People used to talk about them because they were guys they had grown up with. The Chinese boy had only been here for a month or so and one of Radcliffe's homeboys, Gig, was after the Chinese boy. Now Radcliffe didn't like that because some say that the boy liked Radcliffe. He would try to intimidate the boy. Finally, Radcliffe and Gig had some words, but it didn't escalate into anything. A week or two later Gig and the boy were hanging with each other real tough. Gig had tried to move from b-block to c-block. But the counselors weren't going for that. That Gig was nothing but a trouble maker. Gig and the boy would be sitting out on the yard under a tree. The brother and I thought it was very disrespectful for the boy to be playing with that chump, Gig (or anybody else, for that matter). One day, the officers ran down on them.

Once the boy was released from the hole, Rivers was after him. Rivers was a Spanish guy from the Islands. He was doing life for killing a police officer in his country. He claimed that when everything went down, he didn't know that it was a police officer. Turns out, it was an undercover cop during a drug deal. He also claimed that the officer shot him first. He thought that it was some guys trying to rob him. They fired first, and he returned in self-defense. He had been down for about five years currently. He was still fighting his case. Rivers was only 25 years old.

The first time I noticed that Rivers was after the Chinese boy they were talking in the TV room. B-block and c-block TV rooms were connected. They would communicate like that and write each other letters. The half wall and glass were so thick you couldn't really hear through the glass that well. Things were beginning to get real heavy around there about the Chinese boy. I've seen it all before. This is not the first time that chumps were ready to kill or be killed for a homosexual, and it wouldn't be the last.

Now Gig was talking about doing something to Rivers if he didn't leave his boy alone. Rivers was down with the Latin king. Gig was trying to get some of his home boys from D.C. to be down with him. Although he had some that were willing to be down with him, he didn't have the mob because during this time, Radcliffe was still somewhere in the picture, and he had more of the followers. As they put it, Gig was a nobody, and didn't too many like him.

Before it could escalate into something real big, they took the Chinese boy off the compound. Rivers was one of the few guys who wasn't Muslim that I would socialize with. You know, I had to ask him what the hell was thinking. He told me that he never would have done a thing like that; it's just that the Chinese boy looked so much like a woman. I told him it didn't matter what he looked like; he was still a boy. Mind you, I was laughing at him the whole time. He told me now that the boy is gone, he's glad that he didn't get a chance to do anything with him. Jokingly, I told him, "Don't stop there; it's more here." I know I was being mischievous. But I was only playing with him.

he said, "I'm not messing, with you Ziggy." I couldn't invite him to Islam because he already knew that I've done that before, and all he could say is that he's not ready for that right now.

He was always trying to think of a way out. I used to tell him, "Man, I don't want to hear that stuff." He said he didn't care if they shot him or not; he just wanted a chance. Even though I was there with him, I couldn't turn to him and say that I understood because I really didn't know what he was feeling. See, I was going home that year. All I could say was, "I feel you, my brother."

I really felt bad for him, my brothers, and many others that I've come to know. Most of these guys will never see the streets again. And I'm thankful for the opportunity to be in their company and to learn the things that I've learned because I was locked up and had no control over what happened to me. Though it was a violent place, I mean very violent, my most constructive time was done there. Everybody respected each other. It was a world within itself. People were always dying around there. It was always something.

I worked out five days a week. For the past four and half years I'd worked out nonstop. My max was 445 pounds. Oh, Yeah, I was at the top of my game. You had to be to survive at Victorville.

Big Mike wants everybody to know that he's been down for life 20 to 30 years. See he had to be one of the guys to give an interview with HBO. He was telling about some of the things that were going on here. Well that was their whole purpose for being there.

You could always hear the cell doors open, and when they did, you better be up and ready because you would want to prepare yourself, in case someone tried to attack you. On this day, around 4:00 a.m. in the morning, I heard a cell door open, so I got up to see what the fuss was about. Well, what do you know, it was Big time drug dealer, Radcliffe, being escorted by the marshals. I didn't know what was going on, but I knew that if it was Radcliffe, it was something big. As they walked passed my cell, I asked what was up. He replied, "I don't know." I knew it was something, being escorted by the marshals.

He had on a baseball cap, a coffee mug in his hand, and a USA Today newspaper folded under his arm. After the cells were open, there was still no movement.

Minutes later the Colombian Kingpin and his son were being escorted from A-block, which was across from B-block where Radcliffe and I were housed. The Colombian was screaming furiously how he treated Radcliffe like a son and had done everything he could to show friendship and loyalty to him. He said there was nothing he wouldn't do for him. He continued to yell about how could he set his wife up like this. The Colombian said that he was doing life, and it didn't matter about him, but to involve his wife and son like that was a big betrayal.

The Colombian wife would come to visit him and their son, who was also in prison. During one of those visits, she was introduced to Radcliffe and some of the people he knew from D.C. that would be making the transaction for the (drugs), not knowing that Radcliffe was setting him up. Radcliffe had defendants in Victorville. All his defendants took their own weight given the opportunity to testify against Radcliffe to receive a lesser sentence. No one took the deal, so you could see how big of a blow this was to them to hear that Radcliffe had cooperated. It is said that he did it to get his mother, father, and aunts a sentence reduction. The news ripped through the prison like a small storm. The prosecutor said that he didn't care who he was giving up. He was not going to give Radcliffe one less day behind bars. Radcliffe was doing a hundred plus forty years with the L note. After all this, in the newspaper it was stated only his mother and one of the aunts received a few months sentence reduction for all of it. He said he did it for his family. The news said that the transaction lasted about a year. The sale accumulated somewhere around six million dollars.

But was it all worth it? No one has heard from Radcliffe since.

Earlier that year I called my sister, Celes, and asked if she could send me some money. I asked her to call my mom and older brother Jimmy Jr. and ask if each one could send me at least 10 dollars apiece.

She told me it was hard out there. She was talking to me like I never lived in the outside world. She said "I had it made." I asked her what she meant by that. She said that I had a roof over my head, and I got three meals a day. I had no idea that she would turn me down like that. If I had known that, I would have never asked her. I couldn't believe her response. It tore me up. Something rippled through my heart so bad that, for a moment, I couldn't breathe. My feelings were so hurt, that for a long time, I didn't speak to my sister.

In addition to dealing with the blow from my sister, that same year my second oldest brother, Louis, was dying from AIDS. He said that he wanted to see me before he died. He was worse off than he thought. The doctor told him that he was not well enough to travel that far. He had come to West Virginia, and I was in Pennsylvania. I really wanted to see Louis. He had left home when I was about 14 years old. He lived with a family that was helping him because he was going to college. That was the best thing he could have done. Unfortunately, I never got a chance to see him, and weeks later he died. My mom, and sister, Celes, were fighting over who he should leave his insurance money to when he died. My mom and sister had been at odds for years. She had always told my sister that she wasn't good enough for her husband. Well, my mom got the insurance money. She received about $70,000 as my sister said, but my mom said it was only $50,000. At that time, I had learned that she had given my brothers and sisters at least $2,000 or more. Celes wrote me and told me that Mom had given her $3,000 and for me to call and let her know that I needed some money. I wrote her and asked for some money. She wrote me back telling me that she didn't have much left, but she could send me 200 dollars. She had promised me a gold necklace like she had gotten my brother Todd, but I never received that necklace. My mother has never treated me like she did the others. As much as I tried to put our bad relationship between us behind me, she would always do something to keep the bad blood between us. My father must have really broken her heart or something to that fact. She always told me that I looked like my father, and that I would never be anything in life, just like him. And my whole life I believed that. She had nothing good to say about him or me. I was just the kid.

I really tried real hard to have a better relationship with my mother, but she just wouldn't let it be. I was very thankful for the money she sent.

I just couldn't understand why a mother would treat her child like she did me, regardless of what her relationship may have been like with my father or the promises he may have made but didn't keep. I was an innocent child, but I had paid the ultimate price all my life.

Today was a beautiful day, through all the wars. I was still blessed to see it. Officer A.J. came to my cell and told me to pack anything I wish to take with me. I asked, where he was taking me. He told me that I was going to R&D for release. I said, "Don't mess with me!" Now, mind you, we had been at war with the skinheads for some time now, and, believe it or not, these officers were rednecks and would set a black man up quick. I refused to leave with the officer. He told me if I wanted to go home, I better have my stuff packed and needed to be ready in fifteen minutes or I would miss my bus. I didn't think nothing other than the thought I had when he came to my cell. One would have to live this life themselves to really understand what it was like to be in this world. That's right; it's a world all within itself. The officer returned moments later and realized that I hadn't packed. He just looked at me and walked off.

Let me explain why I didn't pack. See, if I was being set up, the officer could easily say that they made a mistake of packing the wrong prisoner out for transfer because this was a normal thing that happened often. By refusing to pack, the officer would have to call a L.T or Sgt. or someone other than himself. Five minutes later he returned with my counselor, Mr. Carton. He told me that I had three minutes to pack my things, or I could spend another weekend in the (big house) Victorville. I then realized that I was a free man. I just had to make it outside of these walls now. I packed what little I was taking with me, and I yelled for the officer like crazy. On my way out, I stopped by Benton's cell.

Benton and Rexton were from Jamaica. Benton and his family had come here some years ago. They lived in Louisiana. Benton was in for drugs and gun, like many others. His cellie, Rexton, was a mixed Jamaican. Both were well known by the Muslims. In fact, Benton was well liked by many of the brothers, couldn't read too good, but he wasn't shy about it with the Muslims. Whenever he would get mail, he would ask me or other Muslims to read his mail to him and help him to respond back to whoever wrote him. One of the brothers worked on his case for him and got one of his charges overturned. He got five years off his sentence for the gun charge. I was happy for Benton.

Whenever there was a riot, they would get the boot camp guys to come over and clean up. They weren't allowed to come inside the prison. You could look out your window and see that they were really upset because anything that wasn't used by anyone would get thrown out the window. The staff was mad. Every lockdown they would have to pull twelve-hour shifts, do all the cooking, well not really cooking; we only got bag lunches on lockdown. They had to do it all: bagged meals, clean the showers, and mop the floors…I mean everything!

~" If a person would just look at themselves as they truly are instead of the image they wish to portray, they would begin to find the truth in life and in themselves, while seeing the illusion and the lie everyone else is trying to live."

Chapter 20

On November 15th, 1996, I was released. I was accepted at the halfway house in Richmond, Virginia. That's where I met Sharon Dilley. Sharon had been down for something to do with credit card. As she explained to me, a friend of hers used a credit card to balance out some dealings with her work.

I didn't get into it much. She started bringing me food to eat when she would come from work. I didn't eat much there at the halfway house because I didn't eat meat, and most of my meals consisted of tuna fish. The cook couldn't find anything better to prepare for me. Still, I didn't give her a hard time. She would always flirt with me, but I never had any type of sex with her, although I could have many times. I would just go into the kitchen and kiss her on her neck, get her hot, talk a little, and go back to the day room.

Her daughter, Tracie, worked there also. She was a college student. We were cool. I think she knew that her mom liked me, but she never said anything.

Terry liked this guy named Mac. He was from Newport News. The Feds had him hiding out because he was testifying against the guys in his gang.

I had only been there two weeks, and my first appointment with my probation officer didn't go well. He talked to me like I was a piece of nothing. I was sitting there in disbelief.

The day after my appointment with my probation officer I went to the Masjid as I often did. I told the Imam what happened yesterday between me and my probation officer.

I mentioned his name, and he asked me to say it again. Once again, I repeated his name "Otis Sharp" He said that if he's not mistaken, Otis

Sharp. was one of the men having something to do with a case in Virginia Beach involving some Muslims years ago.

This probation officer had no respect whatsoever. The director of the halfway house, Mr. Patrick, had it out for me. I knew him, and my probation officer talked after my visit with him that Friday. He stopped me from attending my religious service. I tried to talk to him. He told me that he didn't have time to talk right then; he had a lot of paperwork to do as I was standing right there. He told me to see him on Monday. I told him Monday was too late, that service was today and that I had already been given permission to attend my service. He screamed; "Didn't I tell you, no!!!"

I said to myself, *This fool has no idea*. I wanted to pop his wig. If only he knew, but then the look I gave him should have told him so. I turned and walked out of his office.

Sharon told me that she heard the conversation from the front office and said not to worry about it or let him get to me because that's what he wanted to do, so he could send me back.

The first week of December Mr. Patrick called me to his office and told me that he was the judge around here. I knew then he had received something from the courts in West Virginia. The judge had given me a 60-day extension. He went on telling me, "We'll see about that, Mr. Harper. I'll show you who's the judge around here. I run things around here, not no judge in West Virginia."

I said, "But this is the court. He said I'm the court." I told him that I needed the extension. I didn't have anywhere to go and no money. He told me I went out on my own and didn't ask him anything. I told him that was incorrect. Ms. Sharon Dilly and I asked him if it was okay for her to help me file for the extension, and he said yes. He said he didn't remember saying anything of the sort. I told him I could call Ms. Sharon Dilly. He said that he didn't want to hear it, and that was my problem and come December 16th, he would not be there that weekend.

While watching a movie on the VCR, one of the other tenants named Sandy and her boyfriend came in and started complaining about the movie. They said they wanted to see something else on TV. We told them that we were in the middle of the movie, but she continued. She went over and took the tape out of the VCR. I took the tape from her and put it back in and told her and her boyfriend that I wasn't in the mood for their stuff today, and if either of them touched that VCR again, I was going to break their necks. The boyfriend sat down. She went to the front office and called the police.

They came, and after we had given our side of the story, they told her that there was no reason for them to take me to jail. And, if they were called out again, someone was going to jail. He made it known to her that it could be her.

That Monday morning I was not allowed to go to work. I was told that Patrick, the director, wanted to see me. He made me wait until after lunch before he would see me to ensure I would miss work that day. Finally, he called me in and told me that I would not be able to go to work or anything else because I made trouble over the weekend and had the police called out to the halfway house. I told him that I hadn't done anything, and that Sandy called the police. He said if I didn't put my hands on her, she wouldn't have called the police. I said "You can't be real. If I had put my hands on that woman, I would be in jail."

He said, "You didn't go to jail because you got everybody around here taking up for you."

I asked him if he checked the police report because she had been drinking. He said that wasn't the news he got.

I said, "Of course not. You heard it from her." I told him at the end of the day when everybody was here, I would ask them to tell him what happened. He told me that he didn't need anyone to tell him anything; he made his decision, and that was that!

I said, "I'm missing work for something I didn't do."

Sandy and her boyfriend were able to continue their daily routine, even though his girl had tested positive for drugs from time to time. They had been drinking. By the end of the day, the word had gotten out, so some of the residents expressed their concerns and had their own talk with Mr. Patrick. He called me to the front door as he was leaving for the day and told me that I could go to work.

Sharon was very supportive. She would bring me food and do my laundry. It got to the point that if another woman would talk to me, she would give that look she had. I didn't look at Sharon in that way. She had a good heart, but I was not physically attracted to her. After returning from work that day, Sharon told me that I had a call from my sister, Celes, and that Christy was in jail, and the state had custody of my boys. Immediately,

I called my mom and told her that I'd just talked to Celes. We talked and decided to send my oldest brother, Jimmy, on the bus to get my boys. I had no idea of the task that was ahead of me. Not that it would've stopped me from trying, but it was very difficult.

I called Christy's mom, Miss Lorraine, and for the next few days, we talked and had agreed that she would get the boys, and my brother would come and bring them back to me since I couldn't leave the state. The judge was willing to give her custody, and everything was set, but suddenly Miss Lorraine changed her mind. I didn't understand. I asked what the problem was. She told me that she was not going to get her daughter's children, so I could come and take them away from her. I told her that those were my boys as well, and with Christy being in jail, I needed to get my boys. She said she would think about it. I told her, "Please don't let the state take my boys when you have a chance to get them." She told me to call back in a couple of days. I pleaded with her.

I was already working in Newport News Shipyard, but it was through a temp service. I knew I needed a permanent job to get my boys. Knowing that I needed a job bad, one of my Muslim brothers helped me get a job with him at the Chesapeake Pancake House. At first, I was told that there were no positions open, but I continued to show up for the next week and a half looking for employment. My persistence paid off. I was introduced to Jon, who was the general Manager and his family owned the store. He gave me a job, but the only thing he had open was a dish washing job, which didn't pay much of anything. That went on for about four to six weeks. I took a menu home, before long, I mastered it.

Sharon and I were trying everything to make this work out for me. I was still trying to get Miss Lorraine to get my boys. But she then informed me that she would not be getting them. I knew that I had to do something, so I contacted Mr. Otis. He wasn't in his office. Before I could get him and explain my problem, he called me at the job and told me to come to his office in Norfolk. Before I could say anything, he hung up on me.

I asked Calvin, who was one of the managers at the Pancake House, if he would go with me. I didn't want Sharon to be left without a ride from work. After all, it was her car. I had a bad feeling when I got there and signed in. He didn't even step outside the door; he just leaned his head out and told me that I had 48 hours to leave the state of Virginia and report to

West Virginia Federal Probation office. I was stunned. I couldn't believe this was happening. How could he do this? I knew that there had to be a hearing with good cause to kick me out of the state. 48 hours was not enough time to get anything done. I knew I had to report to West Virginia.

When I got outside, Calvin asked me what was up. I told him that I was just kicked out of the state. He asked if he could he do that. I told him no, but I had no choice at this time. He just shook his head and kind of laughed.

By the end of the day, I was no good after fighting traffic back to the store in Chesapeake. I dropped Calvin off, then drove home and took a shower.

I went to pick Sharon up from her job, and on the way to the halfway house, I told her what took place. She couldn't believe it. She told me to report it to his supervisor. I told her that I already thought of that, but I knew I was supposed to have gotten a hearing to defend myself. Sharon and I had moved into a home in Chesapeake when I was kicked out of the halfway house. But Sharon was still there. She had about two months left to stay at the halfway house. I knew this was Patrick's doing because the court had given me an extension. He got the probation office to kick me out of the state.

For the next two months, I had hearings in the West Virginia Federal Court. The judge was trying to find out why I was kicked out of the state of Virginia. He continued the hearing three times and directed the probation officer to find out what the violations were for, and what's their problem. Each hearing the probation officer said that he was unable to receive a response from the Richmond Probation office. He then asked the probation office to contact them with the information that I had given him about the shipyard in Richmond and the Pancake House in Chesapeake and set the next hearing for May 7, 1997.

That morning during the hearing, the Virginia Probation office was found to be unclear on violations of my rights.

Both jobs were wondering what happened to me and assured the court that I still had employment with them. The court asked the prosecutor if she had anything to say. She said that she just wished me the best and to stay out of trouble. The judge then asked me when I would be able to return to Virginia. I told him that I would need a couple of days. He then told me to report to the Federal Office in Richmond, Virginia. I was ready to leave West Virginia when I got there because I didn't think my brother-in-law wanted me staying there. I didn't have any money to get back, so I went to the Salvation Army. They gave me a one-way nonrefundable bus ticket.

When I arrived in Richmond, I reported to the probation office. I signed in and the secretary, Ms. Small, asked me who my probation officer was. I told her that I didn't know. I explained that I'd just come from Guilford, West Virginia, and was told to report there. She told me to have a seat. While sitting there. wouldn't you know it. Mr. Otis. walked out the door. He had some papers in his hand. He looked up then down and back up again. He noticed me and went in the back where their office was. Then coming out moments later, he asked me what I was doing there. I told him that I was there to report to my probation officer. He asked who told me that. I told him that the court sent me back because I was illegally kicked out of the state. He said, "We'll see about that," and then he told me my probation officer was Mr. John and to check back in a couple of days.

On my next visit I was told to call in everyday to see if the color code that was given to me was taking urine that day. I would come in once a week to check in. This went on for about four to six weeks. Finally, Mr. John told me that my probation officer was Mr. Earnest, and I was to report to him on Monday. I asked Mr. John why he couldn't remain my probation officer. He told me that his boss was the one who appointed my probation officers. Mr. John was alright. I knew that they were trying to give me the worst probation officer they had because I'd come back, and Mr. Otis didn't like that.

When I met with Mr. Earnest, we talked, and I explained what took place with Mr. Otis. He, himself, didn't believe that he had done something like that. We talked about my jobs. He asked if I had my job when Mr. Otis did that. I told him that I had both jobs. He just laughed and shook his head. I went home and told Sharon what happened.

That weekend Sharon and I looked all around, trying to find this movie we wanted to see. We knew it would be hard to find because it was about a slave ship where the slave trader had illegally gone to South Africa and kidnapped people and brought them to the United States to be slaves.

Finally, it was being played at MacArthur Mall. The place was packed. While waiting for a parking spot, this Ford Bronco raced into the space I was waiting for. I said, "Yo', man! I was waiting for that spot." He looked and said something I didn't hear. I got out walked up to the Bronco and told home boy if he didn't move his vehicle, put his fists up. He looked at me and noticed that I was serious. He said, "Okay, my brother." He pulled out, and I got the space. Later, after waiting for the movie, he walked over with his woman and introduced himself. I did the same. Sharon was looking and said, "Please, Ziggy, don't do anything."

He asked if he could talk to me for a minute. I agreed.

I was still upset at Miss Lorraine for not getting my boys. I asked Celes if she would get them, and I would take them off her hands. She told me that she would have to check with her husband. Come to find out, the courts wouldn't give them to anyone but Christy or her mom. I was going through a lot at this time, but let's get back to the matter at hand.

He told me his name was Taylor, and he could use a guy like me in his business. I asked him what kind of business he was in. He told me that he had his own security business. I told him that I had a job but thanks, anyway. He gave me his card and then asked if he could have my number. I looked at him and said, "You probably knew I wouldn't call." He laughed and said that's why he wanted my number, so I gave it to him. We were there to see the same movie.

A few weeks had gone by, and he called and asked if I had thought about working for him. I told him that I was still thinking about it. So, for the next two weeks he would call, so I decided to work for him. I only worked on Thursday, Friday and Saturday. I was still working full time at the Pancake House. It got to the point that I had to let Thursdays go. I was working hard. I had not worked like that since I'd been out. During the security work, I had the opportunity to work with some of the biggest names in the entertainment business. I worked in many clubs: Bottoms Up, Nile, Swingers, The C.J Club, Victor City, and at the Towers in Virginia Beach. That's where I met D' Low. His mother was with him and had too much to drink that night. The name of Taylor's company was ELF Security Service. I was at the top of my game then. I was eating right, exercising, didn't smoke nor eat pork for many years. At this time, you could see why he would want me on his team. It got to the point that I was training everybody on Mondays as well as passing out the payroll. Then he tried to get me to take the responsibility of scheduling everybody for the week. I turned that down. I only took the job because of the under the table pay. That way the probation officer wouldn't get involved. I wasn't supposed to be doing that kind of work anyway, but I needed the money.

I told Taylor, once a month I had to go to West Virginia. I was fighting for custody of my boys. He said no problem. I would miss Friday and Saturday from the security job, and Monday from the Pancake House. Before that, it would be two days from the Pancake House because the judge would have my court days in the middle of the week. After explaining the distance, I came every day to the court hearing and my job. He would only have hearings on Mondays. That really helped because I was losing money. Even though it was one week a month, I still needed the money. Every time I went to court, I also would go to Durham, West Virginia, to see my boys in the group home where they were staying. Litta's daughter, Re-Re, would go with me sometimes.

Durham was four hours the other way. But I would take Re-Re and bring her back home. It was a lot of driving, but I wanted my boys to see any of their family that would come. No one else would take that ride to visit my boys, and I felt bad. I mean Christy 's mom would ask me how the boys were doing, and I would just remain calm and say that they were doing fine. Then I would ask her when she would be going with me to visit. She would say something like, "Maybe next time," or something about my driving. Maria was going to let her two children go with me to see the boys, but after talking with her mother, she changed her mind. I couldn't understand why she didn't really care for my boys. Her son, Earl, had a little girl named Tracie. Miss Lorraine took her and raised her. But she would let the state take my boys. During one of my court hearings, I talked with Christy, and she had agreed that she would get custody and let me have them. We couldn't finish the conversation without her girlfriend/lover jumping in, telling her to come on.

I told her, "You would allow another woman to stop you from getting your children. Y'all live together. While your own children are in the state custody, because you couldn't put the crack pipe down, but you're helping with her children."

I asked Christy, "What in the world happened to you in prison? Some woman went down on you and you lost your mind, or something?" She just stood there looking crazy. I told her that I didn't understand. Was this the mother I knew who loved her children?

Her lover calls out to her: "Chris, let's go."

Back in the day, we didn't know her, but we knew of her. This was a small town. I never thought that Christy would be with another woman. I told her that we were talking about our children, and it was best that she stay out of the conversation.

That Monday Christy came to court and said that she was not ready to get the boys and didn't want me to have them. I was bewildered. I mean, I could not believe that this was happening. I motioned like 'what are you doing.' The Judge set the case for the following month and ordered that I take a psychological evaluation and parental class, of which I finished both and passed. I had to take the psychological evaluation in Guilford, West Virginia, and the parental class in Chesapeake where I lived.

After my return from West Virginia. Sharon as always would ask me how my trip was, and how the boys are doing, and what happened in court? I told her about the conversation I had with Christy about getting the boys, so they can come live with me, but in court that Monday, she changed her mind.

After I took a shower, Sharon said she had something to tell me and made me promise that I wouldn't get upset. I said, "What now?"

She told me that my sister, Celes, had called and told her to tell me as best as she could that her husband, Dante, didn't want me staying with them when I came down anymore. I just shook my head and laughed. The thoughts came running back to when my brothers and I had to share a room while he lived better than we did in our own house. That gave me a headache, so I lay down and went to sleep, but not before I went into Co-co's room to kiss her goodnight. Co-co brought me so much joy here. I loved her just as much as I did all my children.

During all my visits to West Virginia I would always go and get my daughter, Alina. We would hang out and get something to eat. Sometimes I would take her friends with us but not before I went to each house and asked their mother or father.

After I was no longer welcome at my sister's house, I would still go by her job and visit her. Everyone at her job loved me. It was a family business, and they were all white. I liked everyone there because they were nice people, and they would always ask me what happened in court and wish me the best. A couple of women, I think, liked me. You can always tell when a woman likes you. I knew Celes made me promise that I wouldn't mess with anyone on her job, so I didn't.

Whenever I had a court date, I would stay at a cheap motel across the bridge in Cincinnati, Ohio. I only paid 25 dollars a night. I just couldn't believe my brother-in-law. But then, some people you never know until you're in need.

Some of my trips I had my nephew with me in the beginning. One trip I fell asleep. We went off the road to the left, and once I got control of the car, I just kept going and thanked God and laughed. My nephew, Donnald, looked at me crazily. I could only imagine what he was thinking with that look he had on his face. He never went with me again after that.

One weekend while working at the Bottoms Up Club the secretary from the probation office walked up behind me and said, "What are you doing?" I looked and immediately walked off to take my security shirt off. She stopped me and said, "There is no need, Mr. Earnest already saw you."

I said, "Stop playing; you're messing with me, aren't you?"

She said, "Now why would I do that?" Then she smiled and said, "Don't worry he won't say anything tonight. I don't know what he'll do next week, but you are safe tonight. Oh, by the way, Mrs. Bailey is here also. You can put your shirt back on."

I looked for Mrs. Bailey, but I didn't see her, and I had no reason not to believe Ms. Small.

The following week I went to see Mr. Earnest. He asked me what I was doing. I told him that he knew Sharon was violated. He said he knew. I told him that I needed the money to pay my bills. He just told me that I was not to do any kind of work like that. He told me that he was not going to do anything, but I needed to quit that job. I said I would, but then I asked him that if I asked for permission, would he give it, so I could continue that job. He said that my paperwork might restrict me from doing that kind of work. He said he'd get back with me on that. I knew I was just buying time.

"When a man begins to feel what he is without, he
begins to find what he needs within.

Chapter 21

Sharon and I were already married by the Imam, but we needed permission from the probation officer. Not long after, we both ended up with Mrs. Bailey as our probation officer. We asked for permission, and in a matter of weeks we were given permission to live together as a married couple.

We were living together as a family now. I remember the first time I met Co-co; she was so beautiful. Sharon told her that we would be living together. She gave that look she had and said, "What you talking 'bout?"

Boy, I must have laughed my heart out. I met her son, Bill, when I was still in the halfway house. Bill stood about 6'10" and 300 pounds. The boy was built for football and basketball, or maybe both, but he couldn't play that well. Bill was a good guy - real humble. Sometimes I thought he was too humble.

Months later they changed my probation officer again. This time I got Ms. Evert. She was a white woman that had it out for me. I knew that this was coming from Otis. He couldn't get the others because they knew that he had violated my rights by kicking me out of the state. I knew sooner or later he would get somebody to harass me.

They also changed Sharon's probation officer. We now both had white probation officers. She had Mr. Bobby. I was told by Ms. Evert that Sharon and I couldn't be married and that I couldn't see her. I told her that we were already given permission. She told me that she would have to check on that.

One day while Sharon and I were out, Ms. Evert and Sharon's probation officer came by the house and they spoke with Bill. He told them that I was living there. I was real upset, but I shouldn't have been upset with him. Sharon and I had kept everything from him and Co-co.

The next day I went to see my probation officer, and she said that Ms.

Bailey had told us she would check on it but had not given us permission to get married. Now that was a flat out lie by Ms. Evert. She told me, I couldn't get married, and if I go around Sharon again she would violate me and send me back to prison. I filed a motion for a hearing to have another probation officer appointed to my case.

On January 14, 1998 I had my hearing, and Mr. Otis was there. I asked the supervisor why Mr. Otis was here. He told me, "Don't you worry about who's here; you just state your claim."

I explained how I felt I was being harassed after I was given permission to marry Ms. Sharon Dilley by Ms. Bailey. Ms. Evert said that we couldn't be married, and I couldn't visit her either. He told me that Ms. Bailey was not my probation officer anymore, so whatever Ms. Evert said, then that's what I must do. I told him that I wished to appeal, but he told me that he would deny it and not to bring this before him anymore. He said, "In fact, I don't want to see you at all."

I was stunned. This was unbelievable. Mr. Otis and Ms. Evert looked at each other and smiled. The supervisor told me I could leave now. I knew they had it out for me. See how one person can cause a chain of events that lead to a bad reaction? From Mr. Patrick to Mr. Otis, and now it continued.

Sharon worked for a company called Ruffin Mortgage Company. There she became friends with one of the secretaries who eventually ended up getting fired. Sharon tried to get her job back for her, but the supervisor told Sharon that she couldn't even take out the trash for them anymore.

Ms. Evert told me that I had to show my new address and prove that I lived there. So, Sharon got her old secretary to allow me to use her address, and we told her that I would pay $200 a month, but I wouldn't be staying there. It's just an address for the probation officer. So, she agreed.

When Ms. Evert came out to see where I was living, as soon as we sat down in the living room, Ms. Evert started asking all kinds of personal questions. She responded by telling her that she was not going to discuss personal things. Ms. Evert said that she must ask these question as she continued. She asked her things like: Are you married? Who else lives here? How many kids do you have? Etc. I mean all kind of things.

So, I interjected and told Ms. Evert that she was my landlord, not my woman. I didn't think the questions were in order. I thought that her private life was her business and not anyone else's.

As we were sitting there, a mild wind rushed through the window, and it blew the blinds up, and when they came down, it hit the window so hard that Ms. Evert jumped out her seat. She said, "What is that?" The landlord and I looked at each other and laughed. I told Ms. Evert it was just the wind.

"You know, they tell me it's all in how you're living."

She looked at me and asked, "What did you say?"

I said, "Nothing, Ms. Evert.

After the interview Ms. Evert said that we needed to go to the police station. We both asked why. Ms. Evert said that she had to be sure that she didn't have a record. I told the landlord that if she didn't want to, it was okay. She looked at Ms. Evert and said, "No, its okay. Let's go."

When we got to the police station, Ms. Evert wanted the lady to be fingerprinted. I felt that it was enough, but she went through with it.

During this time, we had moved from the house off North Independence St. to Rose Pod Loop.

After living there for a year, Sharon was violated, only after they tried to violate me first. They knew Sharon and I were still together. But to pull us apart, they didn't know how, unless they did something like this.

During one of my trips to court for a hearing in Guilford, West Virginia, Melissa had gone into my glove compartment and had gotten information to my probation officer. Melissa didn't like the idea that I had gotten out of prison and went on with my life, and she was not a part of it. It never occurred to me that she would do something like this though.

I had no idea she was out to get me. My sister, Celes, had called me after this trip and said she was told by Beth and Latrina that Melissa had taken charges out on me for rape. I said, "Rape?"

She said that Latrina told her that Melissa was talking about it because I had used her while I was in prison, then got out and married someone else. I told Celes that she knew very well that our relationship ended years before I got out.

My sister said, "I told you not to see that girl when you come down here." My sister knew I didn't do anything like that. With all the women I could have gotten, now why would I do something like that? I asked my sister to call the police station there in Guilford and inquire about the charge.

Celes called me back and told me that they didn't have any charges on me. I asked her to call Latrina and get back with me tomorrow. The next day I called Celes and asked if she talked with Latrina and Beth yet She told me that Latrina said for me to call her.

I called Latrina and she told me that the three of them were hanging out at Beth's house, as usual, on the weekends, and Melissa would talk about how she was going to get back at me. Latrina told me that Melissa talked about me all the time. She said that if she couldn't have me, nobody else could. Latrina told me she and Beth thought that she was just talking to be talking. Latrina went on to say last week Melissa showed her and Beth a paper from my probation officer stating that if they took me to court, would she testify. Latrina told her that she couldn't be serious, but Melissa told her that she was not playing. I asked Latrina that if I needed her, would she come to court for me and Beth as well. She assured me that if needed, they would come. I thanked her and said that I'd be in touch.

I hung up the phone and sat there in disbelief. How could so much bad shit happen to one person?

A couple days later Ms. Evert called me to her office and told me that I violated my parole. I asked what the charges were. She told me that it would be in my summons. She had no idea I knew about Melissa. The next day she called me to her office. After sitting for about two hours, I was served with my summons. The charges read: Violation: Rape, changing my address and not notifying the probation officer within 72 hours, and a dirty urine.

That weekend I called Latrina and Beth and asked them if they were still willing to testify for me. They both said that they would. That following Monday I went to the federal building and filled out the indigent forms for my witnesses. The clerk notified them of what hotel they would be staying in, how much they were going to get for each mile they traveled, and any food expenses.

Afterwards, Latrina called me and assured me that they would be there the day before court. I was on edge the whole time. After all, so many things had gone wrong so far. They finally called the night before court and told me that they were at a gas station and thought they were lost. I asked her to look at the street signs and tell me where they are. She told me Harpursville Road at the gas station. I told her that they were only two blocks from the hotel and not to worry and stay right there. I was on my way. I drove 32 miles from where I lived just to take them to a hotel two blocks away. I mean, after all, it's the least I could do. they'd just come over 500 miles to help me.

When I pulled into the gas station, once they saw me, they started smiling. You could imagine the joy on my face. I got out and hugged each one and thanked them both for coming.

They followed me to the hotel. Once we got there, they gave the clerk their voucher and freshened up. Afterwards, I took them out to eat. Once we returned to the hotel, I told them that I would pick them up in the morning for court. At that time Latrina stole a little kiss on the lips.

The following morning while waiting to be called in the courtroom, my lawyer, Mr. Williams LA Cross, kept asking me if I see Melissa. Each time a female got off the elevator or the steps, he would look at me. He thought how good it would be if she didn't show up. Shit, he didn't have to tell me.

At that very moment we were called into the courtroom, she was coming off the elevator. Looking at her walk off that elevator like she wasn't doing anything wrong, I couldn't believe that she was going through with this lie.

As Melissa testified, she claimed that I raped her and afterwards, we went to an ice cream parlor and had ice cream. The judge (Ms. Kennedy) asked Melissa to describe how I raped her. She told the judge, "Oh, he didn't have sexual intercourse. Instead, he made me perform oral sex on him."

The Judge then asked her where she lived and how far it was from the police department. As she began, the judge stopped her and said, "I'll tell you how far you live. Fifth Avenue and 20th Street. The police station is on 3rd Avenue and 10th Street. You mean to tell me that you didn't go to your police station and report this information?"

As Melissa started to speak, the judge said, "No, I'll tell you why it never happened."

The prosecutor tried to intervene. The judge told him to sit down, told

Melissa to step down off the stand. She then asked my lawyer who my witness was. My lawyer called Beth first, and she was sworn in.

She testified that she, Latrina, and Melissa were at her house playing cards, as usual, on the weekend, and I had come in town like I did every month. She was going on and on about how I was going to be sorry that I left her and that she, (Melissa) was in touch with my probation officer. She further testified how she, (Melissa) went in my car, got a traveling permit, and contacted my probation officer. She also described how my probation office thanked Melissa so much for calling her, and during the conversation, how both agreed that I needed to be off the streets. The judge thanked her and told her she could step down now. My Lawyer went to call Latrina, but the judge said that she heard enough. She told the prosecutor and Ms. Evert mot to ever use her courtroom as a playground again. The prosecutor tried to speak, but she told him that all she heard was a cry from a scorned woman about a man who didn't want to be with her. She lived two to three blocks from a police station in West Virginia, but instead she traveled over 500 miles to take someone to court in Virginia. It was nonsense. She went on further to tell me that I'd better dot all my I's and cross all my T's. Then she told the prosecutor and the probation officer to get out of her courtroom.

The judge told me to report to the clerk's office. My probation officer told me to report afterwards. When I finally exited the building, the prosecutor was standing outside smoking a cigarette. As I walked down the steps, I kindly mumbled, "Smoking cigarettes can kill at a young age." He looked at me, not knowing how to take my statement.

Months later they violated Sharon. I know it was only because they failed in trying to violate me. Now it's just me and Co-co living in the house. Bill would get Co-co from school for me until I got home from the security job on the weekends. For the next two months I was going to a parenting class, worrying about how well I did on the psychological evaluation that they conducted in Guilford, West Virginia, which was ordered by the judge at family court. I couldn't understand why they were putting me through so much to get custody of my boys.

During this time the wife (Toni), with whom we purchased the house from, had come down from New York. My understanding was Sharon had taken care of the rent for the next six months that she would be away. What pissed me off was that she showed up with the sheriff, giving me two days to move. I can take 30 days by law. By then I was real upset with Sharon. How could she leave me in that situation?

I contacted Bill and told him that I needed him to find some guys who would help us move and I'd pay them 50 dollars each.

About a week and a half later, Toni had been at the neighbors every day. I got tired of seeing her, so I took nothing from the house and put everything in storage except our clothes. I moved back to Norfolk where I took over an apartment that my brother, Jimmy, was living in. I brought all new furniture. The apartment was good because it was across the street from my mom. That way she could help me with Co-co by putting her on the school bus and getting her off. She ended up staying with my mom for the most part. It really worked out.

That weekend I went to the storage to get something. What I saw next was unbelievable. I opened the door. Bill and the guys had everything stacked on top of each other. I mean it was a real mess. I could have killed Bill.

During this time, I was so upset with Sharon, that when she caled my mom to talk with Co-co, I wouldn't speak with her. I knew it was wrong, but most of the time, I would be at work or somewhere else anyway.

~" We must learn to accept a response, rather than expect a response from others that we may have tried to help, or better their condition in life, because what we may understand as help to us, may be understood as harm by them."

Chapter 22

While working at the Nile one night, there was a commotion at the front desk. As I approached, two women were going on about how they shouldn't have to pay the full amount to get into the club because it was after midnight. I told them that if they promised to keep it down out there for five minutes, I would consider letting them in for half price. I turned to walk back outside. Lizzy Smith yelled out, "Damn you're a big mf."

I turned and said, What?"

Her friend said, "She drunk."

I told her, "In that case, you need to go home, not in the club."

At that time Lizzy yelled, "I'm not drunk, and I can go in the club if I want to."

I told her just on that fact alone, I didn't have to let her in. Why did I say that? Oh, boy!

While her friend and I were talking, Lizzy went on and on about how her husband wasn't any good. She continued about how he had left her for a white girl and stole all their money out of the bank.

I told her, "Look, you can go in if you promise not to start any trouble."

She looked at me, smiled, and said, "I promise."

During my rounds in the club, I made it my business to check on her to make sure she was not causing any trouble. I saw that she was dancing with some guy on the floor like she knew him. You see, before I allowed her to come in, not only did she promise not to cause any trouble, but she also gave me her phone number, and I promised to call her as well.

When she saw me, she said something to the guy on the dance floor and stumbled up to me trying to talk. You can imagine trying to hear her drunken voice over the loud music. I couldn't make out a word.

Her friend came up to us and asked me if I would make her leave. Her friend said that she didn't like the fact that Lizzy was dancing with that guy like that and didn't know him. I told Lizzy that I thought it was time for her to go home and get some sleep.

After walking her to the car, once again, she made me promise I would call. They got in the car. Once they pulled off the lot, I threw her number in the trash, like many before hers and those that would come after her. Women were always giving me their phone numbers. I mean, it was like non-stop working this kind of job. it was to be expected.

The next weekend one of my security guys came in the club and told me that some woman was outside asking to speak to me. I told him to tell her I'd be out in a few.

As I walked outside, there was Lizzy and her girlfriend. Lizzy had been drinking again, although not as bad as the last time I saw her, but you could tell she had had enough. I asked her friend why she brought her up here like that. She told me that Lizzy used the longtime girlfriend guilt on her and that if she didn't, she would have driven herself, and she would be sorry if anything happened to her. I just smiled. Lizzy had so much to drink, that at one point she leaned up against the car for the remainder of the time.

I talked with them briefly before walking off. She made me promise that I would call her, but I never did. Everything was coming at me so fast.

It was November of 1998. Sharon had been violated for three months now. We lost the house. I was trying my best to keep up with the bills every month, like child support, which I make sure was paid. I still had Co-co, my car note, insurance, rent and all the household bills that came along with it, not to mention going to West Virginia once a month to court, trying to get custody, getting my boys the things that they needed, and leaving them with spending money, which gave me such pleasure. I thought about them every day and what they may have been going through. They didn't deserve any of this, and I thank God that I didn't have any habits, such as smoking, drinking, and drugs. I mean, anything that would take me away from holding down my responsibilities.

The following weekend Lizzy showed up at the club. This time she was sober. I was standing outside watching my crew shake down. She got out of the car and called out, "Ziggy! Ziggy!"

I looked and saw someone much different from the previous weekends. I called her over and told her she looked much better. I asked if she was going in. She said no, she had just come over to see me, and maybe if she wasn't drunk, then I would take her seriously and call her. She asked if I would come and see her when I get off work. Because she was sober, I couldn't lie to her, so I told her that it might be best if I didn't. She went on about what was wrong with her (with tears in her eyes) and that her husband had left her for a white girl. I told her that I didn't think it had anything to do with the woman being white, nor how she looked. I mean, after all, he married her. In fact, he was the fool. It was his loss.

She smiled and said, "Well, not actually married. We were to be married, but something changed. He started smoking crack, and everything went downhill. I told her that she should be happy then because he couldn't do anything but bring her down, smoking that shit. I couldn't stand out there all night, so I told her that if she would go home, I promised I would come over after work. She gave me that look I saw before and smiled. I assured her that I would. She then asked if I had something that she could take with her to make sure I came. She said that I could give her my watch or something. I gave her my driver's license. I always kept two licenses. She looked at my cell phone and then at me. I told her I needed my phone, so she could guide me to her house. I'd never been to Norton County. In fact, I'd never heard of it until I met her. She laughed and said, "Norton County?" I asked her if it was on the map. She kind of gave me that 'alright now' look.

That night I got to her house about 3:45 a.m. We sat up talking till dawn. Before we knew it, we were kissing and touching each other. She said as bad as she wanted to, she couldn't because this was the first time that we had spent any time together. We needed to talk a little more and go out to eat on a date, do things to get to know one another better. I didn't know if I should get upset or not. I mean, after all, I really had no business being there, but now that I was there, and she had me ready....

I drove home that morning just thinking about what just happened and how I should have not been there. I respected the fact that she didn't give it up, although she wanted to as she mentioned during our foreplay.

That week, I never called her, though she called my cell phone several times. I never answered it nor returned her calls. I just spent the whole week thinking about how this was wrong. Everything that I believed in prohibited me from being with women with such conduct. With Sharon being gone, it made all the prohibited things just that much easier to get in trouble with.

After not returning her calls all week, I knew that she would show up at the club. That following Friday, like I said, I knew she would show up. She pulled in the parking lot and got out of her car. Before she could say anything, I walked up to her and told her that I didn't think that I was the one for her. She gave me that sad looking face again. I told her that I needed to keep an eye on my crew and didn't have time to talk right now. She said okay and that she'd wait until I got off work. I looked at her with a smile and told her that it wasn't necessary and that I'd see her later. I then asked her about her boys, who I met the morning I left. She said that her friend was babysitting for her. I told her that I had to make my rounds.

When I returned outside, she was sitting in her car smoking a cigarette. As I walked towards her car, I could only think what a turn off it was to see a woman smoking. Once again, I told her that I would come by when I got off. She looked with disbelief and said that I was lying to her as I had lied before. I couldn't do anything but laugh. I promised her that I would come by once I was off. She looked at me, turned, and while getting back in her car said, "Whatever."

As she started up her car, I could see the tears in her eyes. I told her to let down her window. I gave her my cell phone. She looked at me and smiled from ear to ear. I told her that if she turned my phone back on and answered it, there would be nothing to talk about. I didn't care how much she came up here. I would never speak to her again. She then said, "I won't, I promise."

~" While the world and everyone in it screams at you to look like this,
feel like that, speak like this, think like that; you must remember to
listen to your own spirit when you feel lost because it whispers to you the
truth that it is okay for you to be yourself and who you really are."

Chapter 23

Whenever I got off work from the Pancake House job, I still made sure that I would spend time with Co-co, even on the days I would go to Lizzy's.

After seeing Lizzy for about three to four weeks, she took me to meet her parents. They lived in a double-wide trailer. That trailer was beautiful. I had never been in a trailer before. I don't know why people talk about trailers in a bad way. This trailer was hooked up, big on the inside.

When Lizzy introduced me to her mother (Roslyn) her mother sat at the kitchen table with her mouth open, finally, she said; Lizzy where in the hell did you find this big as man from? I could do nothing but laugh. Her father Peter shook my hand and asked me what my name was again. At that time her mother said, "I know what I'm going to call you: Big Bastard. She put her hand up in the air and said, "That's if you don't mind." I told her if she didn't tell anyone else to call me that. She said not to worry about that.

Lizzy and her mom were getting things together for the Christmas holidays. I told her that I didn't celebrate pagan holidays, that I was Muslim. She said "Oh, My lord!" She then asked me what I celebrated. I told her that we, as Muslims, had our holidays. I went into details explaining what we celebrated and why. I even went as far as explaining the holiday in which Americans celebrated and where they started. As the conversation continued, she asked me again, "So, you don't eat pork?" Looking at Lizzy, they both started smiling. Finally, I caught on to what they were referring to (oral-sex) and stated how I strongly condemned such an act. I told her that before I became a Muslim that was something that I would never do. Lizzy asked? "So, what is it that you refuse to do?"

I said, "Should we be talking like this on our first date?"

She responded, "Honey, we couldn't be on no date; you don't eat pork." They just laughed their hearts out. I couldn't help but think about how she was putting her business out there like that. I told her it was just the thought of how many men she may have been with. In fact, it didn't matter if she'd only been with one man her whole life. That was something I couldn't bring myself to do.

Roslyn went on to say, "Lizzy, baby, I don't know what you going to do because if you need to be touched like that, you can't cheat, and if you do, don't call me because I don't know anybody that may be willing to go up against a man that big."

Lizzy put her arms around me, laughing, "I don't need another man, mother. Ziggy is all the man I need."

We spent the rest of the day there talking and everything.

I still worked in Chesapeake, so that meant that I would drive 50-some miles one way and over 100 miles two ways. Every day I would stop in Norfolk to spend time with Co-co. As always, women would come in the Pancake House and flirt with me all the time.

One day Selena Harper and a coworker of hers came in to eat. They worked at the medical building on the back street. They billed patients for the hospitals. You name it; they did it. I never intended on having a relationship with her, but so much was going on. After talking with her for the fourth time, within two weeks, she agreed to do my laundry, cook for me, take my clothes to the cleaners, and pick them up. That was her way of keeping me coming by after work sometimes. After our first night out, we went to eat at the Pancake House in Virginia Beach. Jerry worked that store. The family owned the one I worked as well as that one.

Now I had two women that I shouldn't have been with and my wife in prison. Selena had two boys, D and C. She used to talk about how their father needed to be active in their lives, especially Dee. The boy was feminine in everything he did. She got to the point that she asked me to spend time with him, one-on-one, to try and guide him in the right way of doing thing like boys and stop talking and moving the way he did. My first thoughts were, *I have so much on my plate. Do I want to take on this responsibility?* Though the sex was good, I still had too much on my plate. Sharon was in prison, Co-co in Norfolk, Bill was in Newport News. I still had to look out for him. Alina was in Guilford, West Virginia. Mario and Charles were in Durham, West Virginia, which I visited once a month every time I went to court in Guilford, West Virginia, which was four hours the other direction. It didn't matter. I would've driven cross country for them. I tried real hard to get custody. I really did.

Whenever I worked Club Victor City, a strip club, I would stay at Selena's because the club was just two blocks from her apartment. While working at Club Victor City with all those beautiful women and in charge of security, I made all decisions on the do's and don'ts. Having all those women right there in my face all the time half naked, I managed to maintain. You can imagine the many times I was approached by some of these women. I mean, they were like that. Not often, but sometimes girls would come from out of town and other places to dance. See, all the girls had to do was pay the owner to dance, as well as the members.

One day this guy walked up to the door and asked for the owner. I asked if there was a problem. He said that he had some girls who wanted to dance, and they were from New York. I got the owner and they talked. The guy walked out 20 yards to a van in the parking lot and returned with seven women. They were all good looking. He returned outside to the van. I hadn't noticed at first, but there was still a girl in the van. I could see where he had her legs up in the air. One of my crew workers looked at me and I said, "I know damn well this chump isn't doing this mess in my parking lot. Is he trying to get us in trouble?"

I walked over to the van and told the boy that he needed to get a room. I didn't care one way or another, but he had to take that mess out of my lot. He got behind the wheel and moved the van to the other side of the street to another property.

Moments later they both came walking across the lot. I stopped her at the door and told her that she could go in, but she couldn't dance. She and the guy simultaneously said, "Why?"

I looked at her and said, "You got to be joking. You think that I'm going to allow you to go in here and shake your ass in these guys faces, and you hadn't washed your ass."

The girl was so embarrassed.

O boy tried to talk his way in. He had no idea who he was talking to. I told him they could either go in, or they could leave. It was up to them.

Moments later they called me inside the club. The owner was telling O boy that he could book his girl. I could see the dude getting beside himself. I told him that I needed to speak with him outside.

Once I got him outside, I told two of my workers to go in and get his girls. All the time he was trying to talk me into letting his girls stay in the club. I wasn't going to change my mind. I had enough of this guy. They loaded up, and I never saw them again. That's what I liked about this job. I was given control. That way I could handle the situation the way I saw fit.

Back to my routine. Though my hands were already full, I almost started something with one of the girls who worked there. I don't know how it started, but I ended up giving her a ride home after closing, which was 6:00 a.m. Now she lived out at The View, which was in Newport News. I had to end that. I knew it was just a matter of time before I started hitting that. I was spreading myself real thin.

After we closed, I would always sit on the sofa chair right at the door and wait until the girls got their selves together to leave. She would always come and start giving me a lap dance. I would put my hand on her hips to stop her. It didn't matter; whenever I worked the club Victor City, I had to put up with her. She was beautiful; don't get me wrong - and a banging body. But I couldn't handle anymore.

Sometimes I would leave my Pancake House job and stop by to see Selena, spend some time with her, and then I would hit Lizzy. Whenever I tried to get that third one for the night, my testicles would start to hurt … not all the time but enough.

Whenever I didn't show up for the night at Lizzy's, she would want to know where I stayed the night before. I would simply say that I stayed at my apartment with my daughter, Co-co. She would give me that look, and I'd just start sweet talking, kissing, and touching, and I would take her to the bedroom, lay her down, and wax it good for about an hour or so. After that I would take another shower and sleep the better part of the day.

I really liked going to Norton County. It was so quiet, and I could really get some rest until Lizzy felt like she wanted to do something. She liked having sex, that is. The sex would be good. She would do whatever I asked her. She liked it as much as I did. I liked the way she would wake me up in the morning, and she was good.

We would go to her parents' house just about every Saturday and Sunday that I was there. It was something she did before we met. She and her mother would talk and drink coffee. Peter and I were part of the conversation. She had this one aunt that whenever she was around at Lizzy's, she would always run up to me. Lizzy and her mother, playing, would always encourage her yelling, "There's your boyfriend, Ziggy!" I could do nothing but smile and try to keep her hands off me. She would just be hugging and kissing and trying to put my hands on her ass or whatever. Everybody would just be laughing. She would always tell me that Lizzy couldn't do it like she could. The things she would whisper in my ear, I would look at Lizzy and Roslyn and ask them to get her. She was a nice person but not my type. Although she had one aunt that I would have done, had I not met Lizzy. She was high yellow, very good looking, and a body with hips and all. Lizzy was kind of dark skinned and very good looking. Her mom was good looking with a banging body. Her sister, Princess, was bad as hell. She had a very thin waste. Well, they all had very thin wastes, but Princess had an ass like a Stallion.

Back to the aunt, the yellow one. She was a nurse too. Lizzy got to the point that whenever she would come around, she always said with a smile, "Ziggy, here comes your girlfriend." I think they used to talk about me, and somewhere she said some very likeable things about me. She had a son that Lizzy was real close to so, therefore, she would bring him around often. I was good with all the children.

The first time I went to Lizzy's was like a day or two before Christmas. She made me promise to pick her up after work that night once the club closed. I really didn't want to disrespect her parents. Wouldn't you know it; she put her mother on the phone, and she told me that I better pick her up, or I would have to answer to her. When I arrived, some guy whom I have never met, answered the door. He asked me if I was Ziggy. I said, "Yes." He told me to come in. He went to one of the bedrooms, and Lizzy came out. She introduced us. "Ziggy, this is Toby." We shook hands. I would have never thought that he would be working for me weeks later.

During one of the visits to her parents' house, Lizzy told him to ask me about working at the club because they considered him family. I got him on my crew weeks later. He was in the military as well as Princess, her husband and Lizzy's best friend, Rosalinda's husband. Though I never met

Rosalinda's husband because he was stationed out west, we became good friends, especially when she had their baby girl. Rosalinda is Spanish. That baby girl was so adorable. She got real attached to me.

> "When we try to exalt ourselves in the eyes of some at the expense of another person's mistake we show everybody how small we really are.

Chapter 24

After six months Sharon was coming home. I didn't talk to her too much because I was always working, but that's no excuse. I was just into other things that I shouldn't have been. I tried to get my brother, Todd, and his kids' mother, Krista, to go so that they could take Co-co to see her. I told them that I would even pay for everything, but it still never happened. I couldn't keep my brother off crack long enough for anything … like the day I had him help me tune up my car. I knew I shouldn't have paid him until we finished. Anyway, that never happened. I know I was wrong, but I sent my mom to pick her up from the train station. You can imagine my mom going on and on.

When they got home that night, I was sitting on the steps of my apartment, which was across the street from my mom. I had to do that because of Co-co so that my mom was able to take her to the bus stop, pick her up from school, doctors apartments and all that. A-D knew I didn't want to live across the street from my mom.

Sharon walked over, and we talked, but she ended up staying with my mom. For the past three months I knew I didn't feel the same. What I felt wasn't sorry; it was more like pity love, more than anything else. I was not in love with her like I was at one time. Man! I was really losing my mind. I stopped going to the Mosque for Friday Service every Friday. I wasn't making all my prayers. I mean, even though I was sleeping with these women, neither had any problem with me making my prayers or going to the Mosque. In fact, they would even make a place, and that means no pictures on the walls … I mean the whole nine yards.

Now that I think about it, I had no one to blame for that but myself. I mean I would go as far explaining different things about my religion. I knew they were listening because they would ask questions. Anyway, things just didn't seem like they were going to work out, but I was willing to try. Even though she lived with my mom, we would still talk, but the sex wasn't there. I mean, how could it be? I was banging three other women, all beautiful

I was doing my thing now. I had a full and part time job, my own apartment, my car, furniture, and all the up-to-date clothing, everything I needed.

Alright, readers, I'm going to let you in on the real reason why I was not to keyed on keeping this relationship. She was 14 years older than me, but that wasn't the main problem. The real problem? She had a full hysterectomy. That was just one of the things she never told me when we met. I really didn't know as much about her, but she knew everything about me. Talk about a one-sided relationship.

See, for a while, she had me thinking that maybe something was wrong with me. Since I had gone to prison she was the only woman that I had been with. Now, going off the prison theory, they say that when you lift weights, your private part shrinks. All the time she got me thinking that something was wrong with me. You know, I'm thinking of the theory. After finding out it was her, I was furious.

One night after talking to Sharon outside my apartment, she asked me why I changed. I told her that I didn't think I had changed. I'd always been the same. It was just that I find out new things, things that I should have known from the start, and I reacted. (I never told her why. Maybe she'll read this one day and know why. Until then, I'll just keep it to myself.)

As usual I would go to Norton County where Lizzy would be waiting for me every night. Nights that I didn't show up, she would always call my cell phone. Most of the time I would give her that look but wouldn't say too much. She knew I didn't like to argue and fight. She knew I would leave. I guess it's true that some women feel that they aren't loved or cared about if they didn't have a man that would fight with them from time to time. I had enough of that with Christy.

For the next eight months I was juggling Lizzy in Norton County and Selena. Sharon and I had purchased a home in Chesapeake. Yes, readers, it took about six to eight weeks, but she loved me back.

Along with a $200,000 note for a home that I picked out, she kept on calling and sometimes came around my mom's house. She was being real nice. I knew I wasn't doing right and didn't want to put her through that. The look on Co-co 's face hurt more than anything.

Before I go any further, let me go back a little. About the third or fourth day that Sharon was out, as I was coming out of my apartment to head over to Norton County to Lizzy, Sharon was getting into a van with my mom's boyfriend and a friend of his. I didn't pay it any mind, so I got in my car. My mom came storming out of her apartment yelling, "What's going on here?"

I got out of my car and walked across the street. I said, "What's going on?" I tried to calm my mom down, and again I asked what the problem was. My mom's boyfriend claimed that Sharon was just going to drive a car back for his friend. Oh! His friends were in the van as well. My mom looked at me. I told that chump that of all the people he knew around here, he had to ask *her* to do something for him. Everything was quiet. Everyone there knew how I could get. I told Sharon to get out of the van. As she got out, my mom started back up. I told her to please be quiet.

My mom went on and on. I looked at Sharon and shook my head I told her that maybe she should stay at my apartment tonight. Which I think she was trying to do anyway, but instead, my mom got hurt in the process. And I didn't like that one bit. I tried everything not to get back in a relationship with Sharon, but she would always put on a sad emotional trip, and I would fall for it.

So then I was juggling these three women, and at times, when I met someone while working at the club, I would sleep with them and keep moving on. I would always tell 'em from the start that there couldn't be any relationship, but you know women will often try to make you want them, no matter what.

Like Pat for instance. She was from Alexandria City. I met her one night while working at Club Nile. She and her cousin were on vacation. She had divorced her husband and moved to Alexandria, Virginia, from North Carolina.

While trying to clear the parking lot after we closed that night, she pulled up right behind me and got out of her car and just started talking. By then, I had expected anything while working at these clubs. I asked, "What do you think you're doing?"

She just kept talking about how she'd been watching me all night, and she liked my style. I just looked at her and kept directing traffic. She just kept talking. I started laughing. What did I do that for?

She stood right in my face and said, "I made you laugh."

I said, "What's next?"

Her cousin got out of the car and told me that I had to excuse her cousin because she'd been drinking.

I said, "I can see that."

At that time, Pat claimed that she was not drunk and that she liked what she saw. During the conversation, I told her that if I promised to call her, would she please move her car? From there she gave me her home number, cell number, work number, and her pager. I looked at her, and before I could say anything, she said, "I don't want to miss your call." Before she pulled out of the parking lot, she told me that she was staying at the hotel down the street. She gave me her room number and told me that it would be nice if I stopped by before she left the next morning.

While on my way to Lizzy's, I thought about stopping by the hotel. I needed the rest, but I knew if I did, there was no resting.

Getting home the next morning from work was no problem with Sharon because she knew that I also worked in Virginia Beach some weekends. Besides, it was in the beginning while she was trying to lure me back. I would stay with her sometimes. I still had my apartment in Norfolk, so it was easy.

I worked all week at the Pancake House, then the clubs on the weekends. By Sunday, I was so out of it. I never called Pat that weekend like I promised. Hell, I promised a lot of women lots of things but didn't follow through. For some reason I gave her my cell number … I mean the real number. She tried to call me throughout the week, but I never answered her calls.

While standing outside that following weekend watching my crew shake, she walked right up to me. I didn't recognize her at first. I just started laughing. She gave me a half smile, put her hands on her hips, and began to fuss me out. I said, "Hold on, I know you didn't drive all the way down here just to see me."

She said, "Why not? And yes, I did."

I couldn't help but laugh. I told her that she could go back to her hotel and wait for me. I promised that I would come see her.

She said, "If it's okay with you, I'll just wait inside the club until you get off."

What was I to say?

I got to give it to her; not once did she bother me for the rest of the night, other than a smile and a wave of the hand whenever I made my rounds.

When the club closed, I asked her which hotel she was staying at. She told me that she was staying in the Martin hotel on the Ave. in Chesapeake, so I thought it would be better if I had a hotel room in Chesapeake and not out here. I forgot that. I just smiled.

I ended up spending the weekend with her, but I made sure that she understood that I couldn't stay overnight because of other obligations. She said that she understood and wouldn't ask any questions. I liked her already. I never saw Lizzy that weekend. She was under the assumption that I was spending time with Co-co. In some cases, I was, and other times I would tell her that I had to go out of town dealing with something concerning my boys. She was aware that I was trying to get custody.

The following week Pat and I called each other every day. She came down that weekend as well. This time she brought her two sons with her. We hung out and had a good time. I would tell Sharon that I was working the security job. We didn't just work clubs. Sometimes when stars would come to town, even though they had their own bodyguards, they would call us and contract our service, especially for after-parties.

In two weeks on a Monday I had to be in West Virginia in court for my boys. I told Sharon that I would stop by on my way there that weekend. She smiled, kissed me ... the whole nine yards.

After work that Friday, I told Sharon that I'd be leaving for Guilford, West Virginia so that I could spend more time with Mario and Charles, but my whole purpose was to stop in Alexandria to spend some time with Pat. But for the night, I was going to stay in Norton County with Lizzy.

Once I got to Lizzy's, she started complaining about me not spending any more time with her. Until this day, Lizzy has never known anything about Sharon, and Sharon knows nothing about Lizzy. Sharon only knew Selena, and she got that from my mom because she used to call my mom and talk to her. That was my fault, giving her my mom's number. I think Selena was trying to get information that way. I knew better than to let my mom know about my relationship with any woman. Lizzy used to argue that I would never take her to meet my family and friends. I used to tell her that I didn't have any friends. She would say, "What about your family?"

I would always tell her, "One day."

She would get so hot about that and go off about me being ashamed of her. She knew that wasn't the case; she was beautiful, and she knew it. She just wanted to find out what kept me away from her sometimes. By meeting my family, she could start calling and ease her way into information, but I was not about to let that happen.

During this time as well, I was going through something on my job at Pancake House. The general manager was always trying to give me a hard time. He wasn't really about anything. He met the owner's daughter in college, and she claimed that she fell in love with him. Myself, I think he gave her drugs. She was beautiful, about 110 pounds, 5'4". This guy was about 350, easy. I'm talking about fat! Sometimes he would come to work wearing the same clothes he had on the day before with stains on them. Some of the workers used to talk about him under their breath. Me, whenever he had something to say to me, I'd let him know that his lack of change of clothes was noticeable, and he and I would go on for a while.

One day, her sisters, whom I had never met, came to the store. The family owned Pancake House. The son worked at the one on Singleton HWY and Duck Witch Road. Another family member and I worked the Newport News store. She was more beautiful than her sisters, I realized, as I began to talk to her.

The general manager tried to talk to his sister-in-law, so I looked at that fool and went about my business.

The trouble started when his cousin got out of jail and came to work at the store on work release. He was in jail for selling weed.

After about a week I noticed that his main reason for wanting to work here with his cousin was because he really didn't work. He would always go out front and talk with his pregnant girlfriend. I didn't mind him going out there for an hour or something, but he was sitting out there all day. So that meant that I was working for him. Every Monday through Thursday there were only two cooks until lunch or the next shift, which was at 5:00 p.m. I told him that he needed to stay behind the pass bar and help me with the tickets. He had the nerve to tell me not to worry about what he was doing. I told him somebody had to because if he thought for one second that I was there to work for him while he just hung out with his girlfriend, then he was smoking too much of his own stuff, and I wasn't worrying about his weed-head cousin.

By this time, the owner had brought in another general manager. He needed to because O' boy didn't know what the hell he was doing. I mean, the guy was supposed to be a general manager, but he didn't even know how to cook; neither did his cousin, for that matter. After that, every now and then I would have trouble out of him until one day I had a bus come in. He thought he was doing something by refusing to comply with my orders. He was still on eggs he hadn't moved up yet. He was making my orders come out late. So, I told him to stand back. There were about 30-35 people who came in off a school bus. They were elementary students.

It started raining, and like usual, people came from everywhere. I mean, it got packed when it rained. I told O' boy to make toast and stay clear. I handled everything all by myself. I knew he would only try to hinder me. When the new general manager came into work, the waitresses made it a known fact that I handled everything by myself. They were very pleased because waitresses really got their tips by the speed and good work of a good cook. Each one thanked me. After that morning, I really didn't have any more problems out of the work release cousin.

"A small man looks upon the success of others with a jealous heart because all that prospers in the hands of those who work hard make clear to the jealous all they are not doing with their own."

Chapter 25

I was the only guy to come to Pancake House and get the days I was willing to work and the pay I requested. Well, not quite what I asked for, but I got $9.50 an hour. It wasn't that bad, though they offered 10 dollars an hour if I would work on weekends. I worked Sunday through Thursday, but I wouldn't take the weekend. After working at the Chesapeake store from November, 1996 until 1998, I eventually ended up at the Newport News store.

One day a waitress, who was known for having problems with her husband, claimed that she had put a ticket in over an hour ago, and that I was purposely withholding her order. I had no idea what she was talking about. I told her to just tell me what it is that they ordered, and I'd make it for her. She went on and on. Then the name calling started. I just stood there looking at her. I mean, I could not believe this. I told her that I couldn't make anything if I didn't know what the people ordered. She stormed upstairs to the office. The manager was Jose, a man with whom I was cool with, or at least, I thought we were cool. I mean we'd even been at some of the same gatherings, but he came down yelling about her food. I told him to calm down and to let me talk. He just went on, so I said, "Shut up, asshole … the woman never put in a ticket."

He looked at her. She claimed that she did so put in a ticket. I asked her to show me her copy. She started looking, and when she couldn't produce one, she claimed that I must have thrown it in the trash. I was looking at her in disbelief. I was like, "What the hell are you talking about? I don't even have a ticket for you. Where is your copy? You don't even have one because you never put one in. There's no ticket back here for you. How would I know what the customer ordered? Everyone knows that there's a ticket for the cook and the waitress/customer."

Even though she couldn't produce a ticket, the manager took her side and started saying stuff like, "Just fix the food!

I'm told him that I couldn't fix food when I didn't know what it was that she wanted. She just kept saying, "I had the ticket."

I looked at her and told her that she was crazy. She was still going on and on but had yet to tell me what the people ordered. The customer had already asked her once what was taking so long, and that was when it all began. The woman refused to admit that she was wrong and tell me what the customer ordered. Even though I'd been there for two years plus, I knew I was going to get the bad end because she was white, and I was the ex-felon. It didn't matter that she had only been there for four weeks.

Jose wasn't white; he was Spanish and white or something. Still, I thought we were cool. Obviously, I was wrong. Maybe it was the fact that she had interrupted one of his sexual intercourse ventures with a minor, and he was about 30. She made it a known fact to a select few. I just happened to be one of them and not by choice. Anyway, he told me that I was fired. I looked at him then her. By this time, the other waitress was looking on. Then I looked back at him, smiled and told him that he couldn't fire me because I quit, so he could come back there and cook. I was the only cook on at the time and he didn't know how to cook. In fact, the only reason he was one of the managers or even had a job there is because he went to school with Marcus Roberts who was a son of the owner.

From there that same day I went to the Newport News store and applied for a job. Calvin was working there as he worked many Pancake Houses in the area. He had quit the Chesapeake store weeks ago when Don had left to run the Virginia Beach store, and a friend of the family became the general manager at the Chesapeake store. Before I left, Calvin told me to keep coming because they could use someone with experience since the store was new.

So that following Wednesday I went to the store again, and Calvin told me that he would hire me if I were to take some weekends. I told him that I'd spent a long time in, and the weekends with my daughter were all I had. Again, he told me that he'd call.

That Thursday I went back to the store again. Each time I would tell him how experienced I was and would suggest that he call my last job and ask for my boss, in which he would have to call the Chesapeake location to speak with Marcus. He called Calvin to his office. When we finished talking, I was working. I left one job on a Monday, and that Thursday of the same week I had another one. Tell me I'm not about my stuff.

Just the day before Lizzy and I went to the unemployment office because she had gotten laid off, she asked me if she could smoke a cigarette in my car. I looked at her like she sounded crazy and just kept driving. Then she asked me to pull over. Once again, I looked and kept driving. She knew I didn't allow any smoking in my car. Hell, I didn't smoke; why would I let anybody else smoke in my car, apartment or house? It didn't make any difference. As soon as I turned on Route 20, she lit up a cigarette. I told her that she must have lost her mind. She went on about how she asked me to pull over, and I wouldn't. At this time, she told me she was hungry, so we stopped at Taco City. I gave her $20 and told her to get something for everybody to eat. She knew that I didn't eat at Taco City. As soon as she got out and closed the door, I let the window down. I could feel the heat rush in as soon as I did. I said, "I told you not to smoke in my car, didn't I?"

She said, "Ziggy, you better not pull off and leave me!"

I told her to take that $20 and get a cab home. Then I pulled off.

About 45 minutes later I could see her mother pull in the driveway. I saw Lizzy getting out of the car. She walked to the side door (which we used) and stormed in the house. With the look she had on her face, I knew she wanted to kill me. Right behind her was her mother, Roslyn. Both were just talking mess, but Roslyn was laughing the whole time. She knew she was instigating. She was making the situation worse, talking about how she had to leave her TV show and pick up her daughter on the side of the road. I told Roslyn if she didn't stop... She just laughed.

Meanwhile Lizzy in the background was just continuing non-stop with her fussing. Roslyn, still laughing, got up and said that she had to go and pick up Peter from work. I guess so, after she had done put more fuel on the fire.

I was glad to see her grandmother pull up with her boys. But then again, that didn't stop her sometimes.

Later that night somehow it came up again, and Lizzy got really, really upset. Just moments before, her other best friend stopped by. Her name was Venus. She was worse than Rosalinda because Lizzy and Vickie grew up together.

After a while, I had had enough, so, I went to the bedroom. Lizzy followed me, so I got my keys. I tried to leave, but Lizzy refused to let me get in my car. She took my keys out of my hand. So, I just went back into the house to the bedroom and lay down. Venus left, and Lizzy came to bed still trying to act mad. Maybe so, but she couldn't resist me after an argument. The sex was even better.

Two weekends later, Lizzy and I got into another argument. That night Lizzy had some friends and family members over for her birthday. About 12:00 midnight her mom, father, and some of the other guests left. Around 2:15 a.m. I told Lizzy that I was tired. She told me to go lie down. I told her that we still had guests. She gave me a crazy look. I told her, "Well, if you won't tell them, I will."

She started going off about how these were her guests. I told her that it was after two in the morning, and it was time for them to go home. I walked to the living room from the kitchen where we were and told everybody it was time to go. Lizzy stepped around me and told them that they didn't have to go anywhere. At this time one of the guys told me that he wasn't going anywhere. I said, "I know this chump isn't challenging me." I told him he could either walk out, or I could throw his ass out. He stood up. I started at him. Lizzy got between us yelling.

Finally, everybody left, and Lizzy started again, so I tried to leave. She went to the kitchen and got a knife. Terrence, her oldest son, came in the living room, and Lizzy should not have told him to get involved. She knew as well as he did, that I had never and would never put my hands on her or her children. I think the fact that I would never fight with her in that way made her even hotter. Some women feel if a man doesn't put his hands on them, he doesn't care. It's sad, but it's true.

Somebody called the sheriff. He came in and talked to the both of us and said that if he had to come back out there, somebody was going to jail. You know I assured him that everything was under control because I was thinking about my probation. The sheriff looked at me and started talking about football and where he played in high school. I told him where and when I played. "Though I was younger when I played."

Lizzy just broke out. "Excuse me, sir, but we were having an argument. Somebody calls you, and you come out here and start talking about football.

I said, "Oh, shit. I know she didn't."

The sheriff was trying to talk to her, but for some reason, Lizzy got beside herself, and she continued, "You men all stick together." She just kept on until the sheriff told her to put her hands behind her back. He took her to jail. I knew it wouldn't be long before her mom would be calling me to ask what happened. I knew Lizzy would call her but not before Terrence, her oldest son, called her mother. Come to think of it, he may have been the one who called the police in the first place. If so, she would have him to thank.

When she arrived back with her mother, they walked in and immediately Roslyn started laughing. Lizzy's boys came into the living room. Roslyn said, "Why y'all looking at me? I haven't been to jail," she laughed.

Lizzy told the boys to go back to bed as it wasn't time yet. Each one told me goodnight, rather good morning, and went back to bed. By this time, it was about 5:20 a.m.

Her mom looked at me again and started smiling. I asked Roslyn what she was laughing at? I said, "I know you're not laughing at your daughter."

She said, "I'm not laughing at the fact that she went to jail, instead *how* she went."

See, during the argument, she had changed into her nightgown. I really didn't think about it at first. It was skimpy. But they were laughing because she had absolutely nothing underneath. Lizzy started talking about how cold that concrete in that holding cell was on her ass. It was good to see them laughing. I couldn't help but laugh myself. I really wanted to get some sleep then, but I knew that was out of the question. I could see that look in her eyes. Finally, we went to bed, and I put it on her for about an hour.

Once I fell asleep that morning, she did her special that I liked. She used to wake me up in a special way, though she wasn't the best I'd had in my life. But she was right up there in third place. Melissa White was number one without a doubt. Boy, she knew what she was doing.

By this time, I hadn't spoken with Pat for some time. One night, while in Norfolk, I went to a phone booth and called her. She was so happy to hear from me. She tried everything she could to get me to come to Alexandria. With everything that was going on, I knew it was impossible, but I wanted to. I told her I couldn't. She said that if I couldn't commit some time with her, then she would have to find someone else. She went from glad to hear me … to not giving me any sex. Times before, she had asked me to move to Alexandria with her. She expressed that she would move to Chesapeake. But she had a good job down there. She said that I could easily find a job there.

She continued for the next two hours about how she wanted a relationship with me, but if I couldn't give her what she needed, then she would stop talking to me altogether. I was quiet for a moment because I knew she was right. Deep down inside I wanted to go pack my shit and go, but with the probation and all...

I told her that events in my life right then wouldn't allow me to make such a move. She then said that she'd miss me, and I told her likewise. Even till this day I still miss her. I never told her about the probation I was on. She was the only one who I knew that didn't know.

I went on to visit my mom on 32nd Street. As I sat there, I kind of thought how I could make that move, but suddenly I put it out of my mind. Till this day, I've never spoken to her again. I was now trying to decide if I was going home to Chesapeake that night or to Norton County. Finally, after all the women that I had a relationship with, some not even mentioned in this book, Sharon and Lizzy both never knew about each other.

My job kept me around women all the time. Sharon had this friend that was from Jamaica; her name was Jada. The first time Sharon took me to the house, there were about five women there. I looked and thought to myself, was this a setup to find out if I was cheating? All of them were fine as hell, even her friend, and she was pregnant.

It's like they just took right to me. Or was it because most of the women there had men that were in prison for drugs?

Jada had a sister name Uzza. She was dark and beautiful and had a banging body like no other. I mean she was fine as all outdoors. I went outside to sit on the porch with the children because one thing I don't do is sit around with nothing but all women. Jada had two daughters and a son. They made sure that they got real friendly with me. The children were cool.

Sharon came outside with Jada, and I said my goodbyes to everybody. On the way home Sharon asked, "You remember Uzza?"

I said, "Yes."

She then told me that she would be coming over three days a week to clean. With our jobs, we spent a lot of time away from home. We just needed someone to keep the dust down, do the laundry, and clean the bathrooms and bedrooms. Uzza would come over on Mondays, Wednesdays, and Fridays. On Mondays I worked from 8:00 a.m. to 10:00 p.m. and Tuesdays from 8:00 a.m. to 5:00 p.m. The rest of the week I opened from 6:00 a.m. to 2:00 p.m. On those days I would pick Co-co up from school, and sometimes I would pick Uzza up as well.

After two weeks of working for us, she came to work with some short shorts on, and I mean they were calling me. She would make small talk for conversation. Sometimes she would bring her daughter with her to work. She was about five years old. She and Co-co would be in the family room next to the kitchen. So, instead of continuing the conversation, I would excuse myself and go outside to wash my car.

After about two months of her service, we received an outrageous bill from overseas. Knowing neither I nor Sharon made the calls, we soon realized Uzza's boyfriend had been calling our house collect, and she had been accepting the charges. That was a complete violation of housekeeper 101. Uzza had to be let go, and I was kind of glad before anything happened between us.

I used to go and visit my brother Todd and his family all the time. One day I was outside with my brother and some of his friends from the complex. They were always up to no good. This fine woman came out the next row of the apartments. I said, "Yo, man, who's that?"

Everybody started laughing. I asked what was so funny All they could say: "Man, nobody's getting that."

Now, anybody who knew me knows that those were words of challenge, and I loved a good challenge when it came to beautiful women. My brother's friend, Todd, bet me that I couldn't pull her. I told them that I was a Muslim, and I wasn't a gambling man, but I would bet them all a dollar to a dime that by the weekend 'I'd be coming over for dinner. I told them to watch and learn.

As I approached, I must admit, I started to doubt myself. I guess because I had eyes on me. Anyway, she was beautiful, and I had no time to prepare. So, I approached her, and the conversation went like this: "How are you doing today, young lady? Today is a beautiful day,"

She smiled. The conversation continued.

I found it hard to believe that she was single. After about an hour of conversation, she went back to her apartment. When she looked at me with her head tilted as to try and shade her eyes from the sun, she asked me to walk her over to her door. I knew I must have said something right. Usually I wouldn't date women who kept animals in their house, but she was so gorgeous that I had to ask if I could stop by sometime and kick it with her.

She asked me what I was doing later that day. I couldn't tell her that I had to pick up my stepdaughter. I think she probably knew that I wasn't single. That's why she asked me to stop by that night, as if she were testing me. I saw it in her face with that gorgeous smile. But when I agreed, she gave me this surprised look. I was the one smiling now. I knew I had her, but what was I going to do about Co-co? I told her that I was free that night as I touched on her hand and walked off.

I didn't have to be there until 9:00 p.m. When I got there, she had on this short skimpy outfit. Her children were outside when I pulled up. When I came in, I sat on the sofa. The deck led right from the living room, and where I was sitting, gave me a direct look at her standing on the deck with the sliding door pulled open. With her back to me as she smoked, I could see straight through that nightgown, and I could see that monkey looking right at me. I shook my head shockingly. I knew she wanted me to hit that. I got up and walked out on the balcony and walked up behind her.

The way she leaned back on me with her head on my shoulder, I knew she wanted to. She was 5'10", just 110 pounds, high yellow, with a small waist and an ass out of this world. I thought to myself about how I kept meeting all these bad looking women and not keeping them for a long-term thing, but instead allowing Sharon to hold on, even though I hadn't really moved in with her yet.

I returned. She had on something even better. We must have gone on for two and a half hours. I started coming over on the weekdays as well. She liked to smoke weed and lots of it. I used to kick her a few dollars here and there. That made her like it even more.

I picked Co-co up from Ms. Jamieson that lived across the street from us. The bus always let Co-co off right in the front of the house.

Co-co and I went to Sharon's job. Every time I would go to her job it was always nice. Sometimes I would go in and talk to her boss. He was young. His family had money like most white people. They helped him open his own mortgage company. He also had a recording studio on Duck Witch Road in Chesapeake. In fact, that is where I first met the now well-known famous Farrell and his stick man, Chad.

I headed back out to Norton County as Lizzy's family was having their family reunion at the park. Lizzy called herself being upset with me. She knew I wasn't in the mood. We cooked out. Everybody had a great time. Her friend, Rosalinda, was there with her baby. I was playing with her. Then Terrence, Lizzy's oldest son, came over. She was real attached to Terrence. Rosalinda was at Lizzy's a lot because her husband was out on the west coast in the military.

As we were sitting at one of the tables, Lizzy said, "Ou! Ziggy!"

I said, "What?"

She said, "Don't look, but here comes your number one girl."

As I turned around, her crazy aunt just started hugging and kissing me as she always did. Everybody was having a good time, eating and drinking —except myself with the drinking. No one was arguing or anything.

As usual, Lizzy and her mother always wore small skirts. Peter didn't like Roslyn wearing clothes like that, but he really didn't put up too much of a fuss. Lizzy looked up at me with her head slightly down, smiling. Every time she came around I knew she liked me. She was always kind of quiet, but the little things she would say let me know that she liked me. Every time Lizzy walked off to get something, she would always have something to say. To be honest, if she weren't married to Lizzy's uncle, I probably would have knocked her off.

On my way home later that day, I decided to make a stop to see Selena. Once I got there, her best friend was on her way out. Whenever I would show up, she would be so happy to see me and immediately jump my bones. But on this evening her friend was sitting on the living room couch. Selena closed the door and pulled me back into her bedroom. Her friend was shaking her head, chuckling. Selena closed the door and pushed me on the bed. She pulled down my jeans, and we had sex. Every now and then, she would stop and say, "If you marry me, I'll do anything you want me to. You can get it anytime you want."

Selena's friend called out to her. She returned to the bedroom and asked me to stay until she returned. But I had to tell her that I had to go to work, or I would probably be there until the next morning messing around with her.

~" The children of privileged cannot hear the cries of the persecuted and oppressed."

Chapter 26

Finally, in July, after giving Ms. Foxx permission to correspond with the social worker, I was told by my son's lawyer, Ms. Jacqueline, that Sharon needed to show up at this hearing that was requested by the social worker.

Before she went back to West Virginia, she stopped by my job one last time. I fixed her a meal. Although, at the time, I couldn't really put my finger on it, but this woman's attitude had changed. She used to be all for me getting my boys back, but once she visited and saw the $200,000 house, she seemed to change and began telling of her struggles and acting jealous. I didn't know if she would be a help or hinderance.

Every Monday for the past few months we closed at 10:00 p.m. The probation officer was harassing me so bad, it didn't make sense.

In August that year, Sharon, Co-co, and I went to Huntington for court. When we got there, I called Celes. She told me that they were on their way out to the store. I told her that we were in town. She told me to meet them at the drugstore on 14th Street and 12th Avenue.

Once we got there, I formerly introduced them. Celes, Sharon, and the two girls hung out for a while. Dante and I got some beer and just talked. Before that we went to get a room, but we were told that all the rooms were booked.

So, we went down a block to my old job: the Martin Hotel on the Ave. While Sharon was paying for the room, I told the clerk that I was kind of reluctant about staying in their hotel. She asked what the problem was. I told her how I was misled when I trained the new guy who was white, only to have him take my job. She had the most apologetic look on her face.

When we got to court on Thursday morning, I couldn't believe the state's psychiatrist for the boys. She had a tight short skirt that, when she sat down, you could see her underwear. I looked at Sharon, then to my lawyer. She just leaned her head to the side. She was a sister, but I didn't care whose side she was on. She set blacks back another hundred years.

Next on the stand was some guy from the boys' home. He said that he was their counselor. I was so disturbed to see that he was so flamboyant and feminine. The thought of someone like that overseeing a little boys' group home didn't sit well with me at all. When he walked, he had more of a switch than a woman. When he testified, he tried to seem like it was the best thing for the boys to reunite with the mother, or it would be in their best interest to remain in the state's custody. How could this guy get up here and speak like that without even knowing me? He tried to act like he didn't know that Christy lost her parental rights already because she couldn't stay off that crack. For the last nine years I'd never given them a dirty urine sample, and I think that kind of frustrated them. I had been coming from out of town to court for the last two years now faithfully, done everything they had asked me to do, but they continued to fight and refuse to give me custody.

My lawyer called Sharon and even Co-co to the stand to testify. Hell, they even put the boys on the stand, for what, I don't know.

After the hearing was over, the social worker came out all smiles and informed me that I was now able to spend more time with the boys.

When I was called to testify, the Judge, right off the bat, called me disingenuous. I couldn't believe he just said that. I had no idea until later why he said that.

Mario was only 21 months old, and Charles was only four months old. After I testified, and the hearings were over, the social worker came up to me, all smiles, and asked me if I would like to spend more time with the boys before they went back to Durham, West Virginia. I could come out to the social services office and maybe spend an hour or two with them.

As she turned to walk off, she turned back around and said, "I know with everything you guys are paying for the hotel, food, gas and all, why don't you guys just take one car to my office. That way you can save some gas." We had no idea. We thought she was just trying to be helpful. The drive from the courthouse downtown to the social service building is a good three miles.

Once we got to her office, we had brought some food to eat from the Chicken Spot. We played around a little. When it was time to go, Sharon, Co-co and their sister all hugged Mario and Charles and said their goodbyes. They asked earlier if they would they be coming to live with me. I'd always been honest with them. I told them that I doubted that the judge had told the case worker that they could go with me today. As usual, Charles continued to ask why not. Each time it seems like it broke my heart even more.

I couldn't help but wonder all the time why Christy wouldn't help me get custody of our boys. Even her mother had an opportunity to get them. The court in the beginning said that they would give her custody, but she refused, claiming that I would come down and take them from her. Instead, why they would allow the state to take custody, for the life of me, I will never understand that.

The social worker was talking to us as we walked to the door to leave. She was acting like she was in favor of me getting my boys. But something just didn't feel right. I just couldn't put my finger on it.

As we walked to the car, Co-co said, "Dad, that lady is standing in the door watching us."

I turned to Sharon. Then we looked at each other as we got into the car. Sharon said, "What's that all about?"

I wished I knew. We took Alina home. She and Co-co didn't want to leave each other, but it was getting late, and we had packed that morning before court to go back home. They started crying while hugging each other. They spent the whole time together. We had even gotten a room just for them. Before getting in the car, I told Alina that I would be back to get her so that she could spend the summer with us.

In September of 1999, once again, I was being summoned to court for a violation of probation. On this day my probation officer came to my job and told me that I needed to submit a urinalysis by 4:00 p.m. that day, or I'd be in violation for failing to give a urine test. Mind you, there were no tests that day for my color code.

Thinking back, that morning before leaving for work, my wife asked me why I was drinking vinegar. I told her that Lee-lee and the rest were smoking weed while we were watching the game. After getting to work that morning and having it on the counter where it could be seen, the general manager asked me what I needed with vinegar. (Well ex-GM, but he still worked there). I told him that it was something that I ate. He knew better. That was why he was smiling the whole time. Mind you, there are only three people who knew that I was drinking vinegar: Sharon, the general manager and me.

One of the two had to call the probation officer. I started to wonder, could it be Sharon? After all, I didn't do well by her when she violated her parole, and even after she was released, I continued my behavior. When she got out, I tried to end things. In fact, I had in so many ways, but I allowed her to lure me back into the relationship. That was a big mistake because, I believe, I mean, I truly believe in my heart that she called my probation officer that day. It may have been a combination, but I could tell by the way she had been acting. Like I said, I'd been continuing my behavior. I should have left, or better yet, I should 've stayed gone. I knew in my heart that she would leave, but I never thought she would use the probation officer to get back at me. I know about scorned women, but I thought it would be different in my case, simply because she knew what it was like to be in prison. All because I didn't care the same anymore. I never told her, nor did I need to. It really hurt because the both of us had been to prison before, and we vowed never to go back. I guess because she was violated, it really didn't matter to her if I got violated. I mean, I was continuing my relationship with Lizzy whom she never knew anything about, even to this day. I had stopped seeing Selena three months ago, but she knew there was somebody keeping me away from her.

My probation officer, Ms. Foxx, had the United States Marshals come to my job two days later after the urine test. This was during lunch time and, as usual, always very busy. There were three at the front and three at the back. I saw them when they walked in. I just looked and smiled. It was funny that she would request that many Marshals to come and get me. Calvin was standing there whispering, "Big time Ziggy smiling."

She thought that if she could make it look bad enough, that I wouldn't have a job no matter what happened. When the new general manager did say something, it wasn't what she wanted. Instead, he told me that I still had a job whatever happened. The ex-general manager was standing there with a little smile on his face. The waitresses were all saying, "Bye, Ziggy."

Once we got to the federal building, I was put in a holding cell until 4:30 p.m. I went before a Judge for a bond hearing. I had yet to hear the violations. The Judge asked Ms. Foxx what the violation was. Ms. Foxx said, "Mr. Harper has a dirty urine, socializing with a known felon, moving and not notifying me within 72 hours."

Judges don't ask regular questions on a violation hearing. It's almost like they don't have to prove anything. Ms. Foxx just kept on about how much of a problem I've been but had nothing to substantiate that claim.

The Judge said, "Alright, what are you asking for bail?"

Ms. Foxx asked for 10,000-dollar security bond.

I said, "Security bond."

The Judge looked at her like she was crazy. He told her that there was nothing before him that would warrant a bond like that. Ms. Foxx tried to intervene when the Judge asked me if I've ever failed to show up for court. I told him. "No Sir."

Ms. Foxx tried to intervene again. She was very adamant about getting that security bond. She knew I didn't have that money nor property to get out on that. I just looked at her and shook my head.

The Judge said, "Wait just a minute. Do you have any new charges against Mr. Harper?"

"No Sir, your honor, but Mr. Harper…."

"Stop there, Ms. Foxx. Mr. Harper, if I let you go on your own O-R, you will show up for court, right?"

I said "Yes, sir."

"Well, the hearing is set for September 1999."

Once out of the federal building, I started to call the job at a phone booth and tell Calvin to pick me up. Instead, it was so beautiful outside, I decided to walk. It was only six blocks. It was nice. You don't know how good something is until you lose it or are about to. Everybody that was there when I left that morning came up to me smiling, clapping their hands and yelling, "Ziggy!!! The women gave me hugs and a kiss.

I called Sharon at her job and told her what happened. I told her that the violations consisted of a dirty urine, socializing with a known felon, and moving without notifying her within 72 hours. The tone in Sharon's voice didn't sound pleased that I was out. It still hadn't hit me yet.

A few days later I was to meet with the lawyer that the court appointed for me. Later that week when I went to his office, it was unbelievable. It wasn't even an office. I didn't know what it was, but I knew that it was not a lawyer's office. The typewriter was one of those old typewriters. He had no computer. There were no file cabinets or anything. The place needed to be cleaned badly, and the man looked like an alcoholic. Once I had a seat, I knew he was an alcoholic when he started talking. The man couldn't get half his words right. As he continued to talk, or try to talk, I just hung my head. I had to think fast. I was going to court in a week. He didn't even have a copy of the summons. I looked at him and said, "You don't have the summons?"

He kind of smiled and said that he would have to wait until his secretary got back to see where she put my file. I'm like, what file? And where could it be? You know I was thinking, what in the world have they given me for an attorney? I told him that I needed to get back to work. He asked me if I could come in the following day after work. I told him I could.

When I got outside, I looked around and then hung my head. I couldn't believe everything that was happening to me.

When I got back to the store, Calvin asked me how it went. The look I gave him told it all. He started laughing. Calvin laughed about everything. I told him what had happened. The lawyer had told me that if I wanted to, tomorrow I could have him come to the store after 5:00 p.m., and he could get something to eat on the house, while we went over the violations.

I got up called his office, but his secretary said that he had left for the day. I told her to please tell him that I needed to talk to him. She said okay.

The following Friday I called the lawyer around 2:30 p.m. after the noon rush was over. I asked him if he could come to my job around 5:00 p.m. to discuss the case, and I promised him a steak dinner. He agreed.

Earlier that day I called Williams LA Cross, and I explained everything to him. He had defended me in a previous hearing before Judge Ms. Kennedy. But more importantly, he was aware of how bad they were treating me and trying to violate me. I gave him the information. He agreed to meet that evening with us, but I hadn't told my lawyer, Tim Smith.

When he showed up, Calvin started laughing. This man had on some wrinkled slacks with an old shirt, and his shoes were turned over so badly, when he walked, he limped. From the looks of it, he had been drinking again.

Moments later, Williams LA Cross walked in. That's when I told Tim Smith that Mr. Williams LA Cross was going to help us with the case. The look on his face was displeasing. He immediately said, "I didn't think that the court would pay for both to defend me. I smiled and told him that Williams LA Cross was familiar with the whole case and would be helping pro-bono.

Tim Smith came to the meeting with a folder that had about two sheets of paper in it and still unprepared. I knew this guy would be of no help to me and only get in the way.

The following week we went to court. Before going into the court room, we met in a side room. At that time, Tim Smith said, "Judge Ms. Kennedy won't allow Mr. Williams to help with the case.

I asked, "When was this, and why wasn't I notified immediately?"

He told me that Ms. Foxx had come to his office and told him that Mr. Williams wouldn't be able to assist in the case.

I said, "Hold on, Man! What do you mean 'she came by your office the other day?' She can't do that."

He said, "I called her about some papers pertaining to the case, and she told me that she would drop them off later that day."

I asked, "How did she know about Mr. Williams? You must have mentioned it. Why are you discussing my case with the probation officer?"

He just sat there with a dumb look on his face.

Once we entered the courtroom, the prosecutor, my probation officer, her boss, and my old probation officer were there. Everybody that wanted to see me fall was there and then some. As Mr. Williams sat a few rows back, I had Mr. Tim Smith tell the Judge that he and I really hadn't had time to prepare the case. At that time, I raised my hand. Judge Ms. Kennedy asked, "What is it, Mr. Harper?"

I told her that Mr. Williams has offered to assist in the case because he was familiar with it. Judge Ms. Kennedy, at the request of the prosecution and probation officer, dismissed Mr. Williams as my attorney. Judge Ms. Kennedy told me that if I were to bring Mr. Williams in here to defend me, she would make me pay for both. At that time, I told Judge Ms. Kennedy that I would rather have Mr. Williams represent me in my case.

You could hear mumbling from the prosecuting table.

I continued and told her that he would do it for free. Judge Ms.

Kennedy said that if I were to bring Mr. Williams to her courtroom again, she would make me pay for both. While she was talking, I was trying to tell Mr. Smith to let her know that he was willing to give the case over to Mr. Williams. This fool looked at me and said, "I don't think she will like that."

I told him that I did not want him representing me. He told me that he didn't have any choice. It took everything in me to keep from smacking the hell out of this man. I looked at him and told him that he was some real shit.

At that time, Judge Ms. Kennedy rescheduled the hearing for October 19th, 1999.

This guy was a real asshole. I knew I was being set up for a fall. I tried and tried to get him off my case, but he refused. Unbelievable! I just couldn't get over what they were doing to me.

When I got home to Chesapeake, I stopped at Sharon 's job and told her what took place in court. Totally unbelievable.

Later that week I had to be in Guilford, West Virginia for another custody hearing. I left Chesapeake at 2:00 p.m. that Thursday. I had to be in court about 1:00 p.m. Friday. I wanted to stop in Norton County to spend some time with Lizzy and tell her what happened, but by the time she got home, it was about 6:00. With everything that had taken place, I was sleepy. Lizzy started doing her thing. We ended up going at it for a long time. I knew I had to get up and make that run.

On the road I did everything I could to stay awake. I fell asleep a few times. Thank Allah, I didn't have an accident, unlike before, although it wasn't with another car. Running off the road is just the same, if not worse.

Once in Guilford, I got a hotel room and got some much-needed rest. I got there about 10:00 that morning. I had the clerk give me a wake-up call at 12:00 noon.

Once in court that day for custody of my boys, Judge Keith told me that he was going to continue and wait until the outcome of my violation hearing. As I stood there, I couldn't help but reflect about the last hearing where he called me disingenuous. I told him that I'd been coming to court for more than two years, and I had yet to have a chance at my boys. He told me after my next hearing, he would decide. For some reason, nothing seemed right.

Once I left the courtroom, as usual, I would stop by Celes's job and take her to lunch.

Later that day I was just sitting in my hotel room. Usually, after I spend most of the day with my daughter, Alina, I'd go see Melissa White. But that was long over.

That night I went to see Latrina. On my drive over, I couldn't help but think of how Melissa tried to send me back to prison for something that never happened.

Anyway, I ended up sleeping with Latrina.

That Saturday I left Guilford, West Virginia to go to Durham, West Virginia to see Mario and Charles. During this time, as usual, I would go by Renaissance at 4:00 a.m. (as previously agreed) and pick up Re-Re and take her with me. All the time I'd been going up there Re-Re was the only one who went with me. Once Maria was going to let her children go, but her mother said that she wouldn't trust me with her children. I started to say something about how she allowed the state to take custody of her grandchildren when she had the opportunity to get them, and she didn't, but I kept my mouth closed.

After we had pizza, as usual, it was getting late. The boys always looked sad when it was time for me to leave. I sat Mario and Charles down and tried to explain to them as I had before that things were out of my control and that I was trying to do everything I could to get them out of that place. Till this day I can't understand why they were more willing to send me back to prison than help me do the right thing and get my boys and raise them in a family setting. They always talked about keeping families together. I wasn't out there committing any crimes or anything. The people just had it out for me for no real reason at all. It's a shame how one person can get a group to dislike you because they took something personal. But in the end, my boys suffered the most. I still can't believe Christy did this to our boys. All mothers aren't good mothers.

Once back in Guilford, Mississippi, Lorraine asked me how the boys were doing. I told her that they were doing fine. I knew I was lying, but what else could I say? Not what I wanted to tell her.

After dropping Re-Re off, I hugged Litta and thanked her for letting Re-Re go with me to see her cousins.

At 4:00 a.m. Sunday morning I headed back to Virginia. I got to

Norton County to Lizzy's house around 2:15 p.m. That way I could spend the day with her.

When I got to Chesapeake that night, Sharon and I talked about the events that had taken place. I couldn't put my finger on it, but for some reason, things just didn't feel right.

The following week Sharon was heading out somewhere near Tennessee where Bill would be going to school to find an apartment.

That weekend I planned a party. I had Co-co print up the invitations with directions. I had planned it for that Friday night while Sharon, Co-co, and Bill would be out of town. I received a call on my cell phone around 4:00 p.m. It was Sharon. She told me that the car broke down and that she needed me to come and pick them up. I asked where they were. She told me that they were at a shop on Chesapeake Blvd. I asked her how long she had been there. I mean, after all, they had left like two and a half hours ago. I'd been giving out invitations all day.

As I headed to the shop to pick them up, I got on my cell phone and tried to call everyone I could think of to cancel the party. All night, I hoped that no one would come. I was still making calls. It was now 11:00 p.m., and no one had shown up. What a relief.

That night, getting ready for bed, Sharon mentioned the party. Co-co had told her about the invitations I had printed up.

That Saturday morning, I took them back to Chesapeake Blvd. so she could get the car and head out again. We had just gotten that car two weeks ago so that Bill would have some transportation up there.

Around 12:00 noon I got a call from Sharon. Finally, I was in the clear. So, I started making calls and the party was back on. I decided to go and get Terika, Hannah, Tami, and Sadaca since Lee-lee, his cousin, and few others had already arrived for the party.

While Hannah, Tami and Sadaca prepared food, I told everybody that I would be right back. I left to pick Traci up. Once I returned, we started the party all the way up. Everybody was eating, drinking, playing cards and dancing.

Around 3:00 a.m. everybody started leaving after I told them it was that time. Don't you hate when people don't want to leave?

Lee-lee and his cousin had come up together in his cousin's Z-28.

Hannah had come with someone else that she invited. It had been raining. It had been falling all night and very heavy at times.

As everyone was leaving, I noticed that Hannah was getting in the little hatch area. Tami looked at me and pointed to the car. I went over and told Hannah that she didn't need to ride in the hatch like that. She smiled, as she did about everything. I told her that I would take her home. Lee-lee said, "We're going to my apartment." I told him that I would take the both of 'em. Many times, I'd taken him home anyway. I tried to talk to Lee-lee, but his cousin started running his drunken mouth. I tried everything to keep her from riding in that hatch back. I just had a bad feeling about that, and I wasn't the only one.

I took Tami to my bedroom. I must've been crazy! We sat in the chairs and talked for a while. I tried to get her in the bed, but she just kept shaking her head with that look (You must be crazy). I told her about Sharon when I met her. If I didn't show any respect for Sharon at the time, she did.

My cell phone started ringing. I looked at the caller I.D. It was Tiff calling me about 4:30 a.m. When I answered my phone, I knew by her tone (even though I couldn't make out what she was saying) something was wrong. Tami just kept saying, "Hannah is dead," over and over again. I sat there for a moment. I couldn't move. Terika was sitting there with her hands over her mouth. She knew it wasn't good. I hung up the phone, and we headed to Newport News.

As we drove over the overpass, we could look over and see the car on its top. The local police, state troopers, ambulance, and fire department were all at the scene. They wouldn't allow any traffic that way, so I couldn't get a good look at things. I couldn't stop on the ramp with all that traffic behind me.

Once we got to Sophia's apartment, everyone was waiting outside for me. I don't know why, but everyone always looked to me.

They couldn't find Lee-lee. After the accident, he jumped out of the car and ran. He made one phone call to Sophia from a phone booth, and that was it. We drove over to his apartment. Still no sign of him.

It was about 7:30 p.m. Sophia was speaking with the coroners making plans to have Hannah's body shipped to Hampton, Virginia, their hometown. It was a sad day. All we could talk about was how we were all just having a good time, and suddenly, one of us was gone and would never come back. I couldn't help but feel a little guilty. It was my party, and maybe I could 've done more to keep her from getting into that car. Still, none of us knew what was about to happen.

Finally, the coroners got back to Sophia and explained to her that her death was painless. She had told her that Hannah's neck was broken on impact, and she hadn't suffered.

That Tuesday her body was sent home to Hampton. The funeral was that weekend. That Monday when Sharon and Co-co returned home, I told them about Hannah's death, but I mentioned nothing about the party. She knew that it was just one of the women that worked with me.

That weekend most of us drove to Hampton for the funeral. Three of the women rode with me. Tami and some of the others drove themselves. There were three cars.

Once we got there, we went to the grandmother's house where all the family and friends were meeting up for the funeral. We introduced ourselves. Everybody loaded up in the cars and drove to the church. Though I hadn't been to funerals, I never saw so many people at a funeral before. There was not enough room in the church. There were more people outside than in. It took a long time for viewing. That's how many people there were. And it was hot. I didn't think a town that small had that many people. Jim, Tami, and all the girls from the job were crying, of course.

After Hannah was put in the ground, we went to the lodge where everyone was going to eat. Lee-lee, Fisherman, Gavin, Tami, Terika, Tyler, and I were at the back of the line. Because Tami was her family, she got to go to the front of the line.

By the time the rest of us got up front, along with some of the others, all of the main course was gone. Mind you, we hadn't eaten all day. Talk about hungry. We were kind of upset, but it was all good. There was a Chicken spot down the street.

Once we finished eating, we went back to the lodge where everybody was still congregating and listening to music. I kept a camera in my car. We started taking pictures. The pictures Tami and I were taking were a little bit too much for Kaelyn. She had tried to get with me in the past when she arrived on the scene. She was in the halfway house around the corner from the store. Once she got a job with us, I helped her get some things for her new apartment, as well as took her looking for a car. But after finding out that she turned against her husband, the man she was married to for a lesser sentence after playing a major role in the game with him, I kind of had a different outlook on things.

Anyway, Kaelyn called out to Tami and pulled her to the side. (While looking at me with a crazy look). I couldn't really make out what she was saying, but I knew that she was trying to stop anything that may go down that night. I asked Tami what Kaelyn had to say. She told me that Kaelyn told her that I was married. We both laughed as Tami already knew that.

Tami and I had talked about getting a hotel room for the night. After all, it had been a long day. Tami hung onto me for the rest of the evening, hugging and kissing.

Every now and then Kaelyn would give me a look or say something slick while flirting with me. So, I walked over to Kaelyn. I put my arms around her and playfully kissed her while whispering sweet nothings in her ear. She loved every minute of it.

Tami was watching the whole time. She was in love with me. I knew it. When she walked over and told Kaelyn that was enough, Kaelyn smiled with a mixed look on her face.

Finally, as the night began to approach, we decided to go back home instead. The ride on the way back home was in and out of lanes with high speed. We just kept laughing and passing each other. Once we got back to the store in Newport News, Calvin and the ex-general manager came out back where we parked. We all talked and everything. Tami and I were still doing our little thing. We both decided to put it off until another day. Kaelyn had a lot to do with that. I hated the fact that Tiff was her ride home. I knew when Tami took her home, she would do everything to keep her there thinking she would double back to me.

When I got home, Sharon and I talked about the funeral as well as the promise I made to Hannah's boys.

My date for court was coming up real fast. I was still trying to put things together. I would still go to Norton County to Lizzy's house and spend time with her. And at no time did I ever suspected her of anything dealing with my probation problem.

The weekend before court, I placed a call to Mr. Williams LA Cross. He was willing to try and convince this man to give up the case. That weekend before court I spent a good deal of time with Lizzy. I knew that they were going to violate me. I had no idea that I would receive that much time. Under the law which I was sentenced, I should have only received 30 days to six months. Instead, I received 24 months. Unbelievable!! Lizzy asked me to leave her my new car, and she would take over the payments. I knew in my heart she was being honest.

That Sunday night when I left her house, I knew that it was a possibility that I would not see her again for some time.

We stood in the kitchen for a long time holding each other. She was crying and telling me how much she loved me and couldn't wait till all of this was over. I got into my car and made one last stop by her parents. They were good to me. Not once did we fight about anything (Unlike some of my other relationships). I knew that I would miss them.

~" One of the greatest losses and tragedies one can experience in life is the sudden realization that all they believed in, held true and felt that gave one a purpose in life was found out to be a lie."

Chapter 27

Though the distance between Norton County and Chesapeake was about 40-plus miles, it seemed to be longer than that. For the past three months, anytime I was at home at the beach, something seemed wrong. I mean, I just didn't feel right.

The morning of court I said goodbye to Co-co before she left for school. Sharon and I talked for a while. Then we kissed, and I left, but the feeling wasn't right.

Once I got to Newport News, I stopped by the store to pick up Calvin. Though he had agreed to go to court with me and speak on my behalf, he seemed somewhat hesitant. Finally, after walking around the store, we left for court.

Once we got there, and before going into the courtroom, I tried to get this nut, Tim Smith, to give up the case once again. All he could say was, "I don't think Judge Ms. Kennedy will like that very much."

I told him, "Let me worry about that." I couldn't get anything through to this fool. What kind of lawyer stays on your case when you ask him to remove himself? I knew I was being set up for a fall.

Man, I'm telling you, this lawyer never asked for the opportunity to ask this (so-called) witness questions. All they had was their testimony.

How was this fool going to question the very people he's working with? This man had a folder with two sheets of paper in it. I gave him a killer look. I was really upset with this so-called lawyer. He just handed my life over without a fight. Judge Ms. Kennedy asked the prosecutor if they were ready to proceed. The prosecutor said, "Yes, your honor. Is the defendant?"

My lawyer said, "Yes."

I wanted to say HELL NO!!!! But I knew it would only make things worse. I could see the look on the judge's face as the prosecutor called off the alleged violations.

All I could do was shake my head and think about what she (the judge) told me the last time I was in her court room. I knew that they knew that if they brought me back in front of her that there's a pretty good chance that I would be sent back to prison, no matter what the violations were. I could see the look in her eyes that she was fed up, and the only way to end this was to allow the probation officer to be victorious. After all that, the probation officer, Ms. Foxx, told the judge that she felt that I should be placed back on supervisory probation upon my release. Judge Ms. Kennedy gave her a look that sent waves through the whole building.

The judge's response was, "Are you kidding me!!!! Are you serious? Unbelievable! You come in here, and you complain about the man since he's been out of prison. I send him back to prison, and you want me to put him back on three years' supervised probation upon release? It's not going to happen. That's it. I'm ending this now."

As I sat there on the stand and Judge Ms. Kennedy passed sentence on me, I looked abroad at the prosecutor and Ms. Foxx. While the Judge was passing sentence, I was still pleading for the freedom of my boys by pleading that she allow me to remain free. I was literally crying. I had promised my boys that I would do everything that I could to get them out of that place and bring them home where they rightfully belonged. Every time I visited them they would ask how much longer they would have to stay there. I would tell them it wouldn't be long.

While the prosecutor and the probation officer felt great level of satisfaction by the tears falling from my eyes, little did they know the tears were not about the subsequent prison sentence that I just received, but instead, the promise I couldn't keep to my boys.

The Marshall took me to a holding cell where I waited to be transported to whatever jail until I was transferred to prison. A lot of things were spinning through my mind. How could this happen with no proof. But then, during a violation hearing, they don't need to prove it, just claim that it happened. They need to change that!

How was I to know that day would be another turning point of events in my life that I wouldn't have any control over?

On October 19th, 1999, after all the cases were heard, we were all loaded up in a van at the end of the day. Some were dropped off at Newport News jail. The rest of us were taken to Virginia Beach.

During the ride, I couldn't help but think about the cases that took place.

The renegade boys were on trial. This one big Indian renegade received 12 months for cooperating with the government. The judge claimed that the prosecutor had incorrectly presented something in trial. Therefore, the judge had granted them a bond. It never seems to fail. People are always running their mouths about what took place in court. I was trying to understand how they got off by by bond, being charged with guns and meth., and I was given 24 months for alleged violation and no new charge.

Once I got to Virginia Beach jail, I had to spend 48 hours in a cell until my P.P.S. went through.

Everyone who entered the jail had to go through that. At this time, I hadn't spoken with Sharon or anyone for three days. Once the three days were up and I was cleared, I was taken to B-block. That was alright because they were single cells.

When Sharon would come to visit, they wouldn't allow Co-co to come because of her age. I never heard of that before. Depending on who worked that day, they would allow her to come to the window, and I would tell her how much I loved and missed her. Sharon asked me how things were, besides being locked-up again. She asked me about the treatment. Everybody knew that federal prisoners got better treatment than state prisoners. The state didn't care about anyone or their rights.

In my block this guy from New York had been running the TV long before I got there, so I let him continue his little pushing around of others. I was still trying to reduce the anger that I had built up from trial, well violation hearing. I didn't want to end up injuring anybody, but that's how I felt.

After he had beaten up an older guy over the TV, I got involved because the older guy, not only was he older, but he was going through withdrawals ... bad. I guess the young guy thought no one would come along that he would have to deal with. He thought it made him look good to be the winner. By this time, it was lock down for count. During this time the young guy from New York was yelling and screaming what he was going to do to the older guy. The older guy never gave up. That made me want to get involved even more. Though he lost, he still had heart.

Once the cells opened back up, it was time to break his back. I never said a word until the cells opened. Once we were out, I walked over to the guy and said. "Do you want some rec? You like jumping on older men? Don't mind my age, I'll give you all you want right here, right now!"

He then said, "I don't have a problem with you."

I told him that any young punk who puts his hands on an older guy about something as small as that has no respect for anybody. And I said that if he puts his hands on that man about a TV, he would have a problem with me … "And trust me; you don't want any of this."

I told him earlier that day after I got off the phone with Sharon. One of the guys suggested since I put up the fight, to get people off the floor, that I get a cell in that block. Everybody agreed (They wanted someone around who would fight).

It didn't take long after the complaint. I was transferred to FCI Parker. My whole stay at the jail was less then three weeks. I think I may hold the record.

After arriving at FCI Parker, I went through R&D. Afterwards, I was taken to the Alexandria Hall building. With one other receiver, I'd wonder if I would see anybody that I left behind a few years ago.

Once we were assigned to a cell, I made my bunk and came back out to the hallway. That's when I noticed ole Red from the streets. Red was high yellow with green eyes, so you know he thought he was the man.

I went to the TV room where everybody hung out and smoked. That was the only place you could smoke in the building. Once in the TV room, Red looked at me and said, "Don't I know you?"

I told him that he looked familiar too. It didn't take long before he figured it out. I had met so many people doing that job. I could be anywhere, and people would speak to me.

I'd worked nearly all the clubs with a name within the Seven Cities. He looked at me again and started laughing and pointing. He shouted, "Ziggy!"

We talked, and come to find out, he was Pence's cousin. Pence had flossed-out Fridays at club Nile where I supervised security.

As he went on about how people wouldn't believe that I was locked up,

I could only think if he only knew. As he continued, I asked him about Pence. He told me that Pence had lost his clothing store. Yes, the man had that too, as well as flossed-out Friday's at the club. He told me that Pence and his wife were going through a bitter divorce. I couldn't help but reflect on one Friday at the club when Pence and his wife were having an argument. I told him that people were watching, and they had come out on their night to support them because of the activities he had. "How would it look that you and your wife out here fighting?" I told him that some things are meant to be done behind closed doors.

He looked at me and sincerely said, "You're right." He went back inside the club.

Moments later, I thought about what I had said to Pence. I needed to get back with him to clear something up. Once again, I took him into the entrance way. I told him that I was not suggesting that he take his wife home and beat her down. I just want you to understand that.

Jokingly, he said, "I thought that's what you were telling me." He started laughing.

I just smiled.

He, in turn, told me that she accused him of sleeping with her best friend. I kind of smiled and told him that I couldn't tell him what to do, but if I were going to sleep with a woman, certainly it wouldn't be my wife's best friend or anyone else she knew, for that matter. You're only looking for trouble.

His wife was fine as all outdoors. But sometimes we're not satisfied with what we have. And being so, we end up losing what we have and that which we were infatuated with as well.

After that Friday, he and his wife didn't bring their problems to the club. Though she wasn't with him as much anymore, before they left that Friday, she came up to me and thanked me.

After classification, I was assigned to the Jimmy Hall building, the worst building on the compound. I found myself walking past the chapel. I missed two services of Jumu'ah. I was upset but really didn't know why or with whom. I could blame others, but that would be allowing them that much control, and I wasn't going to allow that. I could only be upset with myself.

Working a full and part-time job on the street was my excuse then, not to mention the probation officer riding my back all the time. I would get this bad feeling when I rode by the mosque. I guess it was because I would think about the promise I made. The feeling I would get was unknown and indescribable. It wasn't like the normal feeling of bad.

While running with Red and two other guys, he knew I finally started going back to Jumu'ah service and taleem.

I seemed to be back on track now … back to service and working out Monday-Friday.

Every weekend and holiday Sharon and Co-co would visit. My mom visited two or three times as well as Krista and the girls. Alina visited with them one weekend after Sharon went to West Virginia to get her for the last part of the summer.

Rahim and I were making our Salah together every day except for DHUHR and sometimes ASR, depending on the time ASR came in. Rahim worked in the unit core, so he was gone during the day. Rahim was a good brother from Jamaica. He was being deported upon release. He would talk about how he was going to open a Masjid and that it would be the first where he was from. Rahim was a funny brother as well

In January 2000, during Martin Luther King, Jr.'s birthday, I walked in the chow hall to eat. This guy, Troy, was making eye contact with a grin on his face. I looked behind me to suggest perhaps it was someone else he was looking at. I knew it was me. I asked him what the problem was. He mumbled something. I couldn't hear, so I got out of line. Some of the guys in the line were telling me to let it go and just get back in line. Instead, I sat at the table next to him. I said, "My man, what's the problem?"

Now, mind you, I'd seen him in the visiting room with Leslie, my brother's ex-wife's sister. Before I was violated, I would go over to Leslie's apartment. I used to flirt with her, but we never slept together, although I could have.

Troy claimed that I put my hands on his son. I asked him who his son was. He called Leslie's youngest son's name. I told him, "First, that's not your son by blood, and secondly, my niece, Nakisha Harris, was babysitting for Leslie, as usual, and thirdly, this was done at my apartment where my niece babysat for her most of the time. He was jumping up and down on my sofa. I told him to stop, and he refused so I grabbed him by his arm and pulled him off. I didn't hurt the boy. I've known his family for years. But I don't know you."

I got up to get back in line. Upon doing so, Troy yelled, "Don't put your hands on him anymore."

So, I got out of line again, and I tried to explain to him that I wouldn't do anything to hurt Leslie's boys. "But let's be clear; it's not because you say so."

At that moment, the look he gave was a fighting look. I told him to find somebody else to play with. "This isn't what you're looking for."

He jumped up with a fork in his hand. You know the feds had real forks, knives, and spoons for utensils. So, you see? When he jumped up, I knocked him on his ass like he never had it before.

He never got one punch in. When I knocked him out, and he was lying on the floor, I went to stomp a mud hole in him. Everybody that was somebody said, "Ziggy, please don't do that." My Muslim brothers reached out to me and said, "Ahki, you're wrong if you put your feet on that man while he's out cold." Everybody started yelling, "Get back in line! Get back in line!"

The chow halls in the feds are big, I mean big. I tried to get in line like nothing happened, but one of the officers claimed to have seen what happened. That was moments later, but it was before I was able to move up in the line and get a tray. I just got there in November of 1999, and already I was going to the hole.

In January of 2000, that following weekend, as usual, the both of us had visits. It just so happened my mom was there for one of the few visits she made to me.

When I got into the visiting room, Troy was already visiting with Leslie. Once out there, I made eye contact with her. She had a killer look on her face, mumbling while giving me the middle finger. I just shook my head. Now I got to deal with my mom.

When I entered the visiting room, my mom was over talking to Leslie and Troy. I knew I was going to hear something from her. Like I mentioned before, our families had known each other for twenty some years.

Co-co and I started playing cards. As my mom came over, I could see the look on her face. Once again, she took the defense of someone else besides me. During her little fussing, she mentioned that he was a friend of Todd's and how he's a good boy. I just let her go on fussing. Finally, she stopped, and I was able to enjoy the rest of my visit.

That Monday I went before the hearing office for the charge. I received 45 days isolation, and he received 15 days.

That following weekend, whenever we had visits at the same time, they would allow him out first every time. Sharon got fed up with that and started complaining. She called the administration. After that night, they rotated us.

"I would have never come out to see anybody looking like that. His face was messed up bad.

My mom said that I should be ashamed of myself. Every time after that, when Leslie would come to visit while I was getting visitors first, she would give me a real nasty look. Once again, she gave me the finger. I couldn't hear what she was saying, but I could see her lips saying, "F you."

I would call home twice a day, every day. In the morning at 6:00 or 7:00 a.m. and every night around 8:00 or 9:00 p.m.

She and Co-co would visit every weekend and holidays except Christmas. They would always go to New York to visit her mother and other family members.

Sharon would send about $100 to $150 a month. Her mom and aunt would send a total of $35 to $40 per month. I told her mom and aunt that they didn't need to send me any money. During one visit, Sharon told me to just take the money because I didn't want to hurt anybody's feelings.

I would call Sharon's mom sometimes and talk with her and her Aunt Elaine, as well. They really loved them some Ziggy. I didn't want to hurt her feelings, so I just let them keep on sending it. Don't' get me wrong. I was grateful. I had gotten real close to them in the past two years or more.

In 2001, Rahim was being released. He was being deported back to Jamaica. A few weeks prior, we had a disagreement about something. On his way to R & D, I went behind him. I stopped him and apologized. I told him to hold on to the rope of Allah and if I never got the chance to see him in this life again, Insha'Allah we'll meet in the hereafter. As salaam Alaikum.

I was in the hole for the third time. Someone kept dropping notes on me about regulating the phones and TVs. That's not true, just one phone and TV. See, me and my man, Jake Williams, had gotten used to watching Lifetime. We weren't going to sit there and watch BET all day.

Well, anyway, as usual, the warden and rest of the administration were making their rounds on Thursday. Assistant Warden Mrs. Copeland would come by every time she got to my cell. She would smile, shaking her head, and would mention something about the first fight, which was with Troy. She would say things like, "Mr. Harper, all the time you've done, you're still fighting and beating up people."

I said, "Mrs. Copeland, it's not like that."

She would cut me off. "Yeah, yeah, yeah, Mr. Harper."

I would yell, "Mrs. Copeland, if you get me out of the hole, I will promise you that I will try not to cause any more trouble." But I must be mindful that if people think that all it takes is a note to the administration to get me off the compound and in the hole for no reason, they would do it. See a week ago while they were making their rounds, I asked the chief warden, Mr. Baker, if he would let me out of the hole. At that time, he turned to Mrs. Copeland and said that it was up to her.

He kept walking. Then he turned around and came back and asked me how I got there anyway. I asked him what he meant. He said, "Didn't you come from USP Victorville?"

I told him that that was my last prison before being released and that I was back on a violation, a false violation, I might add. He then said, "But you should be returned to the prison you were released from."

I said, "Correct, but they changed that law during the time I was on the street, or should I say, that policy."

They both laughed. As they walked off, I asked Mrs. Copeland if she was going to let me out. She yelled, "I'll think about it." The only thing about the hole in the feds: You can get some canteen depending on who you know.

The following Thursday I was waiting for Mrs. Copeland to make her rounds. I asked everybody that walked by me if assistant warden, Mrs. Copeland, was here today. All I got was, "I don't know. She may be. I haven't seen her today…" or something like that. I just lay back on my bunk reading a book.

Moments later, somebody yelled, "The floor is wet!" That was one of the ways to let everybody know that someone was coming down the hall.

So, as I was lying there, I looked over my head. What do you know, Mrs. Copeland was standing there, smiling. I said, "Don't be smiling if you're not going to let me out the hole." Of course, I had a smile on my face. I didn't want her to think I was demanding anything.

She replied, "Oh, I can't smile now?" She started walking slowly. I was standing there looking at her. As I began to say something, she said, "If you don't see me tomorrow, then they'll let you out."

I yelled, "But no one comes over here on Fridays!"

I could hear the footsteps of her heels as she continued to walk down the hall. Suddenly, I heard her say, "What did I say, Mr. Harper?"

I just smiled.

The next day I was sweating. The OIC (officer-in-charge) had already made his rounds with a list of inmates who were getting out to pack their property. They had me on edge. That chump came back about an hour later and told me that I had 10 minutes to pack. He said, "I forgot to tell you earlier," but I knew he did it on purpose.

I told him, "There's going to be repercussions and consequences, chump!"

For a moment there, I didn't hear anything. I called out, "OIC. Come on, man. I apologize, chump."

He was standing two cells down, laughing, where I couldn't see him. He walked to my cell, laughing.

I said, "Oh, that's funny. Ha! Ha!"

Once back on the compound, Stan Cochran said he wanted to see me. After I put my things away, I left the Jimmy Hall building and went to the Cincinnati Hall building to see Stan Cochran. We spoke and shook hands. He asked me if I had any intention of fighting with O 'boy Troy again. I told him I had no problem with him. Stan Cochran went on about how we were homeboys, although I didn't tell him I didn't go for that homeboy stuff. Those are the ones who get you. But I went along with it because I'd known him and his brother, Bryant, for years. In fact, Bryant and I went to school together.

~" Most people will accept a lie more readily, than the truth if it's in their best interest to do so, rather than acknowledge a fact that could shatter what they believe in, or benefit from."

Chapter 28

On March 19ᵗʰ, 2000, after working out one Saturday, I went inside the gym to play basketball. During one of the games, I made a lay-up. As I turned around to get back on defense, I immediately heard a "popping" sound as I hit the floor. Suddenly, I found myself sprawled out on the floor. I tried to sit up, but I felt a severe pain up and down the right side of my body. At that point, I could not sit up. About six inmates and a correctional officer got a stretcher and took me to the infirmary.

The physician's assistant who was on duty took x-rays of my back and told me all I had was a pulled muscle. I told him that something was wrong. I was having too much pain. I then asked, "What does the x-ray show?"

He replied, "I don't read x-rays. I would have to show them to the doctor when he comes in Monday."

Unbelievable.

They took me to my building where I lay on the floor rolling from side to side. I didn't eat anything for two days. I was in so much pain. The duty officer of my building had called the chow hall for my dinner as he did all day. After seeing that I was in too much pain to eat that meal as well, he called somebody. They brought some medication to me, and the next day they took me to the VA hospital and had an MRI. Afterwards, they put me back in the wheelchair.

A doctor pointed out on a video screen where I had ruptured two disks. He then told me that he would prescribe some medicine for my pain and that the institution would need to get a specialist that may require surgery soon to evaluate my medical problem.

A couple of weeks later, I met with Dr. Jacob V. Norfleet, M. D., Institutional Contractor surgeon. He told me that he would like to try some physical therapy first. We did for a few weeks. Afterwards, he told me that I would need the surgery.

During the months leading up to that, he had me come to the medical department and did an evaluation by video cam with one of the head doctors in North Carolina. The BOPs doctor said that it was clear that I needed the surgery.

I put back on my shirt, got in the wheelchair, and spoke with the hospital administrator, Ms. Silvia. She told me that she would schedule me to see her before the week was out after she spoke with the doctor.

Two days later Ms. Silvia called me to her office, out back of the medical building, which was a trailer. I've got to tell you, once in the trailer, I didn't like the fact that we were the only ones there. Be mindful, I'd been fighting these people for the longest now.

Ms. Silvia, as usual, all smiles with everybody. She told me to have a seat while she retrieved some papers from the next room.

She returned and said, "Mr. Harper, I sent a sign-off order to Mr. Baker/Warden. Now we'll have to give it some time."

I told her that I appreciated everything she was doing.

A few weeks went by and no answer or feedback from the Warden's office. For the next 13 months I constantly wrote request form/grievance/BPP8-9-10, all the administrative grievances pertaining to my surgery. I even spoke with the warden, warden's assistance, and medical personnel, all to no avail. For the next 13 months no response was given.

In early July, 2001, the new hospital administrator, Ms. Jean Doe, told me in the chow hall during lunch that I was going to get my surgery.

A week later, I was placed in the hole overnight before medical transfer the next morning, which was normal procedure.

After dressing out in the hospital gown, the nurse returned and asked me to get dressed. Once back in the van with the officers, I asked what happened. They said the institution went on lockdown. Therefore, they had to bring me back.

On July 25th, 2001 after lunch I was paged to return to my building. Once I got there, the officer asked me where I had been. You know I gave him the look he deserved, asking a question like that. I was in prison.

They took me to R & D and dressed me out. I was then taken to James Rudolph Medical Center in Housewel, Virginia.

Once I got there, they changed me into a paper gown. The nurse started asking questions. When she asked me when I last had something to eat, I told her that I just finished eating lunch. Her eyes got so wide. She looked at me, then called the doctor and told him that I'd just eaten. He looked at me and asked, "Did you know that you were coming for your surgery today?"

I told him that I had no idea. At the very moment, I learned all about anesthesia, as Dr. Norfleet explained to me what would have happened if I had not been an honest man. I looked at the doctor in disbelief.

My mind was running now. Was the prison trying to kill me because of my complaining? I'd filed every document you could file under the law within the institution. The nurse turned red in the face. Dr. Norfleet was outraged.

Once we returned to the institution, I demanded to see the assistant Warden, Ms. Copeland. I was told that she had left the institution.

I spoke with the physician that was on duty. Once you return to the institution from a medical run, you must go by medical first. He claimed not to know anything.

The following Monday I went to medical to see the hospital administrator, Ms. Jane. After sitting for a while, I was told to go out back to the trailer. She was so nice and friendly. I don't know if she was being nice because they sent me for surgery without holding me overnight in the hole to make sure I didn't eat or drink anything before being put on anesthesia, or if she was nervous or what. But I wished she would have stopped being so nice because there was only the two of us in the trailer. She was starting to make me nervous.

When I came in, she shook my hand. She was a good looking Spanish woman. She told me that I would be going out that week and not to worry. I would be held overnight this time. "We don't want any mistakes again."

Finally, on July 30th, 2001, I was taken to James Rudolph Medical Center. I underwent surgery, which was performed by Doctor Jacob V. Norfleet. M.D.

The next day when I returned to the institution, I was placed in another building as opposed to my original building (Jimmy Hall). My property was given to me in trash bags. I was still kind of out of it, so I didn't go through my things.

August the second, two days later, I was taken to R & D to be released. After going through my property extensively, I noticed that all my documents pertaining to my filings were gone. After inquiring, I was told that my counselor, Ms. Jane, packed my property herself. I thought to myself, *Is that supposed to make me feel better about my missing documents?*

I refused to leave the institution until my property was returned to me. Around 3:00 p.m. I was told that if I was still there in the institution at the 4:00 p.m. count, I would have to remain there until the next business day. Reluctantly, I left the institution. I didn't want to spend any more time than I was sentenced.

The duty officer pushed me outside in the wheelchair to the van.

"Those of you who wish to direct others to fight or war against another must be as willing to lay your own life on the line for the things you say you believe in as easily as you would direct others to do so on your behalf."

Chapter 29

The date was August 2nd, 2001. I was taken to the Greyhound bus station with a back-brace and a walker. They left me to my own accord. The Greyhound bus station attendant had to assist me with getting on and off the bus. While I sat in the bus station, I couldn't help but think about the last few days. The day before, the counselor let me make a call, and I called Sharon for the last time in the institution. The counselor asked her if she would be picking me up. I could tell by the look on her face, Sharon was holding fast to her decision that she had made back in May when she had decided to end the relationship. As I think back on things, it's beginning to become clear now. My relationship and my home, all gone.

My thoughts were interrupted when they called my destination. Once I reached Handen, I called my mom. That was a very hard call to make. Me and my mother never really got along. She answered the phone.

She pulled up smiling and everything. She pretended to be glad that I was home, but I knew that it would only be a matter of time before she was her old self. I got in the car, and she handed me $10 and told me that she wished she had more to give. I told her that I had a little money and for her to keep it. She insisted that I take it. I asked her to stop by a corner store on the way home. The feeling I had was not good. I went in the store and picked up something to drink because at that moment I just wanted to lose myself.

Once we got to the house, I sat on the porch and began to think about Lizzy. I went up the steps and got the phone. I was kind of nervous because I hadn't talked to her since I got violated, except for the first three weeks in Parker, Virginia. I spoke with her on the phone, but she would get upset because I wouldn't let her come visit me. During those three weeks, things began to deteriorate.

The last time I called her was on a Friday. Her youngest son, Jodee, answered the phone. After speaking with him momentarily, I told him to put his mom on the phone. I could hear her in the background asking him who was on the phone. He told her, "Ziggy." I could hear her when she told him to tell me that she didn't have time and that she was running late. I asked him what she was late for. He asked her. She said that she was going out, and that her friend, Venus, was waiting for her.

Until today I hadn't spoken to her. As the phone hung up, I was kind of hesitant because of what may be. After the first two rings, I started to hang up, but she answered the phone. I was surprised at the response I got from her. She was so happy to hear from me, that she was willing to drive over that night. Instead, I told her to wait until tomorrow.

We continued to talk on the phone for another hour or so. While Lizzy and I were talking, she never mentioned anything about being in a relationship. This was my first day out. Maybe she was wondering if she should be honest or not. She didn't know about my injury at that time.

After I got off the phone, a car pulled up, and to my surprise it was Vanessa Carlton. I didn't notice her until she started walking as I could see her face as she turned. Vanessa had gotten out of her car, walked to the back and open her trunk. While I looked on, it was unclear of what she was doing. When it closed, I could see she had a red cup in her hand. This woman was making a drink...wow. Not once did she notice me on the porch, even though it was dark. All she had to do was turn around. I was looking right directly at her. But I never knew it was her until she turned and walked off. I didn't say anything to her because Lizzy was calling me back, and I didn't want Vanessa talking in the background when she did.

Two or three minutes into that, Lizzy had returned my call. So, I never said a word.

The next day (Saturday), Lizzy and the boys came over to see me. She asked me what part of Norfolk I lived in. Before I could tell her, she told me that she was not coming past 49th street. I started laughing. I asked her why. She just went on about how so much killing goes on over here. I couldn't stop laughing. I could understand. After all, she was from Norton County, and you didn't really hear of anything going on over there.

We went to Henry Park, and the boys played in the water. We sat and talked. For some reason she felt that it was her responsibility to stay with me, due to my injuries, because we were together when I got violated, even though we were not together for the better part of my incarceration.

Once she took me back home though, she didn't mention it, but it was evident that we would not be together. I never asked her if she was in a relationship. I felt that if she wanted me to know, or if it was that serious, she would have told me so. They stayed for a while.

As she was leaving, we hugged and kissed, just a peck. The following day I looked through the phone book to look up Keisha first. I couldn't find her, so I look up Vanessa Carlton. Finally, I came across her information.

I called her up and told her that it was Ziggy. She screamed and asked me where I was calling her from. I told her that I was at my mother's house. At that time, I described what she did just the day before. She started laughing and asked me where I was sitting. I told her right behind her on the porch, and that she never looked that way. Where the house sits, the pole light was so dim, it seemed dark. We talked for a while.

Finally, she decided to drive over. When she pulled up, she just looked shaking her head laughing.

After talking for a while, she asked me if it was okay for her to drink. I told her, "Sure, it's okay."

As she was getting the drinks, I went to get something for her to drink out of.

After a few drinks and talking, we went upstairs. We had dated when we were 16 or 17 years old. It's not like we were complete strangers to each other.

For the next few months we were sleeping together. The first night we were together she made it clear that she was involved with someone. I told her that I had no problem with that. After all, the guy was locked up and not due out for another six months.

That Monday I called the social security office to make an appointment. I was scheduled for that Thursday. I called Krista and asked her if she would take me to my appointment. She agreed. When she came to pick me up, she had my two nieces with her. I love those babies very much. My brother can't see the blessing he has. Once we got to the social security office, you had to get in line, or you'd be there all day, so I had to stand there with a two-wheel walker. I had yet to have the staples taken out of my back.

My name was called. The case worker was Ms. Dawn. After the interview, she asked me if I had any of my medical files with me that she could copy. She told me that it would help her process my claim more quickly. As we proceeded to the front, I asked my niece if she would get the medical records out of the car. When she returned with the hand bag, the care worker, Ms. Dawn, looked at me wide eyed and asked, "Are these all medical records?"

I said, "Yes, mam."

She smiled and asked me if I could come back tomorrow and pick up my medical records. I said, "Sure."

While we were leaving, she came to the door and asked if I could wait for 30 to 45 minutes. She had gotten another co-worker to help her run off copies. Once she was finished, she told me that social security turned everybody down the first time, regardless of their condition. During the interview, I had given her the information to Dr. Jacob V. Norfleet M.D.

After we left the social security office, we stopped at the social service office. There I filled out the necessary papers to receive food stamps and a check for $90 a month for having a claim pending with social security.

Once we got home, my brother, Todd, was at my mom's house. I knew he would start something with Krista.

Once I made it up those stairs, I went straight to my room. The girls came to say goodbye. Once they were gone, my mom came to my room and asked for that $10 that she gave me when she picked me up from the bus station. I knew then this would be the starting point of the irreconcilable relationship that my mother and I had since as long as I could remember.

As she continued to fuss, she told me that Todd told her that upon release from the feds, I was given $1,500 to $2,000. Once again, she hurt me so deeply by listening to things from others. She never stopped to ask me; she just took his word for it. I told her that I did not receive money like that. And furthermore, how could he have told her about something or somewhere he'd never been? She just stood there looking crazy. Gladly, I gave her $10, and upon doing so, I told her that when she was giving it to me, I had some money, but she insisted. After all these years, we still couldn't seem to get it right. "What a life." I knew at that moment I had to resort to trying to find somewhere else to live. I wasn't ready, but what choice did I have? We just could not seem to live together.

Later that Thursday after my appointments, I called Vanessa and asked her if she would come pick me up, as we continued to see each other. After she picked me up, we went back to her apartment and, as usual, we would drink, watch TV, or listen to music. All three of her boys still lived with her, so I would interact with them as well, but I hadn't seen them since they were little boys. And her youngest one hadn't even been born yet.

Anyway, I knew it was out of the question, but I would sometimes allude to the possibilities of her, myself and the youngest boy picking up and finding a new life down south somewhere. Of course, each time the conversation came up, we would both laugh. But I was serious. She would say something like, "Ziggy, if only you had come back about two years ago."

I told her that I might just have to move in until I get my own place. I couldn't watch cable over there. She turned to me and said, "Ms. Darlene don't have cable?"

I said, "No." My mom only had one digital cable box. I mean, after all, she lived by herself. At that time, Vanessa told me about a friend of hers that knew this guy they called cable Richard, and that he would hook the cable up at my mom's house.

About an hour later he called, and I spoke with him on the phone. We made an appointment for that Friday. So, I called my mom and told her what I had done and asked if it was okay. She had mentioned getting cable anyway, so she could watch cable as well.

Friday morning Vanessa drove me home before going to work. Around 10:00 that morning cable Richard showed up. Once he got there, we went back outside where he looked for a box. The box was on the side. He opened the lock and hooked it up. Once he was finished, we went back upstairs. He ran a line from the front through my mom's room to mine. Within an hour he was done, and everything was good.

In late August of 2001, I'd been out three weeks. I called Krista and asked her to take me on one of my many appointments. She drove me to the social service office. They gave me $100 worth of food stamps. We left the social service and went to Super Walmart.

I still had a better part of the $500 that I was released with. I was waiting to get the food stamps so that I could do the shopping. I got everything I needed. I spent the $100 food stamps and a $140 of cash. The cash was for all hygiene needs. I made sure I was set for the next two to three months. I got plenty of meat. My mom had a deep freezer. That way I could shop once a month for food. My mom and I didn't' eat the same thing, rather I didn't eat what she ate.

Earlier that week I had run into another one of my old girlfriends, Samantha Andrews. Krista and I were trying to put everything away. We hadn't gotten to the meat yet, so I called Samantha on her job. I knew she wasn't at home. Yes, she had given me her home, work, and cell number. I put all the meat in the refrigerator until she got there.

Once she arrived, she and my mom started a conversation. I'm looking like, if you want to talk, let's get the food bagged up and put away and y'all can talk all you want. I washed my chicken, took the skin off, and bagged three to four pieces. After we were done, we cleaned up.

I was having a drink as we talked and listened to music while the TV was running. Before you knew it, we were playing around. Nothing happened. All she kept saying was, "Your mom in the next room."

Maybe she was reflecting back on when we were younger. One night while we were having sex, my mom walked right in on us. My mom started screaming, "Oh, boy, what are you doing?" I mean she was carrying on like somebody was getting killed or something. I had to look around the room, and I knew we were the only two there.

After messing around for a while, she asked me if I wanted to go to her place. I said sure.

During the first week of September 2001, Sharon, Co-co and Co-co 's friend came by to see me. Sharon came by to bring the rest of my clothes. This was the second time I'd seen her since I'd been out. But I was yet to receive the money that was promised to me. When I got violated, I had money in the bank, and I have no idea what happened to my taxes, which was $4,200. I needed a car.

She told me to go and see this guy named Jaylin that worked for a new dealership on Mars Blvd. She gave me the address and number. When she left, I called Jaylin, and we made plans to come see him that Friday. I called Krista to see if she would be able to take me. My brother, Todd, was just no good whatsoever. Instead, of seeing me through the things I needed to take care of, he was a hindrance.

On Friday Krista, the girls, and I went to the dealership. I met with

Jaylin, and during our conversation, he told me that Sharon owed him $2,000. I knew then I was out back. He took me out back where he had a couple of cars. One needed a transmission; the other one smoked so bad. This man had me test driving this car on one of the busiest Boulevards in the area. Smoked filled the sky. Once back at the dealership, he told me that he could have their mechanic look at it. If not, the other one wouldn't be ready for another four to six weeks. He was waiting for a transmission to come from Carolina.

On the way home, I couldn't help but feel that this wasn't going to happen. It just didn't feel right. Still, I was yet to receive any money from Sharon.

When I got home, I called Sharon on her cell phone as she requested once I had seen Jaylin. She asked me if he had anything for me. I told her what he had to offer was unacceptable. Before getting off the phone, she told me that she may only be able to give me $1,500 of the original $2,400, which was only half of my tax return. As each day went by, I knew the amount would change to smaller and smaller. I told her I'd speak with her later.

On September 11, 2001, I was sitting in front of my TV filling out some forms when a special news report came on. (Twin towers) I watched as the two airplanes smashed into the trade center like everyone else who was watching TV. Immediately, the hatred began.

Thirty minutes later, Sharon called and asked if I was watching TV. I said "Yeah!" She immediately got offended. She started asking me questions in which I had no answers. Because I had no answers, she started alluding to things, blaming me for what was taking place, though none of her family was there at the time. They did work at the Trade Center though. I am like, "Hold on, what do any of this have to do with me?"

"Nothing! Nothing at all!" She just continued talking.

All I could think was she was really in her feelings. I thought this would be a good time to ask her if she was the one who called the probation officer on me.

I said, "Sharon, let me ask you something," after she finally took a breather. I said, "Don't get upset; I'm just looking for answers." I told her that I needed closure of the events that had taken place in my life. I asked, "Did you call my probation officer that day?"

I think I hit a nerve. She started using vulgar language. (You go F yourself). I was shocked. Neither of us had ever used such language towards each other. Once she finished, she just hung up the phone. At that moment, I knew that she called the probation officer. I just sat there for the better part of the day watching CNN-News.

As I reflected on October 19th, 1999, everything was beginning to come clear. When the probation officer, Ms. Foxx, refused to let me travel to Guilford, West Virginia for my custody hearing, after all this time, it was evident that she was up to something, but I had no idea. Especially the fact that the social worker played a part. She allowed Ms. Foxx to talk her into something that was illegal. Ms. Foxx took full advantage of the fact that the social worker was new on the job, just straight out of college. Ms. Foxx knew that it was illegal, so to make it legal, she had to force me to sign a consent form, giving her permission to correspond with the social worker. I had missed two hearings, so I had to give in.

Thinking back to the early days when Sharon once told me that the probation officer asked her what she was doing with a guy like me, that's when the both of us were on probation with Officer Otis, which didn't go well. And now my so-called wife had it out for me because of the events that had unfolded. Yes! Suddenly, the social worker wanted Sharon to come to court as well, now that I think about it. Why was it necessary? She had already made the visit to us in Chesapeake. That was when she claimed that she had a reliable witness, that I was seen socializing with a known felon. How did my wife become a felon that I couldn't socialize with? It's beyond me.

I couldn't stop wondering to what extent of a roll she played. I knew that nothing happens without the will of Allah, and that anything that befalls him is by his own hands.

"Most people spend more time and energy trying to hold on to a past that is gone forever, while dreaming for a future that may not come for them, rather than embracing the present that is right there in the palm of their hands.

Chapter 30

The last week of September 2001 I received a phone call from my case worker, Ms. Dawn, from the social security office, denying my claim. She reassured me that they turned everyone down on their initial claim and encouraged me to refile. She also told me that I needed to contact my surgeon (Dr. Jacob V. Norfleet) MD and tell him that I would need something from him stating that I would be permanently disabled for at least two years or more. That way my claim would surely be processed. She told me that she would be putting a new claim form in the mail for me that day. I thanked her and told her that I would be in touch.

As soon as I hung up, I called to Parker, Virginia where Dr. Jacob's office was located. I spoke with the attending nurse and explained everything to her. She told me that it wouldn't be a problem, and that if I had or could sign a release form, they would forward the information to the social security office. As I continued to explain my situation, she asked if I had a direct number as well as a fax number. I said, "Sure," and I gave her the numbers. She told me that she'd get back with me as soon as she got it done.

I hung up and immediately called my case worker, Ms. Dawn, to inform her. The secretary told me that she was on the phone and asked if I would I like to hold or if there was number where I could be reached. I gave her my name and told her that she had my number.

Twenty minutes later the nurse called me back to assure me that everything on her end was done. Before hanging up, she asked if I would be making my appointment to have the staples taken out. It was kind of overdue. I told her that I would try my best to be there next week to have it done. She told me that if for some reason I couldn't make it, to be sure and call so that they can perhaps arrange a visit with a doctor closer to me because I would need to have them removed. I asked if she had any information handy so that I could contact any doctors near me.

Minutes later she returned to the phone and told me that she had no one in my area; however, if I could find a doctor who would do it, I was to tell them who I was and my situation, then give them their information because they would need to be contacted before doing anything. I thanked her and hung up.

Immediately, I looked through the phone book and started calling doctors trying to make an appointment. After the third doctor's office, I was told by a nurse that she doubted if anyone took on that kind of responsibility. She assured me that, more than likely, no one would take staples out, and if I did find someone, to call her and let her know (jokingly). She laughed. I laughed, and I thanked her. She said, "You're welcome," and we hung up. I knew then that I had to find a way to Housewel, Parker.

The following day I had Krista take me to the hospital to see if I could get a doctor on duty to remove the staples. I was placed in one of the examination rooms.

Minutes later a doctor came in, and I explained my situation to him. He told me that he was sorry, but he couldn't touch another surgeon's work like that. He told me that he doubted it as well that I would ever find a doctor who would take them out. He shook my hand, told me that he wished he could help, but taking the staples out would make him liable if anything were to happen after that point.

As we left the hospital, I knew that I had to get to Parker. So, I asked Krista if she could take me. She told me that she didn't know if her car could make it that far. She said, "We'll see."

My mother was out of the question as I'd already asked her during one of my previous appointments, whereas, I had to ask Samantha Andrews after that one trip. The way she acted, I knew not to ask her again. The way she was driving, speeding and everything, I was glad she didn't get a ticket because I couldn't put anything on it. I was real desperate, so I called Sharon and explained my situation. Ha! To no avail, of course, she refused.

Later that evening, I called Vanessa Carlton. She told me that her car surely wouldn't make it. I kind of knew that, but remember, I was desperate. I just wanted to get those staples out of my back so I could start my physical therapy. The way things were going, I knew that just might be impossible.

I thought about calling Lizzy, but that was out of the question. Around 7:00 that evening Vanessa called me back and asked me to meet her at her mother's apartment. I was kind of reluctant because when we were teenagers, her mom, Miss Eley, used to curse me out sometimes, well, most of the time. Even when I would speak to her, she would reply very nastily, "I am fine." And she would mumble all the way up the stairs. Vanessa would be laughing her heart out.

Once she got to her mom's, she called me and told me that she was at the apartment and that she would be outside watching for me. Her mom lived in Twelve Oaks, which was only one block from my mom's house.

Once I got there, Vanessa was standing on the back steps laughing. She knew I was hesitant because I mentioned it over the phone. When I walked in, her mom immediately asked, "Who is this?"

Vanessa said, "Mom, you remember Ziggy."

She said, "Oh, Yeah, how you do, Ziggy?"

I said, "Fine, Ms. Eley."

She just kept talking. Her sister, Diane, was there. We started drinking and listening to music. Another one of her sisters lived across the court from her mother. They were in and out, her and her husband.

As the night approached, we decided to go to the club right on the corner of 46th and Colley Avenue, the corner street where my mom lived.

Once we got there, I noticed that it was one of those clubs that only served beer and no real alcohol. For some reason, Vanessa was trying to avoid me in the club. Finally, I asked, "Who in here knows your boyfriend?" She looked with those brown eyes, laughing her heart out. She didn't have to say a word. It was written all over her face. I let her do her thing, and I did mine.

Out of all the females that I had a conversation with, this one walked up as I was sitting at the bar. With my back to the bar she walked so close that her butt rubbed against my knees. If I must say, it was nice. She was thick and good looking. I had to give up the conversation to her. In fact, I tried to leave with her instead of Vanessa.

As we were leaving, because I didn't have a car, I ended up going home alone. Vanessa and I had already said our goodbyes for the night just moments before walking out with the stranger. Well, at least I was feeling good. I went in the house, put on some music awhile, and went to sleep.

In October of 2001, one morning after leaving Vanessa's apartment, I called Cable Richard. I talked to him the day before at her apartment about putting cable in for some people I knew. Once he got to my mom's house, we walked to Wallace Place where his girlfriend lived with her best friend.

Once we entered the complex, he stopped at his sister's apartment. I waited on the sidewalk. I didn't know her name at the time, but Mi-mi walked outside, and it appeared that she was throwing up. I walked across the lot and asked her if she was alright. She looked up at me with a look as to say, "Are you kidding me?"

As we continued to talk, Cable Richard walked up, spoke and walked inside. Finally, she asked me in. Once in, she introduced me to her friend, Gina, who was Cable Richard's girlfriend. She told me to have a seat on the sofa. We sat and talked some more.

That Saturday, we were to meet Sheila Johnson to go out and hook up for cable. We were to meet her right there at 16th Street and Colley Avenue where the complex sat. Cable Richard stood and asked me if I was ready to go so that we wouldn't miss Sheila Johnson.

As I got up, Mi-mi's sister, Deena, who I met the last time I was there, walked from the backroom. As Mi-mi attempted to introduce us, Deena smiled and said, "I met him the other day. Hi!"

I turned to Mi-mi and motioned her in my direction. Once we got outside, I asked if it would be alright if I stopped by sometime to kick it with her. She told me that would be fine. As I turned to walk off, she told me that I could stop by later if I wasn't doing anything. I smiled and kept walking.

As we stood about 30 yards from the corner, his sister walked up to catch a bus to work. Once again, I was listening to a guy who was treating her like she was his mother. The conversation was like, I mean, this guy had no control over his own thoughts.

Anyway, she pulled up and Cable Richard and I got in. She drove to Handen Avenue while he was hooking up her cable.

Sheila Johnson and I were conversing. I couldn't help but feel sorry for her. She'd been having a real hard time. Ever since she was married to Johnny Spud, well, her first husband, she'd been hooked on drugs. All those years she's been back and forth to rehab, but most of the time you couldn't really tell unless you came out late at night. She's just another one of my childhood sweethearts.

My thoughts were interrupted by the ring of the phone. She looked toward me and motioned me to be quiet. Her boyfriend was calling from jail. It's funny; I didn't even get the desire to get with her like I used to, even though she was a very beautiful woman.

Once Cable Richard finished, we had a couple of beers. Finally, Cable Richard and I were ready to head back to Norfolk.

Once we got back to Wallace Place, we went to Mi-mi's apartment. Mi-mi and I talked for most of the night. I ended up leaving around 2:00 a.m.

The next morning my mom and I were at it again. My sister, Regina, was going through one of her spells again. I didn't know when, but somewhere she had lost her mind. She comes and goes.

In November of 2001, since I had been seeing Mi-mi, I'd been trying to make that situation livable. See, my sister, Regina, had lost it completely by then. She came to the house and convinced me that her bank had taken her money. As she was talking, I asked her how much money was missing. She said, "Ten thousand dollars." At that very moment I told her that I was going to put on my best suit, and we'd go and talk with the bank's manager together.

Now my mom was laughing. So, I look at my mom and asked her why she was laughing. The whole while she never told me that my sister had lost her mind some time ago and had been committed at one point. My mom didn't tell me until later that day. The whole time she was telling me this, she was cracking up.

My mom had been keeping her children for a few days now. The little boy, Ty, wasn't bad at all. All he liked was to play those video games. The only thing that I found disturbing was the fact that all the games he had were violent.

The girl, on the other hand, just at the age of nine, was out of control. And let me tell you, when I say out of control, I mean out of control. See, I knew I had to find somewhere to go. My niece had already set my mom against me.

One day I came in from an appointment. My niece was walking

through the house with high heels on and some shorts that I am too embarrassed to describe. By the surprised look on her face, she didn't expect to get caught. When I walked through the door, I caught her coming from the kitchen. She didn't know what to do because I stood between her and my mom's room. I looked at her and asked: "What in the world do you think you're doing?"

She said nothing and immediately started crying. I stood to the side to let her by, but I continued to let her have it. Once in my mom's room, I could hear her get louder, and my mom started screaming like somebody was killing the girl or something.

I went to the room and asked, "What's the screaming for?"

My mom started yelling and screaming that I needed to find somewhere else to go. I took a seat right next to her bed and asked my niece to leave the room for a minute. My mom told her that she didn't have to go anywhere.

As I asked my niece to leave once again, my mom started in. "Who do you think you are? You're nobody. That's why Sharon left you. You didn't treat her children right. She told me."

I was stunned. I just took a moment and hung my head. I thought to myself. Once again, instead of defending me or at least asking my side of the story, she took what someone else said at face value rather than defending me. To defend myself was like a flashback of all the bad events in my life, but only worse. It's real. I got up and went to my room. I lay across the bed and let my thoughts wander as these unfortunate, purposefully, intentional events unfolded in my life, by the very people who claimed to care about me. How could Sharon even fix her mouth to say such a thing? I had never mistreated her children or anyone else that I may have been involved with at any time.

It was the middle of November, 2001. I really needed to find somewhere to go. Things in that house were getting even worse. I couldn't help but wonder how my mom could side with a child (my niece) over an adult. This was not what we were taught as children. We were taught to respect adults, no matter who they were. My mom treated my niece as if she were the adult and I was the child. Unbelievable!

It was Thanksgiving Day. I was home alone. Everyone knew that I don't celebrate holidays. I may not have been living like I should, but at least some things hadn't changed. I was invited to a couple of places. I turned them both down.

Respectfully though, Mi-mi kept calling trying to get me to come to her mom's house to eat with them. I told her that she could bring me something back to eat if she wanted to.

That weekend I told Mi-mi that I didn't think it would work out between us. You see, her sister, Deena's, boyfriend, Joe-boy, was at the apartment twenty-four seven. I got tired of running into him whenever I went to the kitchen or bathroom. For the next two weeks she claimed to have handled the situation, but I never saw a change in his activity, so, now that prodded me to seek shelter elsewhere.

I started talking to someone else in the complex. Her name was Karen. She was a pretty girl with three children: two girls and one boy. The first two times, we spoke face to face. For the next few times, we spoke by notes. Only when I was at my mom's, we spoke on the phone, and that wasn't often with everything going on with that situation.

That Friday, when Mi-mi got home from work, she started fussing with me, claiming that I was writing notes to a young lady named Vivian. For a moment, she lost me. I looked at her and started laughing. She gave me a crazy look and said, "Are you messing with that little girl?"

I asked, "How could you fix your mouth to say such a thing? If I thought some old ass was messing with a little girl in our hood, I would break his back."

She started laughing. "I knew that stuff wasn't true."

I asked, "Who told you some crazy stuff like that?"

She said, "Deena and Joe-boy was starting rumors."

You see, the other day when I went looking for Karen, her daughter told me that she was over at Latrina's (Joe-boy's sister) with which whom he lives, well, is supposed to be living with, but he's always at Mi-Mi's in my way.

Anyway, as I rang the bell, he answered the door. When he opened it, I could see her sitting on the sofa with Latrina. I didn't have to say anything. When she saw me, she got up and said her goodbyes. The look on his face gave me much pleasure because I knew he hated on me. We went back to Karen's apartment where we talked and kissed and so on. This went on for a few weeks.

Finally, Karen gave me an ultimatum: her or Mi-mi. Of course, I told her I needed time. The look on her face wasn't too pleasing. I just kind of smiled, but I knew I had to make a choice real soon. I had to get completely out of my mom's house. I was unsure who would be a benefit to me the most. Please, readers, don't get the idea that I was out to use anyone. I told each one that I would handle my share of things.

Well, it was about time for Mi-mi to get off. I got up and told Karen that I'd see her later. We kissed, and I left. Wouldn't you know it; Joe-boy was standing outside with his sister's husband, Bev. That's what they called him. One thing I can say about Bev; he never got involved in any way, and every time he saw me, he spoke. I think he knew that his brother-in-law hated on me.

Once Mi-mi got home, I had already cooked something to eat. I didn't mind that. The only problem I had was everybody eating with us. Well, let me take that back. I had a problem with Deena and Joe-boy. Deena had a job. She worked at the Blue Plant in Handen. The only problem with that was she would spend all her money getting high. She would boil noodles and hot dogs for her children. Yes, that's right. She has three boys, neither of which are his. So, you know he really didn't take charge of making sure that they would eat every day. Hell, he was eating off me. He didn't have a job, nor was he trying to get one.

Just a week prior, one of the guys who Cable Richard's sister's boyfriend knew, told them that he had a job open for four people at the Food Mart across the street. Cable Richard, Joe-boy, all of them claimed they would take the job. They met with the guy, and all were given a job on the graveyard shift. Joe-boy worked one night and never returned to work. That night was just one of the many nights that they fought. See, I don't think Joe-boy could live with the thought that sometimes Deena and I would be the only one's home by ourselves. Of course, I wasn't the only one he would worry about. You see, they both smoked crack. They claimed because they smoked it in a blunt and not in a stem, it wasn't considered smoking crack. Just like a crack head, huh? In denial. Everyone knows that if you leave a crack head alone, sooner or later, she will find others who want to get high.

Well, I can't leave out Mi-mi. She got high too. Mi-mi used a stem. When we first met, she hid it very well. By that time, I was getting used to the fact of not living with my mom, even though I hadn't made that clear with my mom yet. And anyone can see why Mi-mi was what they called a functional crack head. You couldn't tell by looking at her, but living in the same house, you could see it very well. Neither her nor Deena would buy any food. Deena had three boys, and Mi-mi had one. Deena got paid every Thursday and Mi-mi every two weeks.

Joe-boy was nothing but a plain ole leach. I mean this guy was leaching off everybody that let him. His sister and her husband had come over a couple times when they were drinking alcohol and smoking weed. During one of the conversations between Mi-mi and Joe-boy's sister, Latrina, she kind of led on. I couldn't help but hear her. I was sitting right there.

In December of 2001, Mi-mi and I had an argument once again. It was about Joe-boy. I told her that I was tired of running into him whenever I got up to use the bathroom or get something to eat from the kitchen. That following day I packed my things after she left for work. Before I left, I walked over to Karen's apartment and spoke with her briefly. During the conversation, I felt that I was making the wrong choice by choosing Mi-mi, and I think for the wrong reasons (the number of children). I wouldn't be in the position to do what I would like for the children. I love children. I think that if a man is going to be with a woman who has children, he should do as much as he can for them.

Well, I knew I wouldn't be coming over Karen's anytime soon, if at all. I knew it would only be a matter of time before some guy picked her up.

Before leaving, I looked her in her eyes and told her that I felt that the choice I'd made was the wrong one, and I couldn't really explain it right then. I hugged and kissed her. Though she said nothing, her eyes told me that she wished I'd stayed.

Later that night at my mom's, Mi-mi called. She starts fussing about me not being there when she got home from work. I told her that I was not going to argue with her about that situation. She told me that by the time I got to her apartment she would have told Joe-boy again. I told her that it was too cold to be walking back down there tonight. She really threw a fit and hung up the phone on me. That following day, Friday morning, I packed two bags and went back to her apartment.

Once I got there, Cable Richard was there with his girlfriend. They weren't really a problem. Cable Richard, whenever he came by, would probably stay one night, if that. But Joe-boy was there every day. He lived with his sister and her family, which was only three doors down.

I had my mom drop me off. I had two bags of food, as well as my clothes.

As the day began to close, I started cooking so that it would be finished by the time Mi-mi got home. Even though things weren't good between Deena and me, I would still feed Deena's children, as well as her. I mean, after all, the children had nothing to do with anything, and most importantly, they weren't his.

After I started cooking, Joe-boy had started making trips to the kitchen to get beer. This guy was unbelievable. If he hustled a dollar, he would buy beer first. Because we had our fall out weeks ago, we didn't say anything to each other.

Once Mi-mi got home, I was in the bedroom. She came in with this look on her face that she got whenever she didn't get her way. That look like, I am pissed but glad to see you.

Once I finished cooking, I fixed our plates, then the children's. I asked Gina, Cable Richard's girlfriend, if she wanted something to eat. She gladly accepted. Right before I started cooking, Cable Richard had already fixed him something to eat. I believe his girlfriend was waiting for me to finish. She knew that I would offer her something to eat, as usual, which I had no problem with. At this time, Joe-boy entered the kitchen again and then returned to Deena's room.

Deena came to the kitchen. During this course, the children had made it home from school. I told Deena to call her children in to eat. I turned and asked her if she wanted to eat. She started smiling, of course. I paused and looked at her. She tilted her head to one side and started laughing. She knew why I looked at her like that. She was taking my food and sharing it with that leach.

As the night approached, I went across the street to the drugstore and got some beer for Mi-mi and myself.

Deena came to the bedroom and ask for a beer. I told her that she could get one. Once she left the room, I asked Mi-mi if she took care of that problem because I didn't want to get up in the middle of the night or the morning running into him. She got up, smacked her lips, and told me to come with her to the living room. I knew then she hadn't done it. I had a seat on the sofa. She called Deena and Joe-boy into the living room. She told Deena that she had told him before that he couldn't stay overnight anymore. Joe-boy tried to get argumentative with her, claiming that he was not staying overnight. Mi-mi, however, told him that he was lying because I would run into him going to the bathroom. He then attempted to say something to me, but Mi-mi stopped him and told him that she would run into him as well, and that he just needs to leave around 11:00 every night. He then claimed once again that he would come over around 6:00 a.m. to get the children for Deena while she got ready for work. The children were picked up by Deena's ex, to which she was still married but separated from. Furthermore, the baby (Tuck) was being babysat by Gina.

For the next two weeks he walked around with a grit look on his face. When Mi-mi got home that day, I told her that she needed to decide what she wanted to do. The look she had on her face told me that something was wrong. As I looked on, I asked, "What's the problem?"

She told me that she just received a summons to court.

"To court? For what?" I asked.

At that moment, she told me that she hadn't paid her rent for the past three months.

This is unbelievable, I thought to myself. This woman brought home $950 every two weeks. How is it that she couldn't pay $300 a month? Oh, and not to mention she was getting child support from her son's father, her ex-husband. So, I start questioning her about all of this. She had the nerve to try and get defensive. I said, "Hold up! We're talking about moving in together. I got to know that you can better manage your money than that!"

She sat there on the bed, looked up at me and asked, "Will you go to court with me?"

"Sure, why not. I may learn something else."

The following week I went to court with her. When her name was called, she stood before the judge. As the judge read off the summons, did I hear the judge correctly? Did he say a matter of $1,200? I knew she could feel my eyes burning through her back. How many more secrets did she have? It always seemed that when it rained, it poured. I couldn't believe all that I was hearing. It was times like this that I wished I wasn't involved. There were some very attractive women in there. I made eye contact. But then one must wonder, *is this the kind of place you would want to pick up women?* After all, this is a small claims court, and it seems that all the women are on the overdue list for not paying their bills.

My thoughts were interrupted when I heard my old landlord's named called. I had a good mind to walk up to him and demand my deposit that my mom claimed she never got back. But then again, who's believable? Mi-mi was given 30 days to move and six months to pay off the $1200.

As we walked out of the courtroom, I had to make eye contact with this one girl just one more time. She was gorgeous, I mean just perfect. She had shoulder length hair with a great smile, legs out of this world, and a body to live for! As we walked out, I started to stop and ask her for her phone number.

After we got back to Mi-mi's apartment, we sat down and really discussed our move.

During the first week of February 2002, we moved to 1300 Pear Street. Earlier that day, Mi-mi and I had gone to ask her uncle if he would help us move. We told him that we just needed a truck. He agreed but told us that he only had like two hours before he needed to be at work. I knew this was such short notice, but we tried other avenues before asking her uncle, at which time, I only learn myself.

When her uncle showed up, we put the first load on the truck, well, Cable Richard and his girlfriend did. We paid Cable Richard, his girlfriend and Joe-boy to load and take it off to the house. Since Cable Richard and Joe-boy were doing the loading, I would ride in Deena's car with Mi-mi. Before we left the apartment, we put a lot of small things in the car.

As we approached the house, they were on their way back for another load, but something just didn't set well with me. The ride back to the apartment was a long one. When we pulled into the complex and as I got out of the car, I noticed that everything on the truck was Deena's. I stood in the living room and asked, "What's going on?"

No one said a thing. I turned to Deena. "What's going on?" As she tried to justify what was going on, I stopped her and said, "When we asked if you wanted to go in on the payment once we found somebody with a truck, you said that your ex's cousin was going to move your things for you."

She just turned and said, "Well, it's on there now. I don't think they'll take it off." I was the fool. I had already paid them to move the furniture. What could I do?

For the past two weeks Deena has been trying to get Mi-mi to get me to let her move in with us, claiming that she only needed 30 days to save some money to get herself an apartment. Of course, my answer was no!

After the first month of knowing Mi-mi, she disclosed the matter of money owed to her by Deena. She claimed that Deena had agreed to give her $100 a month. After the first three months, she hadn't given her anything for the past 18 months. There was no way she was moving in here. But more importantly, I knew that I would have to deal with Joe-boy, and that wasn't going to happen. He was the main reason why I wanted us to move. That way I could get him out.

As the night approached, we were still trying to get someone to finish moving Mi-mi's things. She didn't have much. It was just the principle.

As the day ended, I realized that Deena and Joe-boy had planned this all along. Deena was at her mom's getting her things together while we were still trying to get somebody with a truck.

Finally, Mi-mi called one of her friends that she worked with. They showed up about 9:00 that night. They helped, and I was grateful. Deena, Mi-Mi's best friend, was gone. No one was left behind to help clean up. I just stood in the doorway and shook my head because I was unsure if I was going to help clean up that mess. They made a bigger mess moving. I kept thinking about how Deena tried to get us to let her come and live with us. Suddenly, I stopped and refused to be used by them any further.

Finally, around midnight, we had everything in order.

The following day I went looking for someone with a truck to help me move. I went up to Colley Avenue and got a couple of guys to move my furniture. My mom was so happy to hear that I was moving. She gave me her practically new furniture. The day before, Deena and Joe-boy hinted around about us not having any furniture. The furniture in Mi-mi's apartment belonged to Deena. I saw that our neighbor had a truck. I went over and knocked on the door. The woman that lived downstairs with her husband answered the door. I said, "I am sorry to bother you, but could you please tell me who owns that truck?"

She replied, "My son, James."

He lived upstairs next to the one she lived in. The houses were joined together, but separate.

As I approached the door, it opened. I asked, "Would it be possible if I could pay you to help me move some furniture?"

He told me that he couldn't lift anything, but he'd be happy to drive me. I thanked him. He told me that he would be ready in 15 minutes.

During the drive to my mom's house, I told him that the guys I had to lift the furniture were on Colley Avenue between 21st and 33rd street from where my mom lived. We hit Colley Avenue and picked up the guys. It took two trips. I told the guys that I would pay them on the second of the month. They trusted me. I told them to be at my mom's house around 12:00 noon. They both said okay.

Later that day when Mi-mi got home from work, she was surprised and happy. She couldn't wait to get on the phone and tell her mom. I knew she did it because she knew that Deena would find out. See, initially, Mi-mi told Deena that she would keep her furniture until she found her an apartment. She was really asking if she could use it. Well, you know what the answer to that was.

Moments later, Deena pulled up with her children, which wasn't a problem, but she had Joe-boy with her, and I had made it clear that neither him nor any of those guys were allowed at our house. He was one of the main reasons for moving, "on my part."

When she came, the first thing she said was, "He's not coming in. I'm taking him over to his mom's house to check on his mail."

I knew there was something more, but she couldn't bring herself to tell it. It wouldn't have done her any good though. As usual, the children hadn't eaten anything. She knew that they would be able to eat over here, even though she now lived with her mom and stepfather.

The following weekend I called Sharon and asked about the money she owed me, as well as my entertainment center. I told her that I'd moved and could use everything. She told me that she knew I had moved. She told me that my furniture that was in the study was given to Bill in college. She went on about how I said it was okay during one of her visits at Parker, Virginia. I thought to myself, you asked that before the following year for school. She asked in March of 2001 but then asked for a divorce in May

2001. Tell me that wasn't planned. Not only did she get the cherry oak wood furniture, but mine from my apartment as well.

In February of 2002, I received my first check. I received everything dealing with my benefits. The only thing I was waiting for now was housing. I had talked to Mi-mi and told her that I had planned on leaving around September. By that time, I should have housing, and that she should consider living with me and leave those problems behind her. She told me that she was thinking about it, but I kind of knew she wasn't going anywhere.

"All stories, even of heroes, villains, tortures and cowards all depend on the point of view of the story-teller."

Chapter 31

It was the last week of February. I thought I would give Sharon a call and ask her about my money and the entertainment center. Once on the phone, she told me that she would need a couple of days to get someone to help her get it out of the house. I also mentioned the money. She told me that she would have to see if she could come up with it. Me being me, I said, fine.

The following weekend, Sharon and Will showed up. She called to let me know that they were pulling up. Once outside, I noticed that they were driving a new-used SUV. If you ask me, it was like they were trying to rub it in my face. Back in 1998 when she got violated upon release (by that time), the only means of transportation was my car. Having to seek employment in Chesapeake, she had to take the bus. Now that I needed transportation, she was going to do her best to keep me from having any. "I knew that!" The $400 she handed me was real short of $1500. She knew all too well with all the business I had to attend to required me having transportation at my disposal. I just smiled. That didn't bother me. I knew what she was doing. The thing that I did have a problem with was the fact that she took personal things and destroyed them.

After taking a couple of items into the house, Bill started taking pieces of the entertainment center out the back. Behold to my eyes when I saw him taking it out piece by piece. I saw nothing but pieces. I really mean pieces. It was in so many pieces. I looked at Sharon and shook my head. I asked, "What am I to do with this?" She told me that she had no one to help her bring it down the steps. I told Bill that he could stop taking it out. There was nothing I could do with it. I leaned against the fence and put my hands over my face. I thought to myself, *This woman really means to destroy me and anything that I own.* It was clear.

Moments later, Mi-mi walked up. As I started to introduce them, they both claimed that they had already met. I had no idea, but everything was beginning to come clear here as well. I could only imagine what they talked about, how the woman that I was somewhat involved with could even entertain anything from ex. Unbelievable!

Briefly, we talked about Co-co. I knew that she wouldn't encourage her to stay in contact with me, rather just the opposite. What could I expect? After all we'd done.

Once Sharon and Bill left, I put the money up and walked to Krista's mother's house (Mrs. Dorothy), as I did regularly. Mrs. Dorothy knew I was in the market for a car. She took me over to a friend of hers. They had just purchased a Lincoln Navigator SUV. They had a couple of cars they were selling.

Mrs. Dorothy introduced me to the couple. Their home was hooked up. It was beautiful. They both had been in the military. The husband and I talked for a while. We had a drink. He told me within the next day or two that we could go to the DMV and get everything changed.

I took the blue Berretta. It was nice and clean.

A few days later I took a ride out to Wallace Place. As I drove into the complex, I noticed Joe-boy and Bev were outside as were others. I had come to see Karen, but I knew that was out now. Why couldn't people just mind their own business? Haters? I looked and waved. Bev waved back.

As I turned around to leave, I stopped and motioned Bev to my car. I had a bottle of liquor. It was about one-fourth left. I handed it to him. He thanked me, and I drove off. I thought I would drive around a little, so I went and picked up Krista and the girls. We went to get something to eat. As we drove, I took 48th Street heading towards Colley Avenue to the 800 block. That's where I had seen her before. When I got out, I took a walk. She and some other females were sitting on the porch. I distinctly remember one being big because I thought to myself, *She should be at home, big is she is.*

As I passed, I blew my horn, slowed down and yelled, "Next time I drive by, I will be stopping!" As she walked from the passenger side of the car she got out of, all I could see was the sudden smile on her face, as well as her female friend who was driving the car.

Later, after I dropped Krista and the girls off, I went home.

Once I got there, Mi-mi had one of her disappointed looks on her face. It could've been about me. She'd been at work all day. She looked at me and told me that I needed to listen to our voicemail. On it was a message from Jerome, Joe-boy, and Cable Richard. They told me that I better stay in the house and never come out. If so, and they saw me anywhere, they were going to mess me up. I picked up my keys and headed for the door. Mi-mi jumped off the sofa and stopped me. She did everything to keep me from walking out the door. Once her son (Don) got home, we had dinner and did our usual. We sat and talked for a while, and then Don went and played video games. I really didn't watch too much TV. Mi-mi watched more than I did, whenever she wasn't smoking. Every two weeks when she got paid, she would smoke heavy. Any other time, only when Deena gave her a little something when she smoked.

One thing I didn't allow was them smoking in the house. Again, I hated the idea that my mom had forced me into this situation. My heart aches every time something happens that reminds me of the failed relationship that my mom and I've had my whole life.

The following day after dropping Mi-mi off at work, I went over to Mrs. Dorothy's house for a while. My niece, Nakisha, my nephew, Donnald, and I played poker for money. Sometimes I would drink with them. All they would drink was cheap beer. All they really seemed to care about was quantity rather than quality. Every now and then I would put extra in to get Budweiser if I was going to drink.

At about 11:00 I headed out to get me something to eat. As I drove down 48th Street, I saw Natalie (though I didn't know her name at the time) standing on her porch with another female. I blew my horn, and she waved. I drove around the block and parked in front of her house. She told me to get out. We introduced ourselves. The other female was her sister. She had two girls as well as her brother's daughter that she was taking care of. Her sister lived next door. Come to find out, the other female was her sister's old-lady. They had two little girls living with them. All the girls ranged from age nine to 14 years old.

After finding out that Natalie went to work at 5:00 p.m. until 11:00 p.m. at the fish market on Colley Avenue, I thought to myself, *This will really work out*, especially because I told her about Mi-mi. She didn't seem to mind. I mean, after all, I told her that I had no intentions of staying with Mi-mi, which was true. I stayed over all day.

As she headed out for work, I went home to get ready to pick up Mi-mi at 6:00 p.m.

The next couple of days, you know I was putting my game down. Natalie was fine! I mean, she looked good, had a banging body.

Finally, that weekend, I spent pretty much the whole evening into the wee hours of the night (2:45 a.m.). I could do that with Mi-mi. Remember, she liked to get high. And everybody knows when people smoke crack, that's all they have on their mind.

The sex with Natalie was good. Of course, you know I took charge. She did everything I wanted her to do. It was great.

When I got home that night, Mi-mi and Deena were still in the back where they smoked. I tell you, people who smoke crack have their own world. They don't ever want that night to end.

I walked in and went straight through the house to the back room. They were looking real crazy, as usual. I turned some music on real low and lay down on the sofa. In Don's room were Deena's boys. Don usually stayed with his father or grandmother on the weekends.

The following day (Sunday) after I cooked for everybody, I headed out to Natalie's house. Once I got there, her daughter, Kenyatta, opened the door. Kenyatta was the oldest of her daughters.

Natalie was still in bed. I went in and lay across her on the bed. She had a smile from ear to ear. We talked and kissed for a while. She got up to go to the bathroom. She always wore t-shirts with no bra and a thong. She had two daughters, but you would have never known she had children. I must tell you, her breasts stood firm, and she had big nipples. I liked everything about her. She stood in front of the TV with her hands on her hips. In the way her hands brought her t-shirt up, I could see the starting point of her vagina and started laughing. She had so much hair, I could see it coming through her thong. Finally, she took her t-shirt off. She came on top of me on her knees and started kissing on my neck. I sat up so that she could take off my shirt. She then motioned me to roll over on her. As she went to take my jeans off, I stood up so that she could get better access at getting them off. I kicked my shoes off. Once she had me standing there with nothing but my socks she started performing for the next two hours. I must say, she was really good, especially when she listened to my instructions. Yes, that's right.

Once we finished, I got up and went to the shower. Moments later she came in and joined me. We hugged, kissed and talked. Before you knew it, we were doing it in the shower.

Once out of the shower, I noticed that she had some areas where her dreads didn't grow in right. I started looking through her hair and told her that she needed to do something about that. She told me that she was intending to have it all cut off and regrow it. I told her that I cut hair. She turned and smiled. "You're lying, what if you can't do is?" While she fondled me, I told her she could stop now. She drained everything I had for the next two weeks. She laughed her ass off. I knew what she was up to. Women try to drain you, especially when they know that there's another woman you have at home. I explained my relationship with Mi-mi the first time that I was over at her house.

I told Natalie that I'd be back later with my clippers. When I walked from the bathroom, Little-e was sitting in the living room. I had my suspicions of him the first time I saw him. Natalie came to the room. Her bedroom was right off the living room when you come into the house, and remember how she liked to walk through the house whenever I was there. Other than me, there were all females. When she closed the door, I asked, "Is O 'boy gay?"

She laughed and said, "Yes."

I asked, "Do he have to be here all the time? I mean, whenever I come over here, he's here." That was led by the fact that I told her that I didn't like the idea of her walking in front of him like that. That's when she claimed he was gay.

At that moment she told me that she would talk to him. I told her not to just talk, but instead, tell him what she needed to tell him. She looked at me and started laughing.

I said, "Alright, you can play if you want to. If my visits become uncomfortable, I will end it before we can get started."

With a smile on her face, she walked over to me, put her arms around my neck and said, "I'll do anything you want me to do; just don't stop coming over."

I looked her in the eyes and said, "I got you whipped already."

She just laughed.

When I got home, Mi-mi and Deena were in the living room looking crazy. Each time I came in, Mi-mi would have that look on her face. She knew I was seeing someone else, but she couldn't really complain. After all, she didn't want to stop smoking crack. As I grabbed my clippers from the bathroom and prepared to leave, Mi-mi started running her mouth. I didn't want to hear it, so I told her that I was going by my mom's. She got up off the sofa and told me that she was going with me. What could I do?

I stopped by my mom's just momentarily. While I was there, I used the phone to call Natalie to tell her that I may not be able to get back over there just yet. But as soon as I could, I'd be over. Now she wanted to talk. So, me being me, I let her talk for a while, then I told her I had to go. After all, Mi-mi was calling from the living room. I think she knew I was on the phone.

When I walked from the back room, Mi-mi gave me that crazy look. It really didn't matter to me. She was doing something I didn't like as well. Besides, Natalie had been hinting around about me moving in with her anyway. I was really considering it. She didn't do anything besides drink every now and then. I could live with that better.

On our way home, we stopped by Mi-Mi's parents' house. While we were there, we decided to eat. That's after her mother (Mrs. Brenda) insisted.

Just moments after we started eating, Joe-boy showed up. He and Deena had gotten into it again. When Mrs. Brenda asked who was at the door, Deena yelled, "Joe-boy! I got it."

Suddenly, we heard yelling. Mrs. Brenda stood up and said, "Not again! I am tired of this Nigga keep coming over here with this mess!"

We all walked to the door except her husband. He never got into any of it. Of course, just like him, I didn't either. I just watched the show each time. There we were, Mrs. Brenda, Deena, Joe-boy, Mi-mi and myself. Mrs. Brenda asked, "What's the problem now?"

As Joe-boy began to talk, Deena walked to the back to get her youngest son (Tuck). Joe-boy continued. Deena had taken his ID card, and that was the only ID he had to cash his check with. Now I thought to myself, Checks? You've only been working two weeks. What? You lost the job already? Well, know it's a matter of time anyway. The man can't hold water.

Deena claimed that she didn't have his ID card, but she did from the smirk on her face. Mrs. Brenda turned to Deena as she returned to the living room. "Deena, if you have that boy's ID, please give it to him so he can get out of my house."

Deena said, "It may be in my bag."

While she was in the back room, Joe-boy was trying to apologize for the damage he caused about a week and a half ago. I had only heard about it, but I was present for this one.

Once Deena returned, she gave him his ID. But he wanted to run his mouth. Mrs. Brenda then asked him to leave. At that time, he wanted to raise his voice. Mrs. Brenda started yelling and using real heavy language, language I never heard her use before. I couldn't help but smile and shake my head. I think that pissed him off even more. I couldn't help it. This guy had been doing this same ole mess ever since I'd known him.

This guy refused to leave. Mrs. Brenda walked to another room and then returned with a bat. At that time Mi-mi said, "Don't worry, Mom. Ziggy, kick his ass."

I looked at Mi-mi, then Mrs. Brenda. I was glad to hear Mrs. Brenda say, "No, I got it. He better get his ass out my house."

Mrs. Brenda had to call the police to get him out of her house. This is unbelievable, I thought to myself.

When the police arrived, he threw his hands up in the air saying, "Mrs. Brenda, you didn't have to call the police."

Mrs. Brenda leaned back and said, "Now I am convinced you really are crazy."

As the police approached the door, he started to plead, but Mrs. Brenda wasn't going for it. She told the police that she had this same problem out of him before, and she wanted them to know that he was not welcome to her home ever again. The police told Mrs. Brenda that she would need to go cross town and get a restraining order against him. All the while he was being slightly argumentative but not so much that it would land him in jail. In fact, he knew when to stop. When he looked back at me, I could see all the hatred in his face. This guy really had a problem.

After the drama, we sat around a little while longer talking about what just happened. Deena got up and went to her bedroom. Mi-mi and I went home. Mi-mi wanted to stop by the store to get something to drink. I was trying to get over to 48th street by 11:00 p.m. when Natalie got home from work. The sex with her had been good. I mean good. Sex with Mi-mi was good at times, but you know when someone smokes crack, that's not going to happen as often as you would like.

After getting home that night and doing some drinking, she wanted to talk shit. She knew I was sleeping with someone else, but what could she do? She was sleeping with the pipe. I must admit, I felt sorry for her that she was on the stuff, especially when she told me that story of how her ex-husband got her hooked on it. But if you see him today, unless you knew, you would never know that he used to smoke crack. He had a fairly good job. He was a manager for a sports wear store and engaged to be married. She really kept an eye on him. Every time he came to pick Jon up for school and drop him off, she was with him. "Trust me, sweetheart, he doesn't want this problem back. If there were anywhere else for me to go before getting into this agreement with her, I wouldn't be here."

I walked out to my car. She came to the door with that sad face asking where I was going. Instead of getting in my car yelling, 'I'll be right back,' I told her that I was just getting a box of Black & Mile out of the car. I walked to the door and put my right arm around her. She looked up at me with those pretty eyes. I kissed her on the lips. We sat down on the sofa. She tried to start a conversation about the other woman. I stopped her and said, "Do you want to argue or enjoy the rest of the night together?" She started smiling. I got up and went to the kitchen and got the rest of the liquor and coke. We drank, listened to music while the TV played, just talking and singing, really enjoying the night. It had gotten to be around 12:30, midnight. We decided to go to bed.

For the past hour we'd been kissing and touching each other, so you know it was on. She went to the bathroom to freshen up. I put the CD in the CD player that we wanted to listen to while we did our thing. There was no one there but us that night, and it felt good.

When Mi-mi entered the bedroom, she crawled on top of me and we started having sex, something she didn't often do, and I never did to her. After that load, we started having sex.

About 35 to 40 minutes later, she said to me, "I want you to do that thing I like." Not often, but this was about the fourth time that she'd asked me to do this to her. I've met some freakish women in my life.

The way the house sat, the street light would shine through with the curtains open. I would pull the curtains, and the way the street light would reflect through the window made it just that much freakier. As I continued my business, I saw a car pull up in the yard. I knew it was Deena. The house had a screen-in-porch, and our bedroom was connected to one side and the living room on the next.

As Deena walked through the screen door onto the porch, I tried to ease up when she knocked on the door. Mi-mi raised her head. I continued. Mi-mi tried to say something, but I started pounding so hard she couldn't get it out. As Deena stood in the second screen door, I knew she could hear us. She leaned just a foot from our window trying to get a glance. With her standing there, knowing that she was trying to get a glimpse, made this night even better. I wondered how much she could see. I tried to reach over and pull the curtain without Mi-mi noticing, so that more light would shine in where Deena could get a real glimpse, and to let her know that I was not going to stop. Mi-mi was breathing real hard by now. That meant I was handling my business, and I was on my second round, which was the longest ... at least an hour or so, especially if I had a drink. Just one good drink, and it was on.

By this time Deena had closed the screen door to the living room and stood at the far end of the porch, which, by the way, was still a good view if she wanted to glance every now and then, which she did.

Once we were done, I made it a point to answer the door. Mi-mi just flopped to the bed as usual. I would always talk to my women during and after. I asked Mi-mi if her night had been filled. She knew what I meant when I said that. She tried to look up at me (while still face down) and chuckled, "You be killing me, but I love it!" You know I put my superman smile on. Once we were done, I put some shorts on and went to open the door for Deena. Mind you, it was 3:25 a.m.

Before walking through the door, she looked at me, slightly smiled, and shook her head. Once again, I put my superman smile on. I knew she got a good glimpse. If not, with just the noise alone, I knew she had to be wet. I turned on the TV and, like any other time, I would ask a crazy question. "What the hell are you doing out this time of night?"

All she could say was, "I was bored."

I thought to myself, *You just need something to smoke.*

I walked back into the bedroom to get some things for a shower. In walked Deena, knocking on the door. She looked at Mi-mi and started laughing. Mi-mi smiled and asked, "What are you laughing at?"

Deena sat on the edge of the bed and asked, "What in the world does he be doing to you?"

That's when I told her it wasn't her business. Then I went to take my shower. When I returned from my shower, Deena was laid out on the sofa. I went to my bedroom and went to sleep.

That following Tuesday I finally got a call back from Mrs. White of JoJo. & Gaidies Law Firm. She told me that they wouldn't be able to take my case, and that she would be mailing my materials back to me today. I thanked her and hung up the phone. I was sitting there thinking how everything seemed to be difficult, but I wasn't going to give up like that. My birthday is March 17th. This particular weekend I would be celebrating my birthday. I didn't tell but a few people like Krista, Todd, and Nakisha, just a few. I didn't want a lot of people over. I drove to Chicken & Steak House, where I shopped for my meats. I needed some steaks, sausages, chicken, and other meats as well.

When I returned home, I saw Deena's car in the yard. As I turned off the street, I could see Joe-boy with a water hose. I could see where he'd been washing her car. I got out of my car, looked at him, got my food out of the car and went inside the house.

Once in the house, I called out for Mi-mi. As I headed towards the kitchen, she was grinning and shaking her head. She knew she was about to get it. Before I could get started, she said, "Deena just stopped by here to wash a couple bags of laundry."

I put the meats on the table and told Mi-mi not to forget to boil the chicken so that I could put it on when I got back. As I walked to the front of the house, I stopped and turned around. I walked back to the kitchen, and I reminded her that Joe-boy was not to come into this house. I didn't like that look she gave me. I told her that I meant what I said.

She said okay. I had to make a run to 48th Street, Natalie's house, before she left for work, which was 5 o'clock. I wanted to let her know that I would be bringing some food off the grill today. Also, earlier that day, she had told me that she needed to see me before she went to work. I always knew what that meant. (Smile)

Before pulling out of the yard at my house, I gave one last look at that leach.

Once I pulled up in front of Natalie's house, a couple of the girls were sitting outside. As usual, the girls were glad to see me. As I got out of my car, both gave me a hug.

Once I got in the house, Natalie was walking from the bathroom, where she'd just taken a shower, to her bedroom. I sat in the living room talking with Kenyatta and the other girls. They always liked when I came around. I'd always been good with children. It was 3:30 p.m. I knew Natalie had to go to work at 5:00 p.m.

Once I got in her room and closed the door, she got on her knees and crawled to me. As she reached out, she called, "Come here." As she had done before, she unzipped my jeans and immediately started having oral sex, and once again, she did it very well.

After 10 or 15 minutes, she stopped, pulled me onto the bed, and took my clothes off, and we started going at it.

After about 20 minutes, I stopped and put her on all fours and I hit it from the back. Then someone knocked on the bedroom door. I stopped. Natalie called out. It was her niece. I lay down on my left side. Natalie was on her side with her back to me. As she gave her niece permission to enter the room, she was positioning herself where she took my penis and put it in her vagina. She threw a sheet across us that landed from my chest to my knees. I felt really awkward. As I whispered in her ear to send her out of the room, she looked back at me and started laughing and said, "She doesn't know you're in me."

Young girls nowadays are too grown, I thought to myself.

Finally, she told her niece to leave and said she'd talk to her when she came out of the room. Just for that, I took her and placed her on her knees. And from the back, I pounded her with every inch. I took two pillows and placed them under her stomach so that it wouldn't be easy for her to straighten to lessen this pounding I was giving her. For a while, I would take my right leg and place my feet on the bed while still on my left knee. Then I'd take my right hand and place it between the blades of her back to keep her positioned, and I would have my left hand at her left waist and the beginning of her hip with a firm grip.

After pounding and pounding, I repositioned myself with the left to the right and pounded some more. All the while she was making noise that I'd never heard her make before.

When I finished with her, she moved the pillows that I had placed under her and mumbled, "Oh, Ziggy, you trying to make me fall in love with you?"

I said nothing and just headed to the bathroom and took a shower. When I got out of the shower, as I walked back to the bedroom, I could see her friend that she worked with, drive off. When I entered the bedroom, I asked if she was going to work.

She got herself together just enough to say, "Real funny."

I told her that I'd see her later that night. I had to get back and put the food on the grill. I leaned over her on the bed, kissed her and left. As I walked out the door, she reminded me that I still needed to cut her hair.

While I drove back home, I stopped to see if Krista and the others were still coming over. They told me that they would be over around 7:00 p.m. I yelled, "See yah!" and took off.

When I got home, I saw Deena's car still parked in the yard. I didn't see Joe-boy, so I was trying to see if her car had moved. It didn't appear so. Once in the house, I could feel that something wasn't right. Once in the kitchen, Mi-mi start running her mouth. But it was okay; she did it with a smile. From the kitchen is the laundry room. I could see these trash bags with laundry in it. So, I walked through the laundry room to the backyard. I could see where Deena had every clothing line full. I looked to my left; the washing and drying machines were going.

I called out to Mi-mi as I walked back to the kitchen. I leaned on the sink and said, "Mi-mi, this girl has five trash bags of laundry back there."

She replied, "Ziggy, she doesn't have five bags of laundry."

"The hell she doesn't. I'll prove it to you."

"No, I believe you. I believe you!" The whole while she was smiling. She knew this girl had all that laundry.

I took the first pan of food out to put on the grill.

Forty-five minutes into my grilling, during one of my walks back to the kitchen, I saw Joe-boy walking out the back door. I yelled out to Mi-mi.

She yelled, "Out here!"

As I walked through the laundry room, she came in the door. She immediately defended herself and said, "Ziggy, I swear I did not know that he had taken a shower."

After she said that, I was furious. I started fussing Mi-mi out. I mean, I really fussed her out. No one wants to do right. She knew this guy was not to be in my house.

By this time, Deena walked in. We were in the dining room. Deena had totally disrespected me. I knew she was behind it. All three of us were standing in the dining room. I told Deena that what she was doing was not right. She had the nerve to get beside herself. When she did that I asked, "Why is it that you can't wash your clothes at your mom's house?"

She answered, "Mi-mi told me that I could wash here."

I looked at Mi-mi. "So, no one has to ask me anything around here, huh?"

At that moment Joe-boy called out from the back door. He could see that we were arguing. I looked up. This fool was walking up in my house. I looked at Mi-mi. What the hell! I looked at this ass and said, "Yo, man, get the hell out of my house."

He started yelling for Deena to tell Mi-mi that I had been trying to get with her. I looked up at the ceiling. Oh! My goodness. Mi-mi looked at me. I looked at Deena and said: "Is this true?"

She looked down at the floor. "No." Then I told that chump that he'd better leave my house and never set foot on the property again. I told him that if he didn't leave immediately, I was going to call the police.

Deena started yelling that I was trying to come between bloods, her and Mi-mi. I told Deena that what she was doing wasn't right, that she couldn't be bringing this guy around peoples' houses and that he was a freeloader. I said, "He's a grown man, and nothing is wrong with him. He needs to get a job or something." Again, she tried to defend this leach.

This woman comes over here. He washes her car. She has five bags of laundry, two which are his, not to mention this guy even had something to eat before I did.

As I was bringing it in, Deena was fixing him plates. I really didn't pay any attention at first. I thought she was only feeding the children. I really got upset when I noticed that this chump had eaten three steaks. I told Deena to take that chump and laundry and get the hell out of my house.

I told her, "Enough is enough. Get your laundry, because two of those big bags are his clothes."

She really started crying with tears running down her face talking about how blood is thicker than water.

As she continued to run her mouth, I said, "Yes, blood is thick and so are these bills around here. Don't ever bring him to my house again, and that's final."

She gathered their things together, even the wet clothes off the line and put them in the bags. As I stood on the front side at the grill, I watched while they pulled off. I was looking at him on the passenger side as they pulled out of the yard. All I could do was shake my head. This guy was completely a full leach. Unbelievable! Before pulling completely out of the driveway, Deena yells, "Blood is thicker than water. I'll show you!"

All I could do was look and shake my head. She really didn't get it.

Later that evening, I put BBQ meats, potato salad, mac & cheese and some rolls on a plate and told Mi-mi that I was taking the food to some family members. By the look on her face, I knew she didn't believe me. Oh well.

When I got to Natalie's house, I took the food in and I told her that I'd be back in a few minutes. She tugged on my shirt pulling me into the bedroom. Once again here she goes with that possessive attitude.

Every time she got like that, I put her in check. But as time went on, I could see that she was beginning to make these small arguments more meaningful by showing more feelings and getting emotional on me, as though we lived together, and I was always gone. (That's why I always explain from the start).

As usual, she asked, "When are you moving? That way we won't have to have these conversations."

I looked at her. "We're not going to continue this, if you don't stop it."

At that moment she started smiling. She pulled me on the bed and said, "I miss you when you're not here. I want to spend all my time with you."

I told her that I had to go, but I'd see her when she got back from work.

Once I got back home, Deena had made it back over. A few of her friends were there. Everybody hung out, listened to music, and danced. Everybody seemed to be enjoying themselves. But we couldn't even finish the night without having some type of disagreement. Wouldn't you know it? It was about Deena. She kept asking Mi-mi to convince me to let Joe-boy come to the cookout. That was not about to happen, and I let her know this once again. I told her that she was lucky I still let her come around!

Before Krista and the girls left, Deena made it a point to let everyone know that she didn't really like Krista, and knew she was up to no good. Mind you, Mi-mi had talked to my mother and Sharon, my ex. Both thought and made claims that Krista and I were sleeping together. They treated us like that even though we told them that no such thing had or would ever happen. We were still made out to be the bad ones.

Everyone had left except Deena and one of Mi-mi's friends, Jannie. Deena was still upset, talking junk, and at some time must have left to call the police.

Not knowing she called the police, we were all surprised when the police arrived. I was shocked because, not only was she the cause of all this, she had the nerve to call the police trying to get me put in jail.

Two officers walked in and asked, "What's going on?"

Mi-mi started running her mouth. One of the officers told her to hold on a minute and asked me what the problem was.

As I began to explain, how it started from earlier that day, I could see where Deena was behind me just off in the living room. At that moment, Mi-mi said, "You're leaving," and just then she picked up a two-liter Pepsi to throw at me. Both officers told her to put her hands behind her back, and she tried to talk herself out of that. One officer told her that what she did was an assault, and they had to take her across town.

Mi-mi told Deena to call Miss Scott, her ex-husband's mom. She worked for the sheriff's department. She only lived a few blocks away.

When she got there, she immediately blamed me. I don't know what Deena told her, but it wasn't good. Miss Scott's daughter, Terrie, who was with her, acted like she had an attitude with me. I just stood there listening to all three run their mouths. Miss Scott and her daughter had no idea that all of this started with Deena and Joe-boy. Miss Scott asked me if I was going down to bond her out when she got a bond. I told her whatever needed to be done. Miss Scott told me to call her as soon as I heard something. I said yes, but I wasn't fooling with her tonight. She put herself there. I did make a call. Just like I thought, they would let her out on her own recognizance.

When they took Mi-mi to jail, I drove over to Natalie's house. After some time there, I drove back to the house to get some beer to drink. When I walked into the house, Mi-mi was standing in the dining room looking crazy. I stopped and looked at her. She walked past me and into the bedroom. I picked up a grocery bag, walked back out on the porch, put 12 beers in it and left. After all we weren't talking at this point.

I sat in the car in front of Natalie's house for a moment, trying to decide if I should just go back to the house. *Hey, I think I'll just go in here and knock her off,* I thought. I didn't feel like dealing with Mi-mi that night. I stayed until three in the morning. The sex, as usual, was the bomb. I don't think you need another description of this banging.

Once back at the house, I went in and lay down on the sofa.

That next morning, I got up and cooked breakfast. I cooked steaks and eggs with cheese, toast, fried potatoes, the whole nine yards. Once she came through the kitchen to the bathroom, she looked at me and starts smiling. I smiled back. Mi-mi said, "I'm still mad at your ass."

When she came from the bathroom, I had everything on the table in the dining room. We sat down and ate. We talked a little about what happened the night before. Basically, she wanted to know if I was going to court. I said, "You're unbelievable! What makes you think I would go to court on you? And besides you should be mad at Deena. She called the police. In fact, you told her to." I couldn't help but laugh. I think I had a right to laugh.

Suddenly, there was a knock on the door. Immediately I knew it was Deena and her children. The children were never a problem. Deena wasn't a real problem. It seems that she just didn't understand about having a leach for a boyfriend or maybe she just didn't care.

Once we finished eating, I went to the living room, put on some soft music and lay on the sofa. Thoughts of my children just kept running through my mind. I wondered what they were doing at that very moment. I wondered if any of them were suffering heart-break of any kind. Not being able to be there for my children has really taking its toll on me, but no one could tell. I'd always been good at hiding my feelings. I dozed off.

Suddenly, I woke up and remembered that I promised to cut Ty's hair, but before I left, I called my mom and told her to bring Ty so that I could cut his hair. My mom dropped him off. I knew she was going over to Mrs. Sissy's house. She only lived a few blocks from me. Ever since we left Baton Rouge, Louisiana, she has spent all her time at Mrs. Sissy's. That and the things she used to say to me took its toll on me more than I could ever know.

Once I finished Ty, I called my mom's house and told my niece, Teresa, to call Mrs. Sissy's house and tell my mom she could pick Ty up. I was kind of unsure if she would. That girl was out of control. She was hard-headed. She was the only child no one could do anything with. That was because my mom aided her, would always come to her defense.

I heard a car pull up, then a horn. I knew it was my mom. When I took Ty to the door, once he was in the car, he started crying. After my mom pulled off, I got my clippers together and headed over to Natalie's house. When I got there, I could see where she walked from the kitchen as I walked onto the porch. I could see through the screen door while the front door itself was wide open. She was smiling from ear to ear.

As I walked in, she approached me and immediately hugged and started kissing me. In one of her usual dress codes, she had on a t-shirt and panties. Once I finished cutting her hair, we went to the bathroom, and I helped her wash it and put a blond-color in it. At first, I didn't like it. In fact, I didn't know that I was to help her with that as well. But once it was done and dried, it looked pretty good on her. It was alright.

Once we finished that, the both of us got into the shower. I kept a few outfits to change into over there. After I dressed, the girls and I walked around the corner to the store. I gave the girls some money for chips and candy. I brought back some beer (Budweiser) for Natalie and myself. Of course, her sister and her sister's girlfriend would always come over and drink with us.

After putting the beer in the refrigerator, I walked up behind Natalie, wrapped my arms around her, kissed her and handed her one of the three beers I had in my hand. She stood tip-toe, placed her ass firmly against me and slowly begin to move. As mentioned before, she had a (10) body with no questions. I had to step back because I immediately began to get excited. She started laughing as I smiled. I stood on the side of the sink. I looked out the kitchen window and tried to think of something else, trying to lose the blood rush she had given me.

Once it was normal again, I walked to the living room and watched

TV with the girls and her sister (fat-mama). While Natalie cooked, every few minutes she would come into the living room. Whenever I needed a beer or when she took a break, she would always sit on my lap. After the second time, she stood slightly over me and pointed to my lap. I could see where my jeans were wet. She laughed and walked off. I immediately followed her to the kitchen. I turned her around to face me. I lifted her t-shirt and ran my middle finger between her thighs from the back of her ass across her vagina to the front. She was so wet that she moaned at my action. My hand was so shiny and smoky. I had to go wash my hands.

I walked out of the bathroom, which was right next to the kitchen, As I headed back to the living room, she walked up behind me and pulled me to the left into her bedroom. She sat on the edge and unzipped my jeans and vigorously had her way with me. In the past, most women that I'd been with couldn't last the time it would take for me to get there, which was 30 to 40 minutes. After which time or sometimes she would stop me, and if she was on her back, she would get in the doggy position and place me into her, and gently she would move me in a soft motion. It seemed the more she made noise, the harder I got. We never worried about the girls or anyone else who may have been over at the time to hear us because we would always turn the music up in the bedroom. But I would be lying if I said they couldn't hear anything.

After three and half hours, I got up and took a shower. Before I got out, she came to the shower. Once again, she pulled one of her moments. She got real sentimental on, me and she was good too. She did it while we stood under the shower. Every now and then, I could feel her vibrate as she talked real softly. I could feel the weakness in her voice.

Once we finished showering, we went back to her bedroom. The girls were sitting out on the porch. We talked and laughed for a while. She got up and heated our dinner up. It was 8:00 but still light outside. I liked this time of year. The time played to my advantage.

Once we ate, I told her that I was leaving, but I'd be back later. I gave her a kiss and hug. I stopped outside with the girls for a while, talking and all. I always liked to leave them laughing and carrying on. I must admit, she was wearing me down. In fact, if our financial situation was different ... I mean, she was receiving assistance to help make up for what she wasn't getting to help her with her two daughters and niece. We had talked about the changes that would be made, nothing we couldn't deal with. I just needed more time. Natalie, she was ready for any changes, just if it meant I would be sleeping there rather than where I was now. Each time I saw her I thought more and more about it, Meaning I gave it some serious thought.

When I got home, Mi-mi, Deena and the children were just pulling in themselves. I never asked where she'd been whenever she went somewhere. Still, that doesn't stop her from asking me questions. I would just look at her, shaking my head, smiling. Playfully, she would come up behind me and put her arms across my shoulders, acting like she was going to jump on my back.

For the rest of the night we sat on the sofa, talked, and watched movies.

As it got late, Deena finally went home. I knew by the way Mi-mi was acting, (kissing and touching) she wanted to have sex. I was burned out. I was going to try and hold out if I could.

Finally, we went to bed. I told her that my back was kind of hurting. She looked at me as she continued to massage me. She undressed me and told me to just lie there. What could I do? She looked at me, then slid down. We started having sex.

The following Monday morning, as I did most of the time, I would iron her son's Don jeans for the day and cook as well. The only thing that was missing was her best friend, Shirley. When we first moved there, and I hadn't gotten a car yet, Mi-mi's best friend used to drop Deena off at work because she would babysit Tuck. Afterwards, she would come and take Mi-mi to work. Every morning I would give her something to eat. It had gotten to the point to where she'd start eating anything she wanted.

When she started eating my cinnamon rolls, I mean every morning now, I had to stop her. I asked nicely, if she didn't mind, after today, please, don't eat anymore of the cinnamon rolls. She had the nerve to get offensive. I stood back and took a good look at her. I said, "Pardon me."

Mi-mi was at the table eating. Shirley looked at Mi-mi. Mi-mi immediately went to her defense. I got up from the table and said, "I don't care what Mi-mi say. Mi-mi don't buy any food in this house. Now I expect for you to honor that. Anything else would be disrespectful."

After that morning, she never ate anything, even when offered. Well, I must admit I did feel bad when she started crying and walked out the door. And once again, Mi-mi was running her mouth. But I had to put my foot down. Those people who she had hanging around were nothing but leaches, including her sister, though I couldn't keep her away. I'd be damned if the rest of them were going to continue leaching off me. Well, once again, I didn't have to worry about anymore after that. It is what it is.

"The accumulation of knowledge can be an effective tool for change; but only if one is willing to take what he has learned and turn it into action."

Chapter 32

Well, today was a good day, hopefully. Every day was a good day above ground. As Mi-mi got ready for work, I helped Don, as usual. His father would always pick him up. I would walk to the door with Don and speak.

After seeing Don off, I went outside and waited. I don't know why she always waited until the last minute. Like most women, I guess.

When she got in the car, she immediately said, "Come on! You going to make me late for work."

Right before pulling out of the yard, I stopped, looked at her and thought, *You have got to be kidding me.*

As I pulled onto the street, she couldn't help but laugh. I leaned to the side, gave her one of those looks, and let her have it. We pulled up in front of her job. You could always see a fine woman at this place. Mi-mi got her things together blew a kiss at me, got out, and looked back at me before going in the door. She said, "Don't be late, Big Head."

On my way to Natalie's house, I stopped by Ms. Dorothy's house as I did all the time. Krista and the girls lived there with her mother. I got my niece, Nakisha, so that she could go and get me a dime bag. Whenever I would smoke weed, like anybody else, I would have the munchies like crazy. I would eat, then sleep.

Once Nakisha got the weed for me, we went back to her grandmother's house, rolled up blunts, and smoked. I took one and put it out with half of it left. I knew that Natalie would want to smoke. Whenever I did something, she wanted to as well.

When I got to 48th Street, Natalie's house, I was as high as gas. I got out of the car and went inside. The girls came up to me as usual. I sat in my chair (the recliner) and leaned back. While I tried to sleep, Natalie would sit in my lap and kiss me or something. She started asking me who was I getting high with instead of her. I told her if she let me get some sleep, I will smoke what I had left with her, just as soon as I got up. She pulled me by the arm and told me to lie in the bed. Before I lay down, I made her promise that she wouldn't bother me, so I could get some sleep. I lay across the bed, and she took my shoes off.

I slept until 2:00 p.m. Boy, after smoking weed, I always ate then slept, unless I drink, which is something I didn't like to mix. I went and used the bathroom. Boy, it felt like I was 10 pounds lighter (as Cube would say). I took a shower and felt new again.

When I got out the shower that joker, Robert-E, was sitting in the living room. I hated that joker. Before long, I was going to stop him from coming around altogether.

Natalie fixed something to eat. Afterwards, we smoked the last of the blunt. While they smoked weed for recreational use, I used it for medical reason. It was better than those pills they were trying to give me. Now I was stacking. I had two 16-ounce Budweisers. I dozed off.

Because I didn't give anyone a time to wake me up, no one did. When I woke up, it was 5:45 p.m. Mi-mi would get off work at 6:00. I jumped up, washed my face, and headed out the door.

I got to Mi-mi's job at 6:12 p.m. I went to the front desk. The receptionist told me that she'd already left the building. I got in my car and drove around the corner to the convenient store. I walked in and asked the clerk if I could please use her phone. It was easy. She was smiling when I walked into the store. I got to use the phone, but afterwards, she asked if it was local. I called Mi-Mi's cell phone. Immediately, she yelled. I tell her, "Hold on now."

Before I could say anything else, she mentioned the clerk. I turned around. She was in the SUV with her friends from work. (The guy and his wife that helped her move from Wallace Place). I turned and thanked the clerk. I walked outside. She was sitting in the back, mean-mugging. I looked at her friend (female). She had the nerve to have an unpleasant look on her face. I am like, *I know this not happening*.

As I headed to my car, I could see where her friend looked back at Mi-mi and said something. When I pulled behind them, the husband motioned me to pull alongside of him. They decided that we should go back to their house and have a couple of beers. (Why? When they ran up on me at the convenient store, they were taking her home.)

I really didn't want to be there, but I also didn't want to be impolite, so I kind of acted like I was listening.

Finally, she was ready to go. It was eight o'clock.

On the way home, she tried to start an argument, but I ignored her. I just let her run her mouth. When I pulled up in the yard, I put the car in park, but I had no intentions of getting out. I didn't want to listen to her noise. Besides, that was a good excuse to spend the better part of the day over at Natalie's house. Mi-mi reached over and turned the car off, took the keys, and got out. She leaned towards the windshield, licked her tongue out and smiled. She said, "See you in the house."

To be honest, between the two of them, they were keeping me drained.

When I walked through the door, she made sure that I knew she had my keys with her while she bathed.

While Mi-mi was in the tub, Deena pulled up. Just what I needed, some mess from her. She and her children came in.

Moments later, Don was dropped off by his father. Oh! The house being full, that didn't matter to Mi-mi.

Natalie worked from 5 p.m. to 11:30 p.m., so, I decided to shower and stay at home for the rest of the night.

Mi-mi came into the living room after dressing. She asked me if I had any money.

"Of course."

Mi-mi said, "I want to smoke some weed." She looked at me, smiling. As she had mentioned, it makes her horny. It wouldn't be long before I wouldn't be able to walk five feet in front of me. Twice I'd had blue-balls from straining myself. I am here to tell you; all those guys who claim to be knocking off a lot of women at the same time are full of it. I'm here to tell you, if you have many, trust me, you're not the only one she's giving it to. That's why I am honest up front. At least the two or three I'm knocking off have agreed to keep it between us. If I keep banging them, I could only hope they would keep it like that. I had great concerns about diseases.

I called Nakisha while we headed to her grandmother's house. I told her I would need her to get me some weed. Once I pulled up, she came to the car and handed me two bags of weed. I gave her $20. Mi-mi tried to strike up a conversation with Nakisha. I glanced over at Mi-mi, then back to Nakisha. I pulled off as I said good-bye. Mi-mi playfully shoved me on the shoulder.

After we got home, we smoked and had a couple of buds. Then we went to bed. Usually, I could go a good two rounds, but for some reason, after sleeping with Natalie earlier that day, I only had one good one in me. Those were the times that she reminded me that there was someone else. Although she knew, she just didn't know who. (Even to this day). Every now and then, I would stop and hold back. I did it if I could. Make no mistake about it; I handled my business. (Smile)

The following week, I received my "number" for the cab service that was given to people on disability. The only thing I was waiting for now was housing. As I'd already dealt with Mi-mi, it is my intention to leave the state of Virginia. No doubt, as usual, she never mentioned that she would leave with me, although she did mention Miracle Land one time.

On April 12th, 2002 it was Mi-Mi's birthday. For the past two weeks leading up to the date, Deena had been trying to get Mi-mi to convince me to let Joe-boy come to the cookout. Just two weeks ago, once again, Mrs. Brenda had to put that asshole off her property again. Deena just kept bringing that leach around people, and she expected people to put up with this guy. My answer had always been the same: "NO!"

Around 3:00 p.m., as I started the grill up, Deena pulled up. Wouldn't you know it? Joe-boy was in the car with her. When she got out, she immediately said, "He isn't staying." I knew she was going inside to continue her plea for that asshole. But I wasn't going for it. I was sticking to my guns. Deena's oldest son stood at the grill with me when they got out of the car. His actions were, more or less, don't change your mind, Ziggy!' Remember all of those fights; the children suffer the most. There's nothing worse than watching your mom get into a fight with your father, but it's even worse when you have to watch the man that's not your father beat your mom and all you can do is watch. You want to do something, but if you did, she would only side with him - bad situation to be in.

Like I thought…here came Mi-mi as Joe-boy got in her car. She yells: "I'll be right back." Mi-mi tells Jon to go in the house with the rest of the kids. Afterwards, she started pleading for that leach. And once again I said,

"No!" She called herself trying to suck up to me now with all the freakish talk. That didn't work because the sex is how I made it each time.

By this time, Mi-Mi's cousin, Pat, and her two children, had pulled up. Pat was beautiful, high yellow with hair past her shoulders that was real. I can say that about each of them; they all had their own hair. Anyway, Pat was fine as all outdoors, man." She stood about 5'5".

When Pat came down, there was this young boy who Mi-mi would get her drugs from. That's how they met in the beginning, and Pat would come down like every two or three months.

Around 4:15 p.m., we got a call from Mi-mi's cousin, Traci. When I heard Mi-mi ask her what kind of car she was driving, I told Mi-mi that she just passed by the house going towards 48th Street. I stepped outside so that Traci could see me when she pulled up. I could see that she was glad to be here from the long drive. Traci drove in from North Carolina, and Pat drove from Miracle Land.

Traci stood 5'7". Her hair was cut short but done up good. She was fine as hell. She had three children, two girls and one boy.

Moments later, as I stood at my grill, Deena pulled up with that asshole in the car again. At the moment, I was walking a pan of food to the kitchen.

Around 5:30 p.m., Mi-mi.'s real father and some of her uncles and aunts came over. Her best friend, Lisa, among others, stopped by for the cookout.

Before the night was over, we had maybe around 18 to 20 people who had stopped by. That was good enough. I didn't want a whole lot of people at my house. That's when you have problems.

I called Krista around 7:00 p.m. She told me that she hadn't made it yet because Todd had Talaia and Melody over at Jimmy's and wouldn't let them go unless she gave him some money. Yes, that's the kind of mess they used to go through. I told her as soon as I got a chance, I'd go and get them.

Around 8:00 p.m., before I left to get the girls, I prepared some BBQ for Natalie and the rest of the family. That meant everybody, sister and all. I stopped on 48th Street at Natalie's house. As usual, I was greeted with lots of hugs and smiles. Natalie's sister's oldest daughter took the food from me and brought it inside. Natalie came to the screen door and motioned for me to come in. I knew if I did, she wasn't about to let me leave right away. But I still had the girls to get and, furthermore, there were still people at the house that I needed to get back to.

I walked in and immediately told her that I had to go and pick up my nieces out at Park View Complex. I promised that I would stop by on my way back, and once everyone was gone, I would be hers for the night.

She laughed, pointing her finger. "You better come back."

"I will. I will."

When I got to Park View Complex, I had to get one of Leslie's sons (Krista's) sisters to go and get Todd. I had never been to Jimmy's apartment. I mean, why should I after what he did? He returned and told me that they were on their way. They came from around the corner of the complex. The girls started running towards the car. I knew they were glad to see me. They got in the back seat. He got in the front. I asked him where he was going. He looked at me like I was crazy. *Damn, I'm not the one on drugs.*

He asked where I was taking the girls. I told him that Krista asked me to pick up the girls, and that he didn't have to bring them home.

I drove back to 48th Street to Natalie's house. Once I got there, we got out of the car. I made a call to Krista. Her mom told me that she was at my house. I called and told Mi-mi to tell her that we were on our way.

After a few minutes, I told the girls to get in the car. Natalie started getting upset. She took my keys and said I had promised that when I came back, it was for the night. After fussing with her for a few minutes, she finally gave me my keys, but only after promising once again.

As I was getting in the car, Todd opened the door to the passenger side. I asked, "Where are you going?" He gave me a crazy look. At that time, I started up the car while he still had the door open. I revved the engine. Actually, I thought I had it in drive. It frightened him so bad, he threw a big rock at me. I had no idea he had that in his hand. I jumped out and ran around the car. As I got to the back of the car, he threw a 40 oz bottle at me. It hit me right on the side of my shin. I tried to run his ass down after that. He was lucky I just had back surgery and the staples recently out. As everybody stood outside, I got back in my car and drove home.

Once we got there, the girls went right to playing with the other children. As I stood in the dining room, I could see out the window. While Joe-boy walked towards the front, I knew he had been in the house. I looked at Mi-mi. She gave me that half-ass sorry look. There was nothing worse than someone lying to you about your place of rest. It was10:05 p.m. All the elderly folks were gone.

If I had known what this night had in store for me, I would have never come back from 48th Street. Everybody that remained in the house: Mi-mi, Pamela, Tabatha, Deena, Krista's boyfriend (Toe) Mi-mi' s best friend, Jannie, her boyfriend, all of the children, which accounted for 11 people and myself. Joe-boy was still hanging around outside somewhere. Deena would go out for a minute then back and forth as we listened to music, laughed, and danced.

I called the kids from Don's room and got everybody in the living room while the women got ready to go out to the club for Mi-mi' s birthday.

About two hours prior, as we drove to the liquor store, they somehow got me to agree that I would babysit while they went out. But it was all good. I walked one of the females that worked with Mi-mi to her car, which was parked in the back. In the back of our house, when night fell, it was dark. From the front door of the house to the backyard outside the fence, I heard her laughing, and somehow explained the relationship that Mi-mi and I were in. I explained that they would be leaving for the club. She said that she would come back for a minute and gave me her number. The night was clean, clear, and the air was just right.

Before opening her door for her as she stood with her back against the car, I placed both of my hands on top of the car while she stood directly in front of me. I complimented her as I moved closer to her cheek where she could feel my breath on her face. She moved just enough to keep eye contact as she continued to smile. I knew then I had her for the night. Her name was Sophia. She wore her hair short, breast was just a mouth full, waist was like a '4' but her ass and hips were a '40'. She stood about 5'5", brown skin. It was on. I slightly leaned towards her again. This time I kissed her on the cheek. I opened the door, and she got in. I said, "See you later."

She replied, "Okay."

I had really planned on getting together.

Anyway, I heard Deena's middle boy and Talaia challenge each other to a dance contest of that popular dance (Harlem Shake) that both had previously exhibited at one point and time. We had the music going, of course. We had to have some rap for them. After about two or three dance offs, Talaia kind of got 'em. Everybody thought so, but me being me, I gave them both some money. I sent the children back to Don's room as the ladies continued to get dressed. Mi-mi and Krista put the food away and straightened up the kitchen. It was 10:35 p.m. I kept checking the clock, trying to get them out so that I could call Natalie before it got too late.

While I continued to put the CDs in the right cases, I sat in my recliner. Suddenly, Deena came busting through the door, and following her was that asshole, Joe-boy. They were fighting again. I said, "Hold up! What's going on?" Both of 'em tried to talk at that time. I told them that they had to take that mess down the street. I called out for Mi-mi to come to the living room. I continued to tell 'em to leave. Still they didn't move.

Once Mi-mi walked up, she started asking what was going on. I looked at Mi-mi, then back at them. Krista had walked up and stood in the doorway of the living room and dining room. I looked at Mi-mi. I was very disappointed in her. She allowed this to get this far. She told him that it was okay for him to hang out in the yard during the cookout. When she asked that, Deena was standing there with her trying to convince me that there would be no trouble. I told them both that I didn't agree, but definitely he was not allowed in the house." At one point, I said to Mi-mi, "See what I mean? See what I meank? Look at this mess."

Deena yelled Y'all are going to put me out there with him, and he's been getting high and drinking all day."

I said, "Man, you got to go home or wherever, and wait for her."

At this point, he started questioning her about going out. She told him that only the females were going out. He then asked who was going to babysit. She told him that I was going to babysit all the children. I'm thinking to myself, *Where in the hell will you babysit? You don't have your own place, a pot to piss in, or a window to throw it out of.*

Joe-boy began, "I can keep them."

Deena asked, "Where? How are you going to keep the kids Joe-boy?"

He replied, "I'll keep them here."

She reiterated, "Joe-boy, you not even supposed to be in this man's house."

He tries to come back, "Well, if you are staying here tonight, I am staying too."

Of course, I say, "Oh no, you're not. There is but one man staying under this roof. That's the man of the house. And that's me!" Why does this fool think we moved in the beginning? To get him and the rest of the leaches out.

Joe-boy said, "I'm not going anywhere unless Mi-mi tells me to leave."

I was blown away by this guy. This dude was unbelievable. I couldn't imagine being like that. This guy had no respect for people or their property.

Mi-mi said, "You heard what Ziggy said, Joe-boy. You can't disrespect this man's house."

He said, "It isn't his house."

Mi-mi replied, "Joe-boy, are you hearing yourself? This is his house. You got to go, Joe-boy. He didn't want you around here at all. I told you, you could come in the yard during the cook-out because you said that you wouldn't start any trouble. Now look at you. Get out my house!"

Just moments prior, Mi-Mi had given Deena her cell phone and told her to call the police. Deena still had her youngest son, Tuck, in her arms, hoping that he wouldn't hit her while she was holding him, but he did lash out at her a couple of times during the incident. Deena took the cell phone and went straight through the house out the back door. She didn't come back in the house during the incident.

Just as Mi-mi continued to tell Joe-boy to leave, at that moment, he yells, "F- y'all." He flipped the glass coffee tables and the ornament shelf with five shelves, all glass. He just kept flipping furniture and breaking up everything he picked up. I was in disbelief. What man could bring himself to do such a thing to another man's house? Only an asshole like this because I refused to let him stay in my house. Unbelievable. I had to jump to keep the furniture from falling on me. When he flipped the entertainment center on the floor, he smashed the TV, VCR; I mean everything until it was broken.

During all this, he charged at me. When we got in the middle of the dining room where all the food that was left over, he flipped the table. Food went flying everywhere. At this point we locked up, and he started choking me. He had me up against the heater, and I was slightly bent backwards on it. Mind you, I just had back surgery. At this point, Mi-mi, Pamela, Tamatha, and Jannie were trying to get this asshole off me. No matter what they did, this fool never let go until I was able to move right in the doorway of the dining room and the kitchen door. We were on the counter, and I tried to grab anything to hit this guy to get him off me. By this time the women had backed off. I ended up grabbing a knife, and I stabbed him in the right eye. All the women disappeared. I still remember the look on Krista's face. As he fell back onto the floor, Joe-boy said, "You didn't have to do this, man."

I am thinking to myself, *Is this guy for real or what?* As I stood over him, I explained to him that things happened to people like him and that he should've left my house when he was asked. He couldn't come to people's houses and do as he pleased. That was one of the main reasons why we moved. I told him that it was a blessing that I didn't kill him.

At that time the police walked in because the door was wide open. They opened the screen door and walked right on in. Mi-mi was standing right behind me. I handed her the knife, and the police walked right up to me, two of them. Right off the top, Joe-boy started yelling, "He stabbed me! He stabbed me!" He just continued running his mouth. I was thinking, *Take it like a man. You were a gorilla moments ago.*

The police called an ambulance. After the EMS got there, they had me stand outside in the yard. As they were bringing him out on the stretcher, he started yelling, "I'm going to get you! I'll get you for this, Ziggy!"

One of the officers told him that if he kept running his mouth, he was going to jail. He continued yelling, "He stabbed me. What are y'all going to do about him stabbing me?" Everybody just looked on as he tried to make it seem like he was innocent and did nothing wrong. Everybody looked on as they shook their heads. One of the officers put me in the back seat of the car.

How was I to know that I wouldn't see the streets again for nearly eight years? One of the officers, after talking to Joe-boy at the ambulance, came to the car and told me that Joe-boy was pressing charges. As the officer placed me in the back seat of the cruiser, Mi-mi sat right on the hill of the yard. As we looked at each other, I shook my head. Though she couldn't hear me, I knew she knew what I was saying as I mumbled; "I told you so, I told you."

> *"If a man hates his life today and where his will has taken him,*
> *on his knees may be the first step that must be taken to begin*
> *the journey to be where he wants to stand tomorrow."*

Chapter 33

I was taken down to Norfolk City Jail. As I sat in the holding tank, all I could do was think of how this guy had ruined my night, with the possibility of no ending anytime soon.

As I was being booked, I asked for a warrant. They asked what I needed with a warrant. I told them that I had a right to file charges against him for damages to my property, trespassing, and assault and battery. The Sheriff that was fingerprinting me told me that he'd get it for me in a little bit.

I was taken back to the holding tank, which was only a few feet from the printing area.

Two hours later, they took me to a cell in the basement to be processed. This process alone takes three to seven days. Once they got me in booking, one of the officers went back to get my cane for me. During booking they took everything, including my prescription for physical therapy from Dr. Norfleet. They put the prescription in a folder for medical.

Norfolk City Jail processing has got to be one of the worst in the country. The living conditions in these cells are inhumane. If the health Department was to walk through there, there is no doubt that they would close it down. It seems that since Keith Wheeler has been president, every entity is just out for money, not really concerned about the people. The only other time I was in this jail was back in 1981, but a lot had changed since then. Not only do these cells have four bunks, at any giving time, they could have five people in a cell. The jails and everything were overcrowded. All they were doing was putting people in jail, even those who should be somewhere else, like for instance, people who have a mental problem, drug problem, and those who didn't commit a crime, like me.

As I sat on my bunk looking around, there was mildew all on the walls, rust on the bunks and everything. Now, I know that there's a law against these living conditions. On the third day, I was called to see the nurse. That's when you know you're getting close to getting a bunk upstairs.

During the visit, she asked a lot of questions. I explained my current condition in detail about my back. I also told her about the prescription by the surgeon for my physical therapy. She told me that she saw it, and it would be in my folder when the doctor got to me. I asked, "How long will it be before I am able to move upstairs?"

She told me it wouldn't be long now. All she had to do was go upstairs, sign some papers, and it was up to the sheriff from there.

It took another two days before I was moved. They moved me to the medical pod, 3-D.

The following week I saw the doctor. When I saw him, I knew I was in trouble. You know how you can look at somebody and get that notion. Plus, the nurse I spoke with the day before, not the one who did my intake, she was black. This woman was white and very nasty. I could see her whisper to the doctor as I walked towards them. I just looked at the deputy and smiled. Most of the deputies were black. So, they understood.

During the examination, the doctor told me that he would have to see about the physical therapy. He ordered me some medication after asking me, what, if any, I was taking on the street. I told him I had been prescribed Percocet.

"I doubt if you can get that in here, but I am going to order you something that should help with your pain. And in the meantime, I'll see about your physical therapy."

I had to wash my own under clothes. Due to my recent back surgery, there was no way I could wash my clothes by hand in the shower as expected.

I filed a complaint to Major Andrews about having my clothes washed because of my inability of my physical condition. A week had gone by, and I still had no answer from him.

For the next two and one-half weeks I complained about the inadequacy of the medical department. That following Thursday I was called to medical again. The medical room was just a few feet from my pod in 3-D. After all, it's the medical pod. Whenever they would bring people to medical, they had a blinder over the little window of the door, so they couldn't see you, but you could still hear them. The deputy had told me to get ready minutes prior. We could hear that it was the females out there. The guys started betting that all of the females would be taken back to their pod before they would let me out.

When the deputy came to get me, before letting me out, he told me that there were still a couple of girls out there and not to make him look bad. As I walked out the door, I turned and smiled at the guys. The girls were sitting on the bench right before you walk through the door to medical. I looked on as I walked past. They whispered amongst themselves. I noticed that one of them was Abbey Gage, so I spoke to her, and she spoke back. When she did, she smiled, and I could see that she only had two or three teeth with the rest missing. Immediately, I knew she had fallen victim to drugs. What a shame. When we were in high school, she was fine as hell. She didn't live on the same block, but we basically hung with the same people. I always liked her but never got up the nerve to go up to her. Have you ever seen a girl years later that you wished you would have said something to? That way you would have at least had a chance to see if anything would have become of it. Well she's one of the ones who got away from me. But it was good seeing her again.

When I first got in the pod. I could see this guy with a full Sunnah. I knew he was probably Muslim. I waited to see if he was going to offer his prayer. After enough time had passed, I got up, made wudu, and made my prayer. Afterwards, he came up to me and greeted me. We talked, and he went into detail about how he came down selling drugs, met a girl, had a baby girl, and things hadn't been the same for him since. When things happen to us, do we need to ask why? It's evident. We stopped living like we should.

Later that day, the deputy stopped by to let us know that we would be receiving a new guy. That was a usual thing. What a surprise. It was to me when in walked Todd. Yes, that's right, my brother.

After he got situated, we sat down and talked. We didn't talk much. For some reason, he, mom, and Sharon all thought that Krista and I were sleeping with each other.

They didn't believe us when we told them that they couldn't have been more wrong. That never seemed to do any good. But if we knew that they were wrong, and we were right, it was all good.

The first call I made was to Mi-mi when I got in the pod. She told me that someone had stolen my air conditioner. I knew that would only be the beginning of bad news. After all, I left all my property in the hands of crack smokers. I questioned Mi-mi about the air conditioner. How could somebody steal a 300-pound air conditioner that's not even sitting in a window, but in the dining room on a corner table? It would take at least three people to carry it. I know; I'd had it for two years.

For the few weeks that I'd been in the Norfolk Jail, Krista and the girls were the only ones to come and visit me. Mi-mi claimed that she didn't have ID. If she didn't have ID, why was she driving my car? Earlier that day, I had asked Krista to go and get her after she got home from work.

Once my visit was over and I was back in the pod, Todd was sitting along the wall looking crazy. He and Krista weren't talking. Her new boyfriend had taken a warrant out on him for an assault and battery. Before I went out to visit with Krista, I had told him that I would talk to her to see what I could do to get her boyfriend to drop the charges. During the visit, I told Krista to have her boyfriend over at her mom's house around 8:00 that night so that I could talk with him. That was a long shot, but I had to try for him.

When I got on the phone, her mom was kind of upset. As usual, he would have the girl on the phone for hours talking about nothing. Finally, I asked Krista if he was there yet. She told me that he was sitting in the back room playing video games but had told her to tell me that he wasn't there. I told her to tell that chump to get on the phone, or he didn't have to worry about Todd. I'd see him myself when I got out. Finally, he got on the phone.

During our conversation I had to move on to plan B and throw some money at him before he would decide to drop the charges or not. I told him that I would give $50; just don't show up to court. He agreed. I told him to put Krista back on the phone and stand by. I told her that I was going to call my mom and tell her that she would be coming over to get $50 of my money from her.

I called my mom and spoke with her briefly. Every time I spoke with my mom, I got those thoughts, you know, the ones where you couldn't protect yourself as a child.

The following week, Todd went to court. Her boyfriend didn't show up like he promised. The prosecutor asked for continuation. The next time, Todd went to court they let him go. He never showed up. He kept his word. Todd never thanked me, but he did promise to help me once he got out.

After weeks of complaining, finally the magistrate called me downstairs.

After a while in the holding cell, he called me in, looked at the warrant, then asked me if I'd seen a picture of Mr. Haley's (Joe-boy) face?

I said, "Sir, I'm here about my warrant. I'm in jail without bail because of Haley.

He looked at me and said, "I'm not going to process this warrant."

He then held up a photo of Joe-boy. I told him that was caused by Joe-boy's actions. Magistrate Mr. Willis looked at me, tore up my warrant, and yelled, "Get out of my office!"

I just stood there in disbelief. I couldn't believe this magistrate just ripped up my warrant.

Call me crazy if you want, but things were beginning to look like the hallmark of Ms. Foxx, the only person who came to mind as things began to unfold. I truly believed that Ms. Foxx still had it out for me and was waiting for my name to appear on anything she could influence.

The female officer that took me back upstairs, just happened to be one of the officers who knew how hard I fought to see the magistrate. It was very critical to my case. I told her what happened. She just looked wide eyed (oh my God).

Once back upstairs, I contacted a lawyer who was willing to take the case. He was black and the only one to take $3,000.00. He wanted $1,500 down and said we could work out the rest in payments. I contacted Mi-mi and told her that my lawyer would be coming by to see her. I told Mi-mi that I may have to sell some of my furniture to pay for the lawyer. I knew that I had to sell my car. At this time, Mi-mi started trying to plea her case. I can't believe she was only thinking of herself.

First, she hadn't been to see me once since I'd been in jail, and besides, everything I was asking for was mine. I didn't understand how she could go on about her being my girl and what she needed. In other words, let her keep everything and take my chance on a court appointed lawyer. I couldn't believe this.

A couple days later I contacted the lawyer. He told me that he hadn't been able to get in contact with Mi-mi, and every time he called, he got the voicemail. He would leave a message, but she had yet to return any of his calls.

"All it takes for one to be able to tell the difference between the truth and a lie is for the wrong word to be heard by the right ear."

Chapter 34

Now I'm having to fight with Mi-mi about my furniture. This couldn't be good. I was trying to be as civil with Mi-mi as I could.

Todd was supposed to get my things and take them to my mom's house. I called my mom and asked her if Todd had been there yet. She told me yes. I asked if he had brought any of my things yet. She said no. I asked if she give him any money yet. She said yes. I was messed up. I told my mother not to give him any money until he brought my things over, especially my white bag that contained my medical records. I got him out of jail to do something for me. I even paid him. Not only did he not do what I asked of him, but he took my money and left me hanging.

During one of my calls to Mi-mi, I asked if my brother had been by there. She told me he came and took one of my VCRs. I said, "What? That's not what I told him to get. I told him to get the white bag with my medical records in it and my photo album with my children in it. I never said anything about a VCR." Before I could finish, she started going off about keeping my furniture.

Weeks later, and I just knew I was not going to get my furniture, but I kept pressing, trying to get my things. Mi-mi didn't know it, but I had some cash stashed away in the briefcase. That was the only way I was able to retrieve the $400.00 I had hidden before any of this took place. This was the only thing she returned to my mom, so I'm told. I almost had to get the sheriff to get my car back. I wondered what role she would play in all this. I knew her sister had been in her ear ever since I got locked up.

I already knew that at least Deena was living in the house. Next I had to go through the process of getting bills out of my name, It's hard when you don't have any help, even harder when the one who claimed to be your help, is giving you the most fight.

After many phone calls and much fighting, I finally got her to give my car to my mother. All I could think of was from one fight to another. Where would it end for me? When would I have peace?

I was trying to coordinate how to get my mom and Mi-mi in the same room while I was on the phone, something that never happened for some reason or another. It always seems to be the other person's fault. I never gave up the fight for my white bag and photo albums. In the end, I just asked her to make sure that my mom got those things. My mom claimed she never received anything, and Mi-mi claimed that she gave these items to her.

My mother claimed that she was supposed to meet Mi-mi. When she got there, there were a lot of things outside on the streets. My heart just collapsed. I knew then, once again, everybody got what they wanted of my things. They just threw the rest in the garbage. The things that meant the most to me were gone. Bags had the first book and contained 186 songs that I had written over the years in prison, and I can't remember how many poems and poetry there were because a good number weren't finished. Photo albums of me and my children, my medical records and many other priceless things. Unbelievable!

In the beginning, I asked my mom to take my car to my brother-in-law, Bo. He could sell it quickly. He sold a lot of cars in the past. After that, it wasn't easy to contact my mother. She had a block put on her phone, even though I was paying for my calls.

She claimed that my brother, Todd, had put a lot of calls on her bill and didn't pay for any. I told her that she accepted the calls. What did that have to do with me? So, in turn, I had to call Krista at her mom's house and have her deliver messages for me. That was more difficult than you could imagine. My mom got back to me and told me that Bo said he couldn't get $1,500.00 for the car. I told her not to worry about it. I'ld just keep my car until this was over with.

As time went on, my mother said that I could get something for it. Something was better than nothing. I know that much, but I would not take less than $1,500. That's what I paid for it, but I'd put $1,200 into it. I put new tires on it and a new radio. I'd only had my car less than a month.

I told my mom to just park it in the yard. My mom would send messages by Krista sometimes. She wanted me to move my car, telling me that her landlord said that my car couldn't sit there. I told my mom that if my tags and everything were good, no one could say anything, and besides, she had a driveway and a yard. If she still lived there, what was wrong with my car sitting there? This had been going on for about three months.

Now that the people stopped sending my checks because I was locked up, she really started pushing me to sell my car. I was also giving her a $100 a month for cashing my checks for the first three months. I was in jail.

Within the next three to four months, she finally forced me to sell my car. We kept going back and forth. She kept giving me numbers. I knew I could get more than the numbers she kept coming up with. I didn't understand why they couldn't see that I was trying to sell my things to get the most money from them so that I could get a paid lawyer. Everybody wanted to do whatever they wanted, but not what was best for me.

I would call Krista's mom's house every other day. If she had something to tell me, she'd accept. If not, she'd just let it go to a dial tone. If I needed her to do something, I'd call right back.

My mom later told me that her landlord told her that she had till the end of the month to move the car. This is the time I needed to speak to my mother directly. No matter what you do, no one will ever deliver a message the way you give it. My mom said the most she could get was $900.00. That hurt! All that money I just put into that car, but I had no choice. I had to take that.

I called Krista about two days later. By the tone in her voice, I knew something was wrong. The first thing she said was, "Don't get mad at me. Your mom said that man only had $500. That was all she could get, and how much do she get for selling if for you?"

I just told Krista that I'd talk to her later.

After complaining about medical, among other things, I was transferred to the Handen Roads City Jail on May 15th, 2002. I sat in the cold ass room intake all day. Finally, I was assigned to a medical unit pod. The rooms were single, but it was cold as hell in that unit. I tried to stay, but it was too cold for me. I requested to be moved to another unit.

After three weeks, I was finally moved to D-3. When I got to the unit, I noticed that they had me on the top floor. I made some noise about that.

One guy came up to me quick. "Hey, man! You can't make it up the steps?"

I told him I wasn't supposed to be going up and down the steps at all. He immediately started trying to get the officer on duty to change our cells.

He was real anxious about helping me. I knew something was wrong. No one, who doesn't know you, is going to go out of his way to help you in this situation, especially a younger guy.

It took about 20 to 30 minutes, but I finally found out what the hell he was trying to do. I didn't know that I was being placed in a single cell whereas the others were two or more to a cell.

The officer called me out to the entry and explained to me what O' boy was up to. I kind of took a step back and smiled. I could see O' boy leaning against the rails of the steps. Finally, I went upstairs. The cells were big. I couldn't help but think of how I would have felt if the cell change had taken place. From that point on, I kept an eye on that guy.

I got on the phone and made my calls to my mom, Mi-mi and Krista's mom's house where Krista and the girls were staying. As usual, Krista's mom was complaining again about Todd calling her house all the time. Now, I knew he smoked crack. But when he was on the street, he was never around unless he was trying to get some money out of Krista. Every time he was in jail though, he acted like he wanted to be a family. (That crack is a mother f.)

I inquired about the GED classes, but I was told that unless my charge changed I wouldn't be eligible. (Isn't that some mess?) All these guys were in there for things that were unimaginable. There was no way I could bring myself to do the things that these guys had done.

The next ten months went something like this: Whenever I was out in the day room, I would make my prayer, along with a couple of other brothers who were new in the den.

Then there was this one guy who would come around whenever we would study, but I would see him while he interacted with the homosexuals. Mind you, the only reason he was allowed is because of another brother who just came in two days ago. He claimed that a man living that life can change and he was to be acceptable.

I understood. I would tell him, "Listen, that's correct, what you're saying. But listen at what you're saying. This guy must change his ways.

The man is not changing his ways if he is continuing the same behavior and is consistently continuing to interact with the homosexuals."

Now I was trying to understand this brother. Why would he allow this guy to bring distinction between us? It was beyond me, but then again, in cases like this, one needed to sit back and let everything come to the forefront. Whenever speaking of this brother, I will refer to him as Joker, especially since he told me to call him "Bismillah." I stopped what I was doing and stood up at the table. I looked at him in the face and said, "What did you say?" He repeated it. I then asked him who gave him his Muslim name. I stood there, and he refused to say. I then said, "You gave yourself that name because no Imam in his right mind, in fact, no one in their right mind would even give themselves that name."

That is not one of the attributes of Allah that man can use. Like I said, all one had to do was sit back, and everything would come out. I told that man he was crazy, and if he wanted me to address him in the future, he needed to give me an appropriate name to call him because the present name wouldn't do. "It's not yours."

He looked at me like I was crazy.

Not long after that, he started hanging with one of those crews on that territory thing. I may have sat at a table with some people who I really didn't care for, but I wouldn't go as far as hanging with a crew. The guys I passed time with were older. Every time you turned around in this pod, somebody was fighting.

Unfortunately, this time it was me. You see, this guy name Mikey Dorsey had been misleading people about his charges. The same white guy I had helping with my case had helped him as well. This went on for a while.

One day everyone was watching the news about a guy who was housed in the pod next to us (Marcus Johnson). Currently, he was getting sentenced. The judge gave him the death penalty. Everybody started talking amongst themselves. When they started talking about his co-defendant, they called Marcus Dorsey's name, and everybody looked back up at the TV. There his mug-shot was on TV. When they started talking about the charges he was charged with as well, everybody just started looking at each other. By this time, he started walking towards the phone. I looked over at the phones. I gave him a look he'd never forget. He had the white guy, myself …. everybody, believing he was in for another kind of murder. He never denied that he was charged with a murder; he just never told us the right person. He told us that he and some guy had gotten into an argument, and the guy pulled out a gun. They started wrestling and the gun went off, and he hit the guy. He had died from the gunshot wound. Now this chump done went and killed some old lady. They put all the information on TV. Man, these guys raped, robbed and murdered that woman. She was 82 years old. Unbelievable. I was just lost for words.

The white guy named Josh came over to my table and just immediately started talking in a way to remove himself from this guy. I only dealt with the guy because of him, so it wasn't hard for me. From that point on, he just seemed to have animosity against me. It was he who had committed the horrendous crime, not me.

In the evening I would always gather with the same older guys D.C., Sunna, Mack (white Guy) and myself. They would always play poker. I played sometimes, and Sunna would always joke throughout the whole game with D.C. and White Mack. Sunna was older than all of us. Once Sunna found out what you were in for, it was a rap. I found out that D.C. was in for raping his two little second cousins. They were around nine and 12 years old. Sunna would stare at you until you would finally just open up. He had a way of making people spill the beans about what they did, or allegedly did. Supposedly, D.C. and some of his other family members had come down from D. C. to Newport News for his wedding. Why would they come all the way from Washington D.C. to Newport News, Virginia, to get married?" Well, I don't know. Anyway, after the wedding, they were at one of the family member's houses. He had taken each of the girls for a ride on his motorcycle back to his hotel room and allegedly raped them one at a time.

Now D.C. claimed that he didn't do it, but the more he talked about it, the more it appeared he did commit the crime. You could always tell by the way someone would act. People like that seemed to get a high or rush or something by letting people know that they had done such a thing. It was beyond me. D.C., would always talk about how his lawyer was going to get him a bond. And once that happened, he would run and there were places he could hide in. D. C. where they could never find him.

We all spoke what we felt at the table. When Sunna began to talk again, I said, "Hold up. D.C., what in the world makes you think that these people are going to finally give you a bond?"

"Now! "Hold on now," he said as he tried to intervene.

I cut him off. "You're in here for not one but two counts of rape. You're on probation from home, and most importantly, you're from out of state. My brother, it's not going to happen. I am from Norfolk, and I can't get a bond. All I did was pull a man out of my house that shouldn't have been in there from the start, but right now, this is about you. My brother, once again, it's not going to happen. Stop fooling yourself. But if that works for you, continue."

Boy, he was hot as a fire cracker. You could have boiled water on his head. The whole time, you know everybody at the table is laughing. D.C. would always bring out his pictures of his wife and daughter. His wife was fine as hell. They had a little girl. When all of this went down, his wife was pregnant. It had been two years at that time. He always had to show his slip whenever he received money. He always talked about the things he owned, but the way he acted with money in here, one would think otherwise. Then again, I guess some people never get used to having things. One thing for sure, he could get used to this life; He's in Virginia.

Everybody at the table would always interject what they thought about each situation. White Mack was allegedly in for child molestation. As he tried to sit there and give his account of what really happened, I was in disbelief. I sat there as White Mack tried to explain. I was looking at this white boy like these people were sick.

He claimed that his niece was being bad. I asked, "Being bad? That's what children do. They get into things." At that moment, I thought I was speaking out like that because I didn't know the situation of my children or whose care they were in.

White Mack continued, he claimed that he just smacked her on the rump.

Sunna was there with these guys long before I got there. At that time Sunna leaned back then forth. Sunna asked Mack what his hand was doing under her dress if he was only spanking her. "You didn't have to go under her dress."

White Mack was sitting there looking crazy.

Where in the heck did they have me? How did I end up in this pod?" I just wondered about the actual account of events that really took place.

I was getting sick, and I had yet to hear about Sunna's case. For some reason though, all we could get from Sunna is that he shot someone, and because he'd been in and out of prison his whole life, this time he won't be getting out. That still didn't tell us what he was in for.

Every now and then, Tillerson would come over to our table. Tillerson was from Norfolk like myself. Sunna would really ride him. You see, Tillerson stiffed a crack head for sex. The price was $10. After Tillerson's little encounter with the girl, he claimed that it was nothing like he thought it would be.

I looked at Tillerson. What the hell did he think it would be like? Come on, Tillerson, man, you got to do better than that, man. I mean, how you really think it would be in here?

We were all over the place cracking up. I kind of felt bad for Tillerson.

Tillerson said that he had seen the girl in passing twice. Each time he would tease the girl. The last time he yelled at her. She yelled back, "I got something for your ass, mother f!"

He had no idea she was talking about taking charges out on him for rape. Had he known that, he said he would've given the chick $20. We fell out laughing. He had to laugh his crazy self.

Sunna started riding him even harder. Tillerson eased on away from the table.

Can you believe it? That man, Tillerson, got 100 years for that. That's right: 100 years, no matter how the judge worded it. Even so, hell, 40 years for a $10 shot of vagina. Unbelievable!

There was another guy in our pod they called Killer James. Killer James was in the drug game. People who hung around him said that killer James started snorting his own product, and within three months, he had changed dramatically. He earned that name because whenever a deal went bad, Killer James just started killing them. He would kill whoever it was. He had a problem. He's go home, take a shower, change clothes, and get back to the crime scene to watch on until they finished. You know, they usually took some time at the scene whenever someone had been killed. I could see how he would have had enough time to go home and take a shower, change clothes, and make it back before they finished.

Killer James was an only child. His mother and father weren't together, but he and his mom were real close. His mom was a school teacher.

During his trial, certain things would come out through the media. The whole time his mom kept claiming that they had the wrong person. I really felt sorry for her. She thought that her son was innocent. She vowed to do everything she could to get him another lawyer for a new trial after the judge sentenced him to 90 years. Yes, these guys were coming back from court with life sentences.

I understood the frustration, but every time one of the young guys came back with all that time, he'd get his crew together and jump someone who didn't have a lot of people who dealt with him. This would go on all the time.

This one time, the guys Killer James and his crew jumped were some guys who Bismillah had hung around. You never knew who they were going to jump until it happened, unless, of course, you were one of them, and even the one calling the shots usually wouldn't tell everyone in his crew until minutes before they jumped someone, with the exception of the one who was closest to him.

Anyway, the brother was involved with that rumble. I didn't involve myself because the brother started hanging with these guys and doing unthinkable things. He was involved with things that were unbecoming of a Muslim from my understanding from the Imam.

He was in there for something that I can't mention, simply because he was Muslim. But his character was unbecoming of a Muslim.

And there was Jerry McCallister. They finally got him for drugs and murder because of who he was or thought he was. He had a crew of guys who would hang around him. One of Sunna 's homeboys who messed with a homosexual in jail got jumped by Jerry McCallister and his crew. That mess was funny. That chump, Jerry McCallister, couldn't fight. He needed all the help he could get. No wonder he had people doing his dirty work for him on the streets. There were like four that jumped the ole boy at that time. Sunna got in it and stopped it, told them that they were wrong to jump the man. It was Jerry McCallister's beef, but of course, he didn't want to fight the man one-on-one.

When he went to trial, he received 20 years in the state. When it came time for him to go to court for the federal charges, I remember reading in the newspaper by Judge Ms. Kennedy, how he thought he would (Jerry McCallister) come into her court and manipulate the system, but she had news for him. Every time his mom and father would come visit before he received any time, he would always tell his boys that he had a date with his baby, his mother, which everyone found touching. You know how a good relationship with your mom is always special. His girl had left him. She must have known he wasn't getting out when he went to trial. Judge, Ms. Kennedy, gave him life.

After the day that Mikey Dorsey's case blasted across the news, the tension between us had been getting thick. You could almost cut it with a knife. His ass was the one who'd been lying to everybody. He had me and the white boy in the Law Library working on a non-existing case. He started keeping his so-called home boys around him all the time. He even kept one white boy with him: White Mack, who was in for molesting his little nephew.

I couldn't believe I was in this pod with all those pedophiles. Another little punk he had with him was Junior, who was in for carjacking. Before the fall out, I asked him what would make him carjack. He told me that he was just sitting around and had nothing to do. He decided to go and take a car.

Another one of his crew members was Mai Mai. He and his home boys on the street used strong arm-robbery, and if anybody that they robbed didn't have any money, they would beat them. Hell, the people they were robbing in their community were just as poor as they were. So, a lot of people were getting their ass kicked. What a shame."

White Mack ended up with 10 years, Junior: 10 years, Mai Mai: 90 years, and Mikey Dorsey, got 135 years from what I heard. He did some real bad things to that old woman. He deserved every day of it.

Finally, they decided they were going to jump me. As soon as I got word, I waited until they were locking down for quiet time.

Once they locked us down, I had D.C. go to the booth and tell the officer anything, just as long as he got me out of my cell while they were cleaning. Both were house men.

When I walked out my cell, Mikey Dorsey knew that I was coming for him. He walked to the far side of the pod as I came down the steps. He knew I was coming for him. I gave him the eye.

Once on the floor, I gave my cane to D.C., then walked towards Mikey Dorsey. He grabbed a chair. As I continued towards him, I tried to convince him that I just wanted to talk and wasn't going to knock his ass out. D.C. started going to doors telling people to look out. People started yelling and screaming. His boy, Junior, was yelling, "You better stop running from that old cripple mf."

I'm like, Yeah! Listen to your boys. You better stop running. I was trying to walk as fast as I could. He was running backwards with the chair. I acted like I was about to run after him, so he picked up the chair and ran. When I fell out laughing, it seemed the whole pod started laughing. His crew was mad as hell. They just kept yelling, "Wait until I get out there!"

D.C. had walked back to the front door to look out. He yelled, "Here they come!"

I grabbed my can and went back to my cell. The officer in the booth closed my door. I could see him talking with the task officers. They walked in momentarily and told the house men to lock down. The white officer that was working really didn't care because he knew that young boys always jumped somebody. I could hear the officer in the booth laughing. They didn't like him anyway because of what he did to that old white lady.

Once quiet time was over, when I got to the floor, Sunna told the cowards that I would fight each of them one at a time.

Junior was the first one. We got into it. I almost had a good slam, but when I picked him up, due to my back injury, I couldn't hold my balance. That was the only thing that saved him. I was going to slam him on his head real hard. Everybody started yelling, "Here come the police!" D.C. and Sunna yelled: "Lay on the floor Ziggy!" I looked quickly, then lay on the floor.

Whenever they had a call like that in the jail, a nurse accompanied them in case of injuries. In this case, it was Ms. Vickie, my sweetheart. They called for a wheel chair and took both of us to the infirmary. It seemed that no matter what I was involved in, the nurse was always fond of me. They were laughing and talking, asking me, "Did you kick his ass? You better have kicked his ass." It was like refreshing for someone of my age and condition to kick one of the young boys' asses because all they did was jump people, and no one liked that.

On the way back to the pod, the officer told me that they put Junior in in-take, and they could take me all the way in with the wheelchair, or I could walk in. He said, "It'll look good if you walk in on your own."

By the time we got back to the pod, everyone was back out of their cells. I told the officer to stop at the door. I got out of the wheelchair. I walked in the pod. Everybody started clapping their hands and making noise.

Once everything was quiet, I went to Mai Mai's cell first. He was in one of the four men's rooms. He came to the cell door, but he wouldn't come out. I knew he didn't have any heart anyway.

At that time everybody was telling me to let it go. But I just had to let everybody know that neither him nor Mack Dorsey wanted any trouble. They didn't have any wins.

From that day on, I didn't really have any more problems, except this one little clown. I mean, the boy only weighed 90 pounds, if that. He ran his mouth for a few minutes until Sunna intervened and got between the ole boy before he got within distance. To be honest, I'm glad he did because I would have punished that boy. I mean punished him. He had only been in the pod for a week and a half, and already he had his ass kicked three times. One guy said that it just showed that he had heart. I told him it only told me one or two things. He couldn't fight, and he liked pain.

The following weekend I was called for a visit. I wondered who it could have been. Whenever Krista and the girls came to see me, it would be in a letter first or I would call. I got upstairs to the visiting room, and once in a booth, Sharon and Co-co sat down. I knew I wouldn't be able to talk to her like I wanted to. She had Co-co with her. I knew she was only there to rub my confinement in my face. I just sat there and let her have her way. She talked like she was concerned about my well-being, but I knew better.

When she started talking about money, I only wondered how far she would go to rub my face in the ground.

That night when she walked away from the visiting booth, I never saw or heard from her again. It has been six years till this date of May 21, 2008. It didn't surprise me any. Though it was a verbal ending at that time, it had really ended years before that. She never got over the fact that I didn't love her like she wanted me to.

Finally, I decided to call Natalie from 48th Street. After sending her money for the phone bill a couple of times, she started asking for $50 for the bill. My calls were only an $11 a call. I knew that there was some guy she knew that was locked up when we met. She and some of the other girls used to go and visit. I didn't mind. It wasn't something I was trying to stop. Anyway, after that, she no longer picked up the phone whenever I called because the money stopped. I was no fool.

Whenever I would call people, I would use a three way.

I talked to Deena, and each time she would assure me that she would come to court for me. After all, this mess happened because of her. I would tell her that all she could speak about was what she knew and saw herself. And I wasn't telling her what to say. I would say something like, "You know he was in the wrong, Deena."

"I know."

Everyone kept telling me that I needed her because she was the girlfriend of that asshole. I knew that. After all, everything took place because of her. Why wouldn't she help me? I helped her; that's why I was in jail. But then again, I wasn't stupid. I knew she had malice against me for not allowing her to come live with us. I could never make her understand that grown people needed to have their own place. It wasn't so much her, but instead, Joe-boy. For the life of me, I couldn't make her understand.

> "The challenges and changes that we experience in life are inevitable, but the pain that we feel from these changes can be caused if we would only realize that our pain is mostly based on loss and a reluctance to release the things of the past, uncertainties of the present and a fear of the future which will bring about more challenge and even relentless change to our lives.

Chapter 35

On January 1, 2003 while in receiving at the Handen Road City Jail, LT. Coxx intercepted legal documents that were important to my trial. LT. Coxx approached the holding tank and called me to the door. Before I could get to him, he asked me to bring my paper work. When he took it, I asked what he was doing. He said my papers were being transported with me to court.

I looked back at the guys in the tank. I was the only one whose paperwork he took.

After getting to Norfolk, I found that my paperwork had been supposedly misplaced.

The sheriff at Norfolk City Jail called back to the Handen Roads City Jail twice to see what happened to my paperwork. He was told that it was sent with me with the transporting officers.

When I was called before Judge J. T. Walker, the first thing I let the court know was that I had written two letters asking that my lawyer, Mr. Kelley, be removed from my case. Out of Everything I'd asked Mr. Kelley, he had yet to bring anything forward. I told him in the beginning about the warrant I filed against Joe-boy. He told me that it would be a lot of red tape, not worry about that right now. I even asked my lawyer to remove himself, and he had refused.

I knew I was being set up for something I just didn't know what. I told the Judge that I asked for a jury trial and that hadn't changed. My lawyer hadn't even talked to the one witness at that time.

The prosecutor spoke up and said, "Ms. Deena is here, your honor."

I looked at the prosecutor as he did a little flexing move.

The Judge said, "Good, then we can move on. Mr. Kelley can speak with her, and we can move forward."

My lawyer returned me back to the holding tank in less than five minutes. I told him I needed a continuance. I didn't even know what Deena was going to say He then told me that the prosecutor was offering a plea of 20 years.

I don't need to tell you what was running through my mind. All my constitutional rights had just been violated. The only other black person in the courtroom was that deputy, and when she took me back to the holding tank, I turned to her and said, "Can you believe what just happened?"

I knew she couldn't say anything, but her face told it all.

When I returned to the Handen Roads City Jail later that day, I was given my file that had mysteriously been lost, which had now somehow been found. It was 12:05 am.

On August 4th, 2006, My cellie and I had a disagreement after we had agreed that he wouldn't smoke in the cell after midnight. About 1:00 a.m. he returned to the cell after doing the shower job. He was at the door smoking, so I turned over after smelling smoke.

I said, "I thought we had an agreement about smoking after 12:00 midnight."

He said, "What do you want to do? I can't smoke out in the pod."

I told him, "You should. During the day you smoke out there."

He told me that I needed to move over to 200-pod, which was the non-smoking pod! The tone is what set me off. As I rose up off my bunk, I continued by telling him that I'd been in the same cell since I'd been there, which was nearly three years.

He cut me off and said, "I don't care how long you been here."

Before he could finish, I was out of the bed. I smacked him in his face. He started screaming, "Get your hands off me! Don't put your hands on me. I got something for you; just wait."

I sat down to put my boots on. This chump pushed the button, and the officer in the booth opened the door. He ran out to the booth. Next, he went through the port. He returned to the cell, and they counted. As I got up to confront him, the door opened, and the female sergeant took him upstairs to 300-pod. The next morning during breakfast (I was on bed rest so I would eat in the pod), Officer Mr. Wade came to the table and told me that I was needed upstairs.

Once up there, Sgt. Griffin and Captain Hughes were in the office.

Once Captain Hughes noticed that it was me, he immediately said, "Not this guy." (with a smile). I sat down.

He said, "I know you're not into anything."

I looked at him and said, "What's going on?"

At that moment, he started asking me what happened last night? I told him everything accept about the smack in the face. I continued by saying that this is the first time that anyone had to pull me in the office like this.

He looked at me and said, "Alright, I'm letting you go this time. You're free to roam."

Sgt. Griffin immediately asked me to wait outside the office. I could hear the conversation. The captain was not about to give into Sgt. Griffin.

Sgt. Griffin was tremendously trying to persuade the captain to lock me up. After his failed attempt, he got very defensive and told me that he didn't have any time for my shenanigans. As he walked toward the elevator, I could see that this man really had it out for me. He displayed great frustration.

Once down on the first floor, the captain told me to stay out of trouble as he left the building.

When I entered my pod, brother Hajj and Abdul asked me what happened. I explained as I heated my food up. Once I finished, I went and got into bed.

Forty-five minutes later, Officer Ms. Kacey came to my cell and told me that Sgt. Griffin said for me to pack my property. Once back up the elevator on the 3rd floor, Sgt. Griffin was writing. I asked him what was going on.

He replied, "You'll find out in a minute." So, I engaged him in a conversation.

I told him that I was free to roam by the captain. "You forgot he told me I was free to roam."

He then said, "I made some phone calls, and it's been a change of plans for you. See how that works?" He had a smile, so I smiled with him. (Realizing that I was the prisoner).

Then from nowhere he stated, "Osama bin Laden and Hez, they might get away but you won't."

Immediately, I was devastated and tremendously disturbed by his accusation, and under these circumstance and conditions, very illegal statement. He continued. "They claimed they didn't do anything either. They got away, but you won't. I got you." He had a big smile on his face.

I looked at Officer Ms. Kacey. "Did he just call me a terrorist? Because I am Muslim?" I looked at him and asked, "Did you just call me a terrorist?"

He just looked with a half-smile on his face with no answer. The look on my face told him not to repeat that. I just leaned over with my head and placed my face in my hands. This man was very adamant about trying to get me on something. I looked toward the elevator. I saw Lt. White. This man hated me since the day he took over the building.

It was no secret that he disliked Muslims. I can go as far as saying that he really hated Muslims, as he was quoted. This was a weekend. This man came in on his day off to put me in the hole with his street clothes on.

This man really doesn't have a life on the streets. (I thought to myself). Officer Ms. Kacey was told she could go downstairs and send officer John Doe up, which was a male officer. Once he was there, Sgt. Griffin told him to pack my property. He started taking everything out of the individual binders.

I said, "Hold on, man. What's up?"

He looked at me like I was crazy.

I said, "Don't take them out."

This chump started screaming. Now, mind you, this was not one of our regular officers. I had never talked with this man before this day. I didn't mean to laugh, but I couldn't help myself. His speech was messed up. I mean, really messed up. Lt. White came in with that "we got you look." I couldn't do anything but think how sad it must be to leave your family, wife, or something else that you had to be doing on such a beautiful sun shining day, simply to place a man, that's already locked up, in the hole. Some people will go to extreme measures, my brother.

One of the Muslim brothers came up and asked what was up? I told him, "Fighting," by motioning my hands. He looked disappointed in me. I was like, *can you make me feel any worse?*

During the walk to 10 building, once in front of the building itself, Sgt. Griffin told me that we were in the area where everybody always confessed. I immediately reversed it on him. I asked why he was so adamant about locking me up.

He pauses for a minute and said, "Harper, I wouldn't be able to sleep tonight knowing that I didn't lock you up."

Knowing that he couldn't charge me because it happened on another shift, I asked, "What's the charge?"

He knew I knew because I was an inmate adviser. That was my job. He said somebody would come see me once I was in building 10. I noticed that my cellie was on the other side, as I could see across through the windows.

I couldn't help but think how he came out of his mouth like he had a really good fight game. Instead, he ran to the police. I hate chumps like that. Once in my cell, 303, I cleaned the place up and just read. I went outside one time during the 10 days that I was in there. They had nowhere for me to sit outside.

On August 11, 2006, one of the Lieutenants came by my cell and asked me how long I had been Muslim. I thought that was strange. I got up and went to the door and called out for him because I wanted to know why.

That weekend two guys got into a fight out in recreation. I didn't understand these young boys. Fighting over a stamp. One stamp.

We cannot fulfill our needs today by thinking about yesterday, the past can bring knowledge and a sense of accomplishment that we made then, but that memory cannot fulfill the needs of ourselves or anyone else who wishes for a change today...if we want change to come today, we must begin to act today utilizing past, present, and the future to facilitate change now."

Chapter 36

On Monday, August 14, 2006, the property lady came by and told me to pack up. The following day I was transferred to the Queensboro correctional center. I had heard, but never detailed fully, but I can tell you from experience, the place was nothing but a hell hole. There were more drugs there than I'd seen in any camp. And this was a TC program or supposed to be.

I didn't understand how these guys could tell on each other, but when the U.S. Senate and legislators came walking through a week ago, they had everybody standing by their bunks like they were in the military or something, so I was told, and I believed it. The guy who told me, didn't like this program himself. Why would he lie? He went on to tell me that whenever they stopped and asked an inmate how he liked it, instead of telling the truth, the chump would actually tell the people that he liked the program, and it worked.

The guy told me it was unbelievable. He said that the warden and the major would stand there with a look on their faces.

I strongly believed that if something wasn't right, you should stand against it. if you don't, you've become a part of the problem and should be dealt with accordingly. But under these circumstances, it makes it just that much more difficult.

One day I asked C.O. Curry to order enough trays so that Jonnie Mitchell and I could have two apiece. There were three of us, so he ordered six trays. By the time the trays arrived, the workers showed up.

One day, Jonnie Mitchell had warned me about a guy named Mujett. One of the guys wrote a book, and from my understanding, he thought because he was in this book telling their story, that he was a big guy. He and I had our words. Let me stop trying to play this down. If Officer Mr.

White had opened my door, I would have killed that chump. The man went on about who he was, started pulling up his shirt sleeve and pointing to a tattoo on his arm as if that was supposed to mean something to me.

Oh, man! I lost it. C.O. White looked at me and said, "O'boy, come on up front."

I was yelling. I told that sucker just because somebody wrote a book and put him in it, about him and some sucker terrorizing his community, I was supposed to care? The confrontation between him and me was out of control. Jonnie Mitchell came to his door. I mean, the nurses and everybody were looking. We were going back and forth.

He really set if off when he said to the other inmate workers, "Give me his name and number." He had a meeting with the Warden. I really lost it then. I told that chump that what he had done in his community didn't impress me.

"You want to impress me, sucker? Stop going around here spying on people so you can go back and tell. And furthermore, the best story has not been told yet. If so, I would be sitting on death row right now."

He got up and left the building.

Sam, another inmate, and I were sitting in the room. Suddenly, one captain, three lieutenants, about four sergeants, and I don't know how many officers, came to the door. The captain looked at Sam and called him to the door. At that time, the older guy in there with us had walked across the floor to the bathroom, knowing that something was about to go down. He wanted to make himself scarce. The Captain told him once he finished to step outside the room. I looked at Sam. He looked at me, and we both knew that they were coming for me. Once they were out of the room, I just knew that they had come to beat my ass. Otherwise, why would all these police come down here? The Captain was talking to Lt. Jacob.

I said, "Hold on; everybody is coming at me all at once?"

They were trying to interrogate me or something. I had already had one run-in with the captain because earlier I was talking to him and C.O. White about Ramadan. The night before, I had received a hot tray instead of a Sunni. There was a big miscommunication about my meal for Ramadan, so I told them that I would take my name off the list and fast on my own. I had asked Captain Workman if it was okay for me to hold my food during the day until it was time for me to break my fast. He said that he didn't have a problem with that, but I would have to give the tray back so that it could be returned to the kitchen with the rest of the trays. I said, okay.

Mujett ran up to the command center and told them that I had threatened him. I told the captain and the rest of them exactly what happened, well not exactly. Of course, I didn't say anything about the threatening part.

Once everything came down, one lieutenant said, "I just want to know one thing." He got C.O. White's attention. "Did he, or did not threaten you?" He asked C.O. White.

C.O. White said, "Well, I don't know anything about no threat."

Mujett had a lot of pull with the administration because he was the best snitch on campus. After the lieutenant ask C.O. White that, C.O. White started telling him that I was taking trays when I was supposed to be fasting. He continued saying that I kept going into the chemical closet, taking the chemicals. He also claimed that I had a medication stash. The captain asked what happened to make me run the guy I ran out of the room. C.O. White told him that I didn't run him out, and the guy had a real snoring problem, and he was asked to be moved. So, the captain and his crew walked out.

Sam and the older guy came in looking like they had just seen a ghost. They had asked what that was all about. I told them it was about that punk, Mujett.

Later that day, Jonnie Mitchell came over with that look on his face. I said, "What's up, man?"

He said, "You," pointing his finger. He said, "Listen, if you come over my house, and I had my dog sitting over there, and I told you not to pet my dog, but you wanted to pet him anyway, and he bites you...who is to blame?" He said, "I told you not to pet my dog." He was smiling. "I told you not to mess with that boy, didn't I?"

I told him that I didn't know that chump was in with these people like that. "Whatever happened to the real convicts," I was thinking aloud. Ever since that took place, I couldn't get anything done. I could see what Jonnie Mitchell was saying then.

The problem didn't stop there. In fact, it continued and got worse. After that incident with Mujett, I didn't know what he said to Officer

Mr. Curry, but my door stayed locked, and every time pork was served on his shift, he would refuse to call the kitchen for me to get a veggie tray, knowing that I was Muslim. Those days I went without my meal. I filed an informal complaint, but the response was in his favor, so I filed a grievance. Those people refused to help you, even if you were right. Meanwhile, I had another follow-up with the doctor.

> "The enemy uses that which we desire and lust for within our hearts to trap us into intentionally submitting to their will, allowing us to falsely believe that if we do, we will be able to keep what we have been deceived with."

Chapter 37

Dr. Songo was from Africa. During my follow up, the head Nurse, Ms. Oliana, was holding my medical file. As I was speaking to the doctor, she interrupted, stating that none of the things I claimed were in my medical file. I asked her if she had the right file. She looked at me like I had said something wrong. She said, "I'm looking in your file right here."

I looked at Doctor Songo and said, "Well, maybe someone at Arlington Correctional Facility deleted critical information from my medical file.

Doctor Songo leaned back in his chair and said, "No! No! They won't do that."

I leaned forward and looked at Doctor Songo and said, "Welcome to America, Doc."

He looked at Ms. Oliana then back to me. If you could see the look on his face, you would've laughed your ass off.

Ms. Oliana said, "Well, I'm going to call Arlington back and see what they say."

I told her that my claim was irrefutable.

She said, "Okay, we'll see."

I had too many things coming at the same time. I was also dealing with those inmates and staff. I had heard somewhat about this institution, but I had never experienced anything like it. I mean, having done time in places like USP, Victorville and then end up somewhere like this. You just can't adjust to the way they do time here.

Once back in my room in the infirmary, I was thinking who I could get to check this out. I didn't want to accuse the Arlington Correctional Facility in case they hadn't done anything like that.

Those are great accusations. I talked with Jonnie Mitchell later that day. He told me that I should think about writing the psychologist. The only thing about writing the psychologist was you needed to be careful of what you say. You could find yourself in a straight jacket or in a dry cell. You didn't want that. So, I sent him a request form. He came that same day.

When he walked in, he had my medical file with him. See, I explained on the request the problem I had with the medical head nurse, Ms. Oliana. He came in and we went over my file, and everything that I told him that Ms. Oliana said wasn't in my file. He flipped the pages, calling them out. I continued, and he did likewise.

Once we were finished, he said that he was going to get copies of those pages, and he was going to go see the department head. This made Nurse Ms. Oliana not like me even more.

Because of the lies from inmate Milo, Carter, and Baxter, they harassed me. I tell you, one day inmate Baxter was picking up trays from the rooms. When he got to my room, only Scott's tray was on the small trash can. He looked around and left. I was reading the newspaper. Officer Mr. Morgan was at the door. I noticed that he had gloves on his hands. He was in my cell before I could get up. Once more, I didn't know what he was looking for. He walked towards me and asked, "Where is the tray?" I told him that I had it. He said, "Where is it?" I pointed over on the wall on the top of the next bed. I got up, walked over, and removed the pillow and the heating pad (I was keeping my trays warm). I told him to let me get my food off the tray. He tried to snatch my tray, but I pulled away. He looked and got real upset, yelling, "Give me the tray!"

I told him that Captain Workman told me that I could hold my food until it was time to break my fast. He said, "I don't care who told you nothing," with his African accent, and snatched the trays out of my hand, and just that second, I caught myself. I was about to take his head off. He knew it. He looked at me and said, "Okay." I wanted to do something to him bad, I mean bad. He would always yell, "Jesus Christ!" He didn't know how bad I wanted to break his face.

Inmate Carter used to come in the room, talk for a while or lie down and get some sleep. Ever since the incident with the trays, he didn't come in like he used to. He even dropped dime and told the people about the chemicals I kept in my cell, even though he knew all I was doing was cleaning with them. It's not like I was going to sell or drink them. They probably would be happy if I did drink them. It would have been easier for them! He snitched that I was holding pills in a bag. What he didn't tell was that I was giving him the pills. He didn't mention that, of course, because that was of benefit to him.

Jonnie Mitchell and I were shaken down twice. We never knew why until that day we were sitting out in the hallway. Carter was also out there with us. He knew all the time. Jonnie and I both asked him if he knew what was going on. He just shrugged his shoulders and said, "No." He then got up and walked up front.

Until what was previously mentioned about Officer White, we had no idea of what was going on. Let me put it this way; I had no idea. Each one of those guys stayed up in Jonnie Mitchell 's room. The more I think about, how he told me this place was when he first came here in the late 1990's, it made me wonder. I'd always given him the benefit of the doubt, but maybe he was just playing both sides. I couldn't say anything until I saw otherwise, but you can bet I was keeping my ear to the floor. He had spent four and one-half years here before. That's a long time, with lots of history. Still, I wanted to give him the benefit of the doubt, but still, I couldn't put anything past anybody I didn't know.

On another day, inmate Baxter and I had it out. This man was really some "mess." One thing I'd learned is that you can't beat these guys who were programming. It was a set-up. And the administration was behind it. To hear the truth, ask anybody that bucked the program there, but someone who completed the program is like asking the warden herself, with the exception of my Muslim brothers. We didn't get involved with that snitching stuff.

On November 2, 2006, I had an argument with Baxter about the cleaning supplies. He told me that he didn't work for me. "Nobody said anything about working for them. I just asked you for the cleaning supplies." That's why I hate dealing with people on dope and drugs. They are chemically unbalanced after getting high for a long time.

"When a man tries to fill the void within himself, with things outside himself, he moves further away from himself.

Chapter 38

I feel in order to be complete, I must bring my children together as a whole before my time on this earth is up. I'm determined to make it happen. There would be great grief if, for some reason, I couldn't pull this off. My fear is that my children would live their lives with hatred in their hearts for me, and I just can't live with that. So, I continue my struggle.

Thinking back on one of the court proceedings in Guilford, West Virginia, being that I couldn't be in the courtroom while the boys testified, I didn't learn until I was all the way back home in Chesapeake, Virginia, that that my oldest son, Mario, was of age and could think for himself. They had coerced my youngest son, Charles. He testified that I used to beat him bad and placed him in a closet. Why my lawyer, Ms. Jacklin, didn't tell me that before we left the court house is an indescribable pain that still haunts me. This lie was a major factor in me not getting my boys back. Had I known that this was said, without a doubt, I would have stopped the proceedings and explained that there's no way possible that could have even taken place. Charles was only four months old when I got locked up. When I was released, I went back home to Virginia. After learning that his mother had turned lesbian during the 18 months she did in prison, she and I never reconciled.

By January 18, 2007 it had been more than a year since I'd heard from my daughter. Well, at least it seemed like it. I guess she was really upset because I couldn't get her to write me back. Sometimes I set into my thoughts so deep that tears would fall from my eyes before realizing, but I am thankful to God that my children do know their father. That way if they want to, they could look me up and talk about whatever ill feelings they have. I could ease their minds if only I have the chance that I'm fighting for so diligently today.

My niece, Nakisha, is trying to help me locate her these days. Engaged in this controversial approach with my oldest has been critical growth for me. I just wonder what she has learned from this. I just wanted her to know that it's very important to me that she's safe out there in the world. I applauded her taking the approach she did in trying to understand how things work in life, even though it's impossible for her to know everything. I myself don't even know all there is to know; however, I do know someone could have the best of intentions at heart, but things don't always play out the way we want them to.

It's been six weeks since I sent her a 14-page letter and two birthday cards. I guess she's really upset with me. There's nothing worse than trying to be a parent from prison. Occasionally, I would pull out the pictures I had of Alina. It was so painful, even to just look at them. I'm really struggling with this cutting edge of my life. If only she knew the pain I have felt and the many tears that have fallen. There's no doubt she'd be more understanding.

I know that she has her own life to live, but I was crushed to find out that her boyfriend had talked her into leaving and moving to Madison, Wisconsin. I had hoped by this time in my life I could have her on a computer looking for her brothers. Now that they are coming of age, the courts can't get involved. I can't describe the pain I feel knowing that someone has had that much control over her when it came to me. After my divorce from Sharon my daughter was all I had. I have always stressed the importance of education and encouraged her to stay in school. She has kept her promise and made it through high school without any children. My fear was that this move would hinder her continuance.

I had no idea that I was on a crash course with Alina like this. This is a memorable lesson. I had only tried to encourage her to do her best in whatever it is she chooses to do in life. But more importantly, be careful of the road she chooses to obtain that which she sought. Listen, use logic and occupy your mind with good concepts. I had hoped that she would grasp my constructive way of putting things. I had been critical of her moving away from home at such a young age. It's so burdensome because she moved to another state where neither side has family. After examining my approach, putting myself under heavy scrutiny, I feel really bad. I did not mean to anger her, but I felt it equally important that I remain her father and not come across as her friend, especially since it seems that her mother acted like her friend instead of a parent. "I'm assuming now, which isn't good.

I tried to expound on the virtues of life as I knew them. Judging by her response, somehow our communication gave off bad body gestures. To be separated by hundreds of miles and to set that kind of feeling just consumed my heart completely with an abstract feeling that I never felt before. If she could only understand what I was going through, I really think that she would change some of the things in the way she presents them. I was only trying to protect, not ruin her life.

Rejection for a parent under these conditions can be admittingly fearful. Why? I tell you, God forbid, but if one of life's obstacles sharply approaches, left without remedies, it could ultimately end lives. And who would be the first to blame? Me. Because at that very moment the parent will automatically come to mind of that child. It really means a great deal to me that I patch up my relationship with my children. This has been a quick eye-opening experience, though it took me some months to try and reconcile with her.

She's taking our difference real hard, from the looks of it, which could lead me to believe that perhaps the relationship between her and him didn't work out, but she refused to tell me, fearing that I may throw what I said in the past in her face. How incorrect that would be. I would only suggest that we pick up the pieces and continue to move forward.

Each day I beat myself up because I wasn't there to raise her and her brothers. I could only imagine what kind of names I may be. Too often in situations like this, once reconciliation occurs, there are always hidden injuries endured. I know that it will be a huge obstacle, but it's my responsibility to reach out and clinch the opportunity to bring my children together. I often wonder where each of them is and where life has taken them. Not every day, but often enough, I try to understand where Christy's motherly love was that every mother is supposed to have for her children. I then often reflect on my childhood. Even though my mom wasn't really there for us like she should've been, she kept us all. Too many times, I know that she wished she could have done something with me altogether.

Reflecting on the things that everyone has done to make me fail makes me a very hateful and dangerous man. But I know that I will only lose if I carry out any of my thoughts. I long for the day I can embrace my children. We have a lot to talk about, and I have a lot of explaining, but I'm ready!

I guess my life and the way it turned out is what makes me more determined to save my children. I feel that if I don't save them from the wrong path of life, then my life has been in vain. There must be something good to come out of this.

On January 21, 2007, I wrote Krista, and I asked Celes to use her resources to help me find Mario and Charles. They were at the age where the courts couldn't get involved, well at least Mario was. I'd been trying to get my niece, Nakisha, to contact my daughter for me now for a few weeks. Also, I put her phone number in so that I could call, but she hadn't accepted it yet. Therefore, I was unable to call. My mom's number had been temporarily disconnected, and I couldn't seem to get anyone.

I wrote, and no one wrote back. Perhaps I should have just let it go. Each time I came up with this concept, I felt like a failure, and that I couldn't live with, even though someday I may have to but not yet, as I continue to pull my family together.

2008: I have less than four months left before my release day.

In 2008 with only four months left before my release date, I was writing to the Hajid house. It was a place like a halfway house. The only thing is that it was only for Muslims. I wrote and requested an application, and a week later I received it. I filled it out and mailed it right back. I didn't have much time to work with. Normally one would start preparing for release six months prior, but I had nowhere to request placement till now.

I received a letter telling me that someone would be out to interview me. I received a memorandum on June 11th, 2008, letting me know that on Friday, June 20th, 2008 at 11:00 a.m.-12:00 p.m. Mr. Bill Bullock from the halfway house would show up and conduct the interview.

Once we were finished, I reminded him that I had less than two months before my release, and that I needed something in place with the administration so they would know I had somewhere to go. He said he understood. We shook hands. Afterwards, he attended Jumu'ah and the prayer.

About a week later, I wrote a letter to Mr. Eli Malik, the director. He responded by requesting a letter from the institutional Imam. I felt that this was not going to be good. I just had that feeling. I say that because, at the time, the brothers were at differences about who would be the Imam. The brother hadn't been a Muslim for a year and was temporarily in place by some of the brothers in the community. During the votes, I remained neutral due to his arrogance and boastful ways, in addition to his continued acquaintances with his prior gang affiliations. I'd seen it all before. In fact, the Qur'an says when someone is trying to secure the Imam position, Islamicly you should try and make sure that person does not become the Imam.

During rec., I went to the yard to speak with the brother. As I approached him, he turned and started walking the other direction with the brother he was talking to. So, I called out to him. He said he didn't have time right now. The last thing I like is having to go to another brother for approval for anything. These brothers do not adhere to the Qur'an and the Sunni like the brothers I left in the feds. So, I waited until the next movement, which was an hour. He never got back to me.

So, I Salaam the brother I was talking with, and I went back to my pod. I waited until Friday, Jumu'ah, to speak with the brother.

After the prayer, as I approached the brother, again he started to walk off. I called out to the brother again. He stopped and wouldn't even look me in the eye. Brothers who come to prison and accept Islam, after a while, learn a little Arabic. These brothers think they know what they are doing. Some of these guys think they are in control of another man's life. I feel sorry for the individual because he really doesn't understand what it is that he's fighting to become. A pious man would be running the other way. I showed the letter from Mr. Eli Malik where he was requesting a letter from the brother for me to be accepted in the program. I told the brother that I had nowhere to go upon release, and I needed this with my disability. The brother said that he was not going to write a letter for me, turned, and started to walk off. I stopped him and asked him what the problem was with him writing a letter for a Muslim being released from prison.

He said that I hadn't been to classes in the last month. I looked at him and said, "Really!" This is what you get when brothers don't understand the religion. This is Islam, not someone running for office. I told the brother that he'd been here two months, if that, and already he found it necessary to be harmful to an elderly Muslim. He didn't understand the religion. I told the brother the right thing for him to do was to write Mr.

Eli Malik and tell him that there was nothing that he could tell him about me because he had only been here for six weeks and really didn't know me, which was true. The brother still refused.

The brother hadn't been Muslim a year yet and already managed to cause harm. At that time, I had been around the Deen (Islamic teaching) about 16 years. I was 44 years old and needed the approval of a 23-year-old brother who had only been Muslim a few months. I told the brother that it was not his place to deny me or watch over me or another brother for that matter. I went on to tell him that I'd been locked up for over 15 years, and I'd been to more classes than he could fathom and never missed jumaa" ah service unless we were on lock-down for a killing. I went on telling him that I didn't remember giving a pledge to a brother for nothing. I only came to him because Eli Malik requested a letter from him. (Which I had never heard of before). I told the brother that his actions were unbecoming of a Muslim. The brother never exhibited the right attitude to be the Imam. He acted like he just received a rank and a medal or something.

I went back to my pod and wrote a letter to Mr. Eli Malik trying to explain what was going on here at the institution. They wrote me back denying me because the brother refused to write a letter. I couldn't believe a brother wouldn't write a letter because I wouldn't get involved with that mess they had going on. It was unbelievable that a Muslim would not help another Muslim get some help being released from prison. In fact, our age difference should have been enough, if only the brother understood the (Religion). There's a level of respect that goes with age difference in Islam, and the brother didn't give me my rights. There was so much conflict and confusion going on here with the brothers. Brothers were about to fight, having to be pulled apart.

This Ummah was going through something. I never saw so many brothers fighting for a position. The community was divided. Brothers acted like I should be more concerned about what was going on in there. I was leaving.

My release date was July 29, 2008, and now I needed a birth certificate, social security card, and an I.D. You need all those documents in the world to get your life back on track.

The last week of June, after trying to get the brother to write the letter, due to his gang affiliation, he now managed to get into a fight and was shipped back to Jefferson County state prison, which is a max level institution where most of us came from. In so many ways, he still had that street mentality. Brothers like him get positions because of their recitation, and this is one of things Islam tells you to look out for. It states to be careful and mindful of the one with the beautiful Islamic recitation.

But still, just under a year … he really didn't understand what he was reciting. The brother was giving classes as well. I know that the brother didn't understand the deen that well by the things he would say sometimes. This is really what you call blind following. No one there had been anywhere before coming to prison to learn the deen correctly.

> *"If you have question about whether you are right or wrong in your actions towards others, all you have to do is ask yourself; how you would feel if it was being done to you by them."*

Chapter 39

In June 2008, I was called to R & D (receiving & departure). I knew it was time to pack out.

Once back at my pod, I started packing. The brothers in the pod came to my cell wishing me the best. I was transferred to the Norfolk City Jail. I hated this jail. I don't like any jails, but I really hated this jail.

I went back to my old block, 3rd floor medical. I was hungry every day with no commissary. I asked if my money was there yet. Although the money was there, there were more than two weeks before they put it on the books, just so they could tax me. They had taken a dollar a day totaling $16 of my $48, which I had intended on spending on my personal hygiene items. They claimed I owed them for being in their jail when truthfully the new law stated that inmates who had to pay didn't even apply to me because that law came into effect after I was locked up. It seems that anyone who has a little power can do the people any kind of way they want. They held my money, so they could get a piece of it. Everyone is trying to capitalize for their gain nowadays. When I got locked up, you didn't have to pay to be in jail.

July 29, 2008, was my release date. I was in a metro program known as VASA. They helped people get the necessary documents needed to start living again.

As I prepared to leave, I really didn't know what to expect. Just the day before I learned that I could stay with Krista, but I had to use her mother's address. It was good news, but I must admit, there were some concerns about living with my brother and her because she also had a boyfriend who was always around. Now that's some crazy stuff.

It was 8:30 a.m., and I'd just finished taking a shower, trying to get my head right for the world once again. It seems I'd left a good impression on the other guys.

As I sat there gathering my things together, everybody started forming around me, shaking my hand, wishing me the best and telling me to keep my head up.

When I was released, Ms. Kimberly and the staff from the VASA program took me to all the places I needed to go. It took nearly all day to take care of this stuff.

Finally, she took me to Krista's apartment. When we got there, no one was home. We tried calling the number she gave but no answer. I knew this was the work of my brother. If you knew my brother, you would understand what I mean. Ms. Kimberly told me it was getting late and she'd been off work for two hours. I told her that it was okay; she could leave. She said that she needed to see me walk in the door.

At that moment my niece, Talaia, walked up, and I asked where her mom was.

She said she was in Handen over at Sheila Johnson's house. Sheila was my childhood sweetheart. I asked Talaia if she had her number. She called Sheila, and I spoke with Krista. She was trying to tell me where Sheila lived. I handed the phone to Ms. Kimberly. She got off the phone and told me she knew where they were.

We got in the car and drove to Handen. We pulled up to this apartment. Krista and Sheila were standing outside. I told Ms. Kimberly that I appreciated everything, and I'd see her next week.

I was running out of medication, so I was referred to the free clinic. I was grateful. They were the only ones willing to help me.

Ever since I've been out, the free clinic and I have been trying to get my medical records from Ms. McCaster, RN, at Alberto Prison. I filed four months prior to my release date, and I never received them before I left. I called Virginia Beach (Department of Corrections). I spoke with Mrs. D. Starling from Health Services. She told me that she had a chance to speak with Ms. McCaster and was informed that she mailed my records. Before I could say anything, Mrs. D. Starling told me that she also called the free clinic, and they hadn't received anything pertaining to my back condition, which I needed for them to treat me and for my SSI. This was just more of her actions against me because I filed a grievance on her before I left the institution.

On November 2008, I volunteered to the non-profit organization around the corner where I lived with my sister-in law. I knew I would need everything I could get on my side once I finished the first year of supervised probation. I had planned to ask to be relieved from the supervised probation even though the restitution was not paid in full, because upon sentencing, the judge also ordered that after the first mandatory year of supervised probation, I would have to remain on supervised probation until which time the restitution was PAID IN FULL! That would have taken me the rest of my life to pay this. I was on disability and couldn't work so that meant I could only pay $50 a month. I owed $13,828.36. Like I said, it would take the rest of my life.

After a year on probation, I asked my probation officer, Mrs. M. Gallow, if she was going to keep me on supervised probation. She told me that I didn't need to be supervised, but it would be up to the judge. She wanted to know if there was anything that I could think of that would help.

I told her that I could get a letter from "Real Seed Real Ground." where I had been volunteering for the last year. She said it would help. Then I asked, "What if I could get Mr. Ken Griffin (head common wealth attorney) to assist with filing?"

She looked up at me and said, "Are you sure?"

I told her that I was going to his office from there. She said okay.

She didn't know that I'd already been talking to him about my case because I was also trying to get housing as well. On September 8, 2009, Mrs. Padgett at the non-profit organization wrote a letter for me.

I had an appointment on August 8, 2008, to re-file for my social security benefits. When you file for social security, while you wait, you can get renewal relief. It wasn't much, but I was thankful for the general relief I was getting. I was getting $45 a month.

On October 2, 2008, it more than doubled. It changed to $96. I would have to make this work for me every month.

On that same day, I was approved for snap $176. That was great help. On October 10, 2008, I had an appointment with the Social Security

Administration doctor for a complete examination. From there I awaited their decision about my benefits that would help me get back on my feet.

~" A small man's fears of the unknown compels him to leave a sign in the world for the eyes of other men before they die, because they feel that if they don't leave a mark they will soon be forgotten."

Chapter 40

When I first filed for public housing, I was turned down because of the charge I had gotten from Joe-boy. I'd been living with Ms. Kathy for a while.

Between 2009 and 2010 I got married to a sister. We were having a function at the Masjid. The brother already knew that I was trying to get married. The Imam introduced me to a young lady. After meeting the sister, I had a chance to meet and speak to her two boys. Qur'an, he's the youngest. His only concern was if would we still take vacations. I told him sure.

I talked to her for the next two weeks. After courting her for a while, we set a date for the marriage. It was to be in December, 2009.

On December 7, 2009, I had my informal hearing with public housing. Like I said, I filed for everything when I got out of prison. I was turned down, but I appealed. On December 17, 2009, I received a letter telling me that they reviewed statements and information that I provided and ruled to reinstate my application.

On June 4, 2010, I received a letter letting me know that I'd been placed on the list for a one-bedroom. That was good news because, by this time, things between my sister and I were not good, and I had given up my living quarters with Ms. Kathy. I still had my washer and electronics there. They were wrapped in plastic.

I went by one day just to check on Ms. Kathy and my things. When I got there, she was out. I still had a key because I was paying Ms. Kathy for storage. As I walked to the back of the house where my room was, I could see the lock that I put on the door. The door and lock and all was snatched off the door. I had the key. I went to open the door, and her granddaughter and the great granddaughter were in there having a ball.

Everything I had was new. Her granddaughter lived there sometimes when I was there. She was cool. she finished her first year of college but never went back. She had taken the plastic off everything. I came to get some of it, but I didn't want her to think I was taking it because she was using it. So, I just talked with them for a little while. Then I left. I drove all the way down there for nothing. I was upset about that.

I wrote a letter back to housing requesting retroactive pay from the date of my application. On June 10, 2010, I received a response. They told me that I was reassigned to the preference category. I was glad to hear that. I asked Ms. Kathy to look out for me on my mail.

On July 1, 2010, I received a letter giving me three choices. I picked Bay Point. It was the best out of the three. During the walk through, I noticed that whoever lived there before really smoked a lot. When I opened the door, it just hit me, so the workers said that they would clean the walls, but they would need a week to get it done. So, I went back to Virginia Beach. My wife didn't know that I had gotten my apartment. Things had gotten bad with her. Without going into much of the details; it was bad.

A Muslim marriage between a man and a woman is far different than other marriages, or at least I thought so. One night my wife left the house like she did many times. She would leave the house without taking one of her sons. Sometimes she would literally start an argument just to make it more of a reason to leave. This sister would go whether there was an argument or not. From time to time, I would have to call a brother of knowledge because she wouldn't take it from me, but I'm her husband, and I would show her the Islamic proof, and she still wouldn't listen. I guess she got tired of the brothers telling her that I was correct so one night she left the house, but this time she took her boys with her.

I didn't think anything of it. I thought it was a good thing. About two hours later, I got a call from one of the brothers I was locked up with. He gave me the usual greeting, and I replied to him. The brother proceeded by telling me that my wife was at his house, complaining. I told the brother, "First of all, my wife shouldn't be at your home this time of night by herself." I went on to tell the brother that he knew that it was un-Islamic. He said I was right and told her to leave.

About 45 minutes later, I got a phone call from another brother. He didn't greet me. He just went on about how I didn't have a job or money and how I was just lying around. First of all, in case he didn't know it, the sister and I had a contract for the amount I would give out of my social security check. Not only that, but when the boys had games, I made sure we went to them because it meant so much to her and Qur'an. I took him to every practice he had. Besides that, whenever they needed to go somewhere, I took them. Who cooked the meals? I made her breakfast every morning before she went to work, and when she didn't feel like driving, I took her and picked her up.

At the start of the school year we had let both schools know that I would be picking up each of the boys every other Friday during lunch for Jumu'ah. Everything was fine. That the brother didn't know, and besides, the brother knew better than to do it this way. That's not the way we do things in Islam, and he was very knowledgeable.

An hour later, my wife made her way to another brother's house. (I mean, this is really a shame.)

This brother called me and told me that my wife was complaining to them about my mistreatment of them. I told the brother that there was no validity to what she was saying. I asked the brother why I wasn't given the opportunity to defend myself. In Islam, the husband has a right to be present if his wife has a complaint about him, and the same goes for the wife. I didn't get that right. She didn't come home that night, so I just left.

I will not speak about all the things that the sister did, but they were not of our teachings. If I wasn't trying to live according to the Sunni, I wouldn't have stayed with my wife because of all the things she was doing. I moved back to Norfolk from Virginia Beach.

Not long after I moved into my new apartment, I received a letter from my ex letting me know that it was over, and she had moved. Months later we got re-married but divorced again.

After that, I don't know what she was saying to the sisters because I couldn't get a sit down. It seemed things really got bad for me with the Islam community over the last three years.

I'd been trying to get married again.

In Islam, when you reference, you should never call names, so I will refer to this brother as so & so. There was one brother who helped brothers get married. He was around my age or a little older.

After more than a year, I started going to the brother like every other week. All he would say was, "Okay, brother."

After three years it was obvious that I was not going to get a wife there at that Masjid. Not only at that Masjid, but I couldn't get a wife at another Masjid because I would have to go through the brother to try and meet a sister there as well. It was just the way things worked between us. You just can't walk up to a sister and start talking. I began to feel like I had given someone control over whether or not I would find happiness in this life.

For the past three years I felt like brothers were coming from prison and getting married. Some were getting married and making babies with nowhere to go. Now, if a sister already has those things and wished to give up her rights as far as the husband being able to furnish the roof (somewhere to live), food and garments, then the woman had a right.

As I said before, my questions is, how are these brothers having sit downs when I was told before that I needed to have these things in place? At least income. Some of these brothers didn't have anything. Just making babies, then going back to jail. There would be times when the brother would ask another brother in my presence because we would hang out after Jumu'ah and talk all the time. I was standing right there, and the brother knew that I was trying to get married, but he approached another brother that I was talking to who wasn't anyhere ready for marriage.

I wanted to say something to the brother, but I knew that some of the brothers didn't like me because of some of the things that brother had said to me. For instance, one of my close companions and I were talking about marriage, among other things as well. The brother told me that I might not be getting a wife because of the way I lived in my house. I was heartbroken to hear that from him. This was the same brother who has been asked four times and each time would decline. I'll tell you why. He had a girlfriend, that's why. You have some brothers in the community that are asked whether they were ready for marriage. There was a lot of favoritism going on with that. In the past three years the brother had yet to ask me if I was ready for marriage.

One day after Jumu'ah, I was threatened by a brother. The brother finished giving the Khutbah, and then we lined up for prayer. The brother always asked to make sure the lines were straight hill to hill, shoulder to shoulder. Even though he threatened me inside, once outside as the brother began to talk about what took place, all of a sudden another brother eased alongside me and said if I hit him, all the brothers were going to jump me. In my early days, before really understanding Islam, he would have to make good on that. But I was shocked that the brother would say something like that. That was further notice that he wasn't trying to help me ever get married. I know what the sister did in Richmond played a part also.

Another brother began to elaborate on the story of two companions of the prophet. He told me that the companions never got married, that they were busy studying all the time. I just looked at the brother and gave a good smile but was hurt. Why wouldn't that brother want for me what he wanted for himself? Is it not true that the completion of our religion is marriage? If the brother wanted to be praised for reciting that portion of the Sunni, he should have completed the entire story. Had he, those who didn't know better would have known that marriage is absolutely encouraged and completes oneself. It is through marriage that alleviates fornication and other things that are detrimental.

Marriage is the other half of our deen. For brothers to take it upon themselves to say who should be married and who shouldn't be is not their place … not to talk about a lot of things that drove me away from that Masjid and it was the only Salafi Masjid within the seven cities. Though I lived 30 miles one way from the Masjid, I made it a point to be at Jumu'ah every Friday. I made sure any brother who wished to go had a ride.

~"To have vision is to be able to see what others cannot: to become a visionary is to have the ability to allow others to see through your eyes.

Chapter 41

On August 20, 2011, I received a letter from my ex. She informed me that they had moved and was giving me an updated address, so I could continue my payments for the vehicle. I responded, and from there we ended up getting married again. That didn't last long.

Some brothers had indicated that I was not living accordingly to the Deen in my house. What goes on in my household is between me and Allah (subhanahu wa ta 'ala). I never put my hands on anybody in that house. Abu Uwais (rahimahullaah).

"We need a Ramadan."

"Where?" he said that brothers should not worry nor concern themselves with what the next brother may not be doing, not just during the month of Ramadan but all year round. Also Stop the Discord. Brotherhood is of utmost importance. When we don't understand the real meaning of something, we lose the importance of it. When we don't understand how heavy and the greatness of brotherhood is, that leaves room for the Shata to cause distinction amongst the ranks. It was clarified in the book of Allah (subhanahu wa Ta 'ala) and the Sunnah of Prophet Muhammad (saws). Say that it's so inviolable, so scared that when you step up on it, you trespass, and you transgress. Then you have done a great disservice.

To Islam and the Muslims many brothers take it casual, "I can be like this, or I can be like that. I can get along with the brother. I don't have to get along with the brother. I like the brother. I don't have to like the brother. He's okay with me; maybe he's not.

That's not how Islam is taught. It has taught us that as long as there's a brother on the face of the earth that believes in the wonders of Allah (subhanahu Wa ta 'ala) and his magnificent names, attributes, and singles him out alone in worship and does not set up partners with Allah. Verily the believers are brothers.

After I returned back to Norfolk, on December 24, 2011, I got divorced. We lost our Masjid in Norfolk, so, the few brothers on this side started going to Masjid about 30 miles one way.

From December 24, 2011 until February of 2014, I had been going across the water for Jumu'ah every Friday, still looking for a wife. For the last four years I'd been treated as anything other than a Muslim brother. I'd been trying to get married ever since I left Virginia Beach.

In the beginning, once I came back, brothers would always stop by. In fact, we used to have classes in my apartment. The only thing I didn't like about that was this one particular brother would appoint who would lead prayer in my apartment when the prayer came in. The brother was clearly out of order. Islam teaches us that whenever a brother is visited at his home, he is to lead the prayers in his own house unless his visitor is a sScholar, Shaikh or a student of knowledge, and then only if the man of the house asks him to do so. Other than that, it is a blessing for the man of the house to lead the prayer. The brothers knew this. I was trying to figure it out for a long time. But after a while, it became clear to me. The brothers in the community had been speaking badly about me, and he was one of them.

This brother was one of my closest companions. I really had love for the brother. This is the same brother who was asked twice in my presence if he was trying to get married, but he declined. I was standing there, but the brother hadn't asked me for the last three years. And Islam teaches us that one should have a place to live, be able to feed the sister and provide clothing. I had all of that. Yet others didn't have those things and were coming out of prison getting married like nothing.

This particular brother lived with his mother and didn't have a job. He sold oils each day to get his money. And for three years I'd been sitting in my apartment allowing those brothers to run my life.

The time was May 31, 2014. I won't tell everything that had happened to me at Masjid Ash-Shura. But they ran me away from the Masjid. I don't know if they understand what they had done. I'm not the only one who they've run out of the Masjid. If I had a girlfriend, I wouldn't be trying to get married either. I was trying every Friday. It didn't make sense to stick around, knowing that the brothers had taken it upon themselves to keep me from getting married.

Twice I was told not to marry a Christian. I was on the phone with another one of my good brothers, and I told the brother that I may have to try and find a Christian wife.

The brother stopped me and said, "Oh, no, ahki, you don't want to do that. I was married to a Christian. Let me tell you, ahki. You don't want that." But the brother had just told me that he was dealing with this shorty, which is the word he used. I was wondering if the brother understood what he was saying to me.

The brother was confused or something. This brother used to be an Imam in prison too. Yeah, right! The concise manual of Marriage Imam Muhammad Ibn Saalih Al-uthagmeeh [d.14214] [Qq]: What is the ruling on marrying a Jewish or Christian Woman? Are the Jewish and Christian women permissible?

They are regarded as "People of the Book" or as polytheists. [Aq]: Marrying a Jewish or Christian woman is allowable according to the view of the majority of the Scholars. Al-Imam Ibn Qudaamah said in al-mughnee") 7/99); there is no differing amongst the Scholar concerning the acceptability of marrying free women of the people of the book.

The key proof regarding that is the verse in which Allah says, made lawful to you this day are at-Tayyibaat (all kinds of Halaal (law-full) foods which Allah has made lawful (meat of slaughtered Eatable animals, milk products, fats, vegetables and fruits). The [slaughtered cattle, eatable-animals] of the people of the scripture [Jews and Christians] is lawful to you and yours is lawful to them [Lawful to you in marriage] are chaste women from the believers and chaste women from those who were given the scripture [Jews and Christians].

Both brothers couldn't have been more wrong. Unbelievable! You know what? I've seen it too many times now. I can believe it. But it hurts.

I'd been sitting in my apartment now for nearly four years. I'd been trying to get married the whole time. I didn't, and I don't have a girlfriend. I'd been married to a Christian woman before, and in fact, my marriage to the Christian woman was more beneficial. Preservation and protection of both mates the Prophet (sallallaahu 'alayhi wa sallam) said.

Regardless of the treatment from my so-called brothers in Islam, they could never shake my faith or belief in religion. So many of the brothers that had gone to prison read a few Islamic books, speak a little Arabic, come back to the streets, have not learned the religion correctly, which consists of going abroad and sitting at the foot of the scholars, Shaikhs and the students of knowledge. Most brothers will spend 10 years at best before given a title of Imam and a student of knowledge. When you don't have those things in place, you get what is happening in the Masjid in the black communities resulting in turmoil simply because no one has actually put in the work. When that happens, you no longer have Islam; you have Hislam. Fortunately for me, Allah(swa) has given me the ability to understand and to tell the difference between right and wrong and apply this daily.

So, here's my life's story, an open book for all to see, not to judge, not to scrutinize, not to impress, or even to stun you. But I stand here a man willing to share my life, the racism, the injustices of our legal system, the back stabbing of family, friends, so-called friends, loved ones, people who are supposed to have your back, all to let you know that no matter what life throws your way or how many hurdles you have to jump through, you can overcome them. Don't let anyone ascribe you with the title MOOT!

I challenge you to move forward in your life to be prosperous, humble, and always be true to yourself because it is only then that you can be true to others.

~" If the truth one speaks, or the truth that life shows you...shakes the faith, belief and purpose in life that you have chosen for yourself, release them and you lose nothing, because the foundation upon which you first believe in was only based on lies and illusion... THE ONLY CONSTANT IN EXISTENCE IS CHANGE!"

Acknowledgements

First, I would like to thank the creator for allowing me the ability to do this work. My mother who loved me enough to carry me for nine months and gave birth to me. I'd like to give thanks to Mrs. Judge Forrester, Mr. Howard Gwynn and Mrs. Gallagher for giving me the opportunity to do this work. Had it not been initiated by

Mrs. Gallagher from the beginning, there's no doubt in my mind that I wouldn't have made it this far.

I would like to thank Mr. Carl Williams, the director of NNRHA for the opportunity before a panel to show the injustice of the court that had been perpetrated against me, time and time again…and after two and a half years overturned their previous decision and grant me housing.

Mrs. Mae Coxx who went to extreme measures to make sure that I remained in the penal system for the rest of my life… Well, you know what they say: "haters make you greater!"

Once again, Thanks.

I would like to give a special thank you to Jacqueline "Jackie" Bonner for her love and support.

From the Heart

Wishing they were here to see me overcoming the hurdles and obstacles in life.

Love & Miss You, Brothers

Jim Bell Jr. (Deceased, January 2014)

Larry Donnell Bell (Deceased, May 1996)

Surviving siblings:

Sally Ann Turner; thanks for encouraging me to do this book, Henry James Bell, Elisha Renee Bell-Williams

My Children

Alexia Canada, Marcus Brown, Christopher Brown, Whitney Avery- Love You Always!

My Mom

Dorothy Ree Cooper- Thank you and Love You! -Your son Ziggy.

Printed in the United States
By Bookmasters